ADDRESSING MISCONCEPTIONS ABOUT AFRICA'S DEVELOPMENT

Addressing Misconceptions About Africa's Development

Seeing Beyond the Veil

Edited by
Senyo B-S. K. Adjibolosoo
and
Benjamin Ofori-Amoah

Studies in African Economic and Social Development
Volume 11

The Edwin Mellen Press
Lewiston•Queenston•Lampeter

Library of Congress Cataloging-in-Publication Data

Addressing misconceptions about Africa's development : seeing beyond the veil / edited by Senyo B-S. K. Adjibolosoo and Benjamin Ofori-Amoah.
p. cm. -- (Studies in African economic and social development ; v. 11))
Includes bibliographical references and index.
ISBN 0-7734-8350-0 (hc)
I. Africa--Economic conditions--1960- 2. Africa--Social conditions. 3. Structural adjustment (Economic policy)--Africa. I. Adjibolosoo, Senyo B-S. K. II. Ofori-Amoah, Benjamin. III. Series.
HC800.A5427 1998
338.96--DC21 98-11845
CIP

This is volume 11 in the continuing series
Studies in African Economic & Social Development
Volume 11 ISBN 0-7734-8350-0
SAESD Series ISBN 0-88946-514-2

A CIP catalog record for this book is available from the British Library.

The Edwin Mellen Press
Box 450
Lewiston, New York
USA 14092-0450

The Edwin Mellen Press
Box 67
Queenston, Ontario
CANADA L0S 1L0

The Edwin Mellen Press, Ltd.
Lampeter, Ceredigion, Wales
UNITED KINGDOM SA48 8LT

Printed in the United States of America

To the generations that have a genuine concern for Africa's economic development

CONTENTS

ILLUSTRATIONS

FIGURES

TABLES

PREFACE

The purpose of this book is to re-open the debate and discussion on certain accepted notions about Africa's economic underdevelopment problems, and critically examine the validity of these notions, preferably in human factor terms. The rationale and the impetus for writing this book lie in the observation that these accepted and/or entrenched notions about Africa's economic underdevelopment are misconceptions that create, place and entrench psychological, social, intellectual, economic and political impediments on the development process in Africa. The need to address these issues is therefore, imperative for the development process in Africa.

The main contribution of this book to the existing literature on Africa's development is its conclusion. The book concludes that many positions held by scholars on the problems of economic underdevelopment in Africa are purely misconceptions that need to be dropped; and that Africa has a golden chance to develop, and this will surely happen. Each contributor carefully articulates what the actual misconception is, the problems of underdevelopment it has created, and offers recommendations regarding how these misconceptions must be fully debunked in order to pursue successfully development planning and policy. This book is the first of its kind and will create an extraordinary interest in international development and immense impact on the international development community.

We are indebted to many people for making this book a reality. First and foremost are the seven contributors who bore patiently with us as we struggled to get a publisher for this work. They never gave up and responded favorably to our frequent and infrequent demands. Thus we acknowledge Dr. Francis Adu-Febiri, Dr. Joe W. Essuman, Dr. Boniface Gebe, Dr. Godson Obia, Dr. Joseph Oppong, Dr. William Osei, and Dr. J. Henry Owusu.

Second, we are grateful to our two families, Sabina, Selassie and Selorm Adjibolosoo and Agnes, David, Jonathan and Abigail Ofori-Amoah. Their support and encouragement pushed us through our frustration and despair as we labored through this collection.

Third, we are grateful to our academic departments, the Department of Economics and Business, Trinity Western University, Langley, BC Canada and the Department of Geography and Geology, University of Wisconsin-Stevens Point, Stevens Point, Wisconsin. We appreciate and cherish the support we have received from colleagues and administrative staff in these two departments.

Finally, we want to thank the Edwin Mellen Press for agreeing to publish this work. Without them the ideas expressed in this book might never see daylight.

Benjamin Ofori-Amoah
Univ. of Wisconsin-Stevens Point
Stevens Point, WI, USA

Senyo B-S. K. Adjibolosoo
Trinity Western University
Langley, BC, Canada

PART I

GENERAL INTRODUCTION

1

MISCONCEPTIONS ABOUT AFRICA'S UNDERDEVELOPMENT AND DEVELOPMENT

Senyo B-S. K. Adjibolosoo
Faculty of Business & Economics
Trinity Western University

And

Benjamin Ofori-Amoah
Department of Geography and Geology
University of Wisconsin-Stevens-Point

INTRODUCTION

African countries have suffered economic decline for many decades. After the achievement of political independence in the late 1950s and early 1960s, many African countries pursued massive development planning and economic policies based on orthodox neoclassical economic theory and/or socialistic principles. By the late 1960s and early 1970s, it was, however, apparent that development planning and existing policies and programs were failing to achieve their intended objectives. This situation led many scholars to seek relevant explanations for the failure. Within a short period of time, a massive development literature, rationalizing why the African development planning and policies have failed to achieve the intended goals, emerged. Among the obstacles identified by this literature, are overpopulation, the suppression of women, lack of grassroots participation and democratization, outmoded traditional and cultural practices, the inability of African countries to trade among themselves, excessive corruption, massive social inequality, the pursuit of socialism, abject poverty due to low incomes, environmental degradation, poor land tenure systems and ineffective agricultural practices, problems of regional integration, and ethnic strife, and so on. As is often the case, it is usually argued that unless African countries overcome these hindrances successfully, no development can take place on the continent.

In the light of this argument, many African countries have tried feverishly in the last three or four decades to develop and implement relevant policies that could help them to deal successfully with each of these problems, but to no avail. Obviously, this raises the question as to why all the attempts made in the past to deal with these problems as recommended by economic development experts have failed to bring about development in African countries

The contributors to this volume believe that a lot of these so-called problems to Africa's economic underdevelopment are based on misconceptions that must be debunked to free the African development psyche and mentality from a position that is hopeless and self-defeating. This chapter presents the main themes discussed by all the contributors and their policy suggestions regarding why and how African countries should reject these misconceptions successfully in order to proceed with their development program. The contributions cover a wide range of development topics including social, cultural, economic, political, environmental issues as well as sectoral and regional issues. In each case, every author addresses a particular form of misconception, debunks it, and offers policy recommendations.

In Chapter 2, Ofori-Amoah and Adjibolosoo take to task the view that Africa's population and its rapid growth rate have contributed significantly to its underdevelopment and excessive poverty. In this chapter, they provide an historical overview of the population-development debate to show that the issues are not new at all. Ofori-Amoah and Adjibolosoo then turn their attention to various arguments that have been put forward to support the detrimental effects of Africa's population size and growth on its economic development. Ofori-Amoah and Adjibolosoo maintain that Africa's development problem is neither due to too many people nor rapid population growth. In fact, Africa may have to increase the size of its population, educate and train its people in order to exploit effectively and efficiently its available resources to its best advantage. Thus the population argument is a hoax and scholars who have always used this argument to explain Africa's inability to develop are oblivious to the fact that there are other factors that contribute to Africa's development problems. In view of this, the authors maintain that current population policies being designed for and implemented in African countries will create more problems than they are designed to solve. As such, African countries that desire development must have to abandon immediately some of these policies and proceed with their own development program as is commensurate with the acquisition of the basic necessities of life.

Adu-Febiri discusses existing views regarding social inequality and underdevelopment in Africa in Chapter 3. Adu-Febiri points out that many developing countries' governments always begin their development programs with the objective of creating income equality. This is due to the fact development scholars have always maintained that social inequality has been one of the major hindrances to development programs in Africa. As such, if

African countries can create programs that will deal successfully with this problem, they will develop. In his discussions, Adu-Febiri maintains that this view is not only a myth, but also wrong. He argues that the emphasis placed on issues relating to income inequality and their impact on sub-Saharan Africa's economic underdevelopment is misplaced because even in the presence of excessive income inequalities, many developed countries have been able to achieve economic development. Thus, in the case of Africa's underdevelopment, the real issue is that there is just not enough to go round due to low productivity. This is one critical reason why the view that underdevelopment in Africa is being caused by continuing inequality is untenable.

Chapter 4, also written by Adu-Febiri, focuses on issues related to what scholars have come to label as *African Socialism*. Adu-Febiri points out that the pursuit of the socialist development agenda in African countries is based on the view that African societies operate on the basis of continuing group participation, egalitarianism, and collectivism. Adu-Febiri argues that this is the primary reason why the Marxist-Leninist development agenda has been very appealing to different African leaders and/or helpers. Yet, regardless of this view, many programs based on the socialist model have all failed in all African countries that attempted them. This being the case, one is faced with the question: "If African societies were essentially socialist, why have well-meaning socialist programs failed in making development happen in Africa?" Adu-Febiri maintains that the failure of the socialist agenda in Africa is not necessarily due to its inability to recognize that African societies are essentially socialist. Instead, this failure is due to the inability to recognize the significance of the human factor (HF) to the national development program. As such, they concentrate on plans, policies, programs, and projects that do not have the necessary ingredients that make development happen in nations.

Ofori-Amoah's Chapter 5 discusses the critical issues relating to the environment and gender-based development strategies. He maintains that development strategies that attribute Africa's development problems to neglect of the environment and women issues in the development process do not necessarily constitute a new development strategy. Instead, Ofori-Amoah views each of these so-called new development strategies as a new series of false starts for African countries. This, Ofori-Amoah argues, is because the type of environment and gender-based development strategies being advocated has some very serious theoretical and practical flaws. These flaws make the applicability of the strategies to Africa's development program very doubtful. While not discounting the general need to address environmental and women's concerns, Ofori-Amoah cautions about the belief that the key to Africa's future economic development lies in addressing these issues.

In Chapter 6, Osei focuses on the gender factor in rural energy systems in Africa. Osei examines the inconclusive reporting and controversy that cloud women's work in rural energy production systems and the dynamics of socio-economic relationship of rural food and energy systems in Africa. Four issues constitute the core of this examination. These are the relationship between rural energy and women's socio-economic opportunities; the relationship between women domination in rural energy systems and its low-valued task status; exclusion of male in the rural energy system as a sign of women subordination and the relationship between rural energy systems and women health. Using case studies from Ghana, Osei shows that while women dominate the rural energy system, they do not suffer any real significant socio-economic impacts from being engaged in the system yet. Health implications are real but not limited to women only while power and control rarely enter into fuel needs decision-making at the rural level. Osei recommends the need for continuous site-level research to provide support for planning and policy.

Oppong discusses the various myths about Africa's traditional medicine in Chapter 7, and presents arguments to explain whether African traditional medicine is dangerous, anachronistic or panacea. Oppong traces the various orthodox views regarding traditional African medicine and presents detailed arguments and/or analysis to substantiate the view that the orthodox conceptualization about indigenous African medicine is either dangerous or anachronistic. He maintains that traditional medicine has a great deal of substance to it. Its potentials are extremely high. For this reason, Oppong suggests that what has been known of traditional Africa medicine should serve as the basis for further development in an area, which has been grossly misunderstood and neglected.

In Chapter 8, Obia presents a detailed analysis of some of the misconceptions about Africa's agricultural production, population and land resources and also about their interrelationships. He does this by evaluating the conditions of Africa's land resources, population growth, and agricultural production. With respect to conditions of land resources, Obia takes the notion of poor tropical and erodable soils to task and shows that these conditions are not peculiar to Africa. He argues that there is therefore more to Africa's declining productivity than limitations of its physical environment. In the case of population, Obia challenges the indiscriminate use of rapid population growth rates as the inevitable time bomb that will destabilize the continent. He argues that the real source of Africa's problem is its inability to enhance agricultural production. Obia then explores the interplay among Africa's land resources base, its population growth, and agricultural production. He concludes that the focus of development needs to change from emphasis on population control to a restructuring of agricultural production and resource conservation.

Adjibolosoo's Chapter 9 deals with how African countries can achieve regional integration in Africa, successfully. Adjibolosoo reviews the literature on previous attempts regarding regional and/or economic integration in Africa and argues that all these efforts failed because they pursued regional integration in the wrong way. He then dismisses the view that Africa is too diverse to achieve any meaningful form of regional integration on the continent. Adjibolosoo argues that African countries can achieve integration through the piecemeal harmonization approach. He concludes that by developing the human factor (HF) and using it effectively, African countries would be successful in this regard.

In Chapter 10 Ofori-Amoah revives the debate on growth center theory and regional development, whether it was a failure or an opportunity missed. Growth center theory, in its beginning years in the 1950s, was viewed as a blueprint for resolving regional economic disparities and also reducing costs of regional economic development. Throughout the 1960s and early 1970s, growth center ideas flourished as scholars and regional planners recommended it to African, as well as other developing countries, to accelerate regional economic development. However, as the high hopes expected from the theory did not materialize, enthusiastic support to the theory declined, and by late 1970s and early 1980s the theory had been abandoned never to be mentioned again because it was largely considered as a failure. Ofori-Amoah does not agree with this view. In this chapter, he discusses the ascendancy and decline of the growth center approach as it was practiced in Africa. He argues that the growth center approach was necessarily more of a window of opportunity missed rather than a failure. Ofori-Amoah argues further that this approach was not given time and the chance to prove itself. The best use made of it was having it neatly enshrined in development plans that even never got off the ground. He encourages African countries to reexamine the growth center idea as a strategy for regional economic development.

Gebe discusses the cold war and its accompanying impacts on African countries in Chapter 11. He reviews the various events that led to this war and how African countries became the real battleground for the war. Gebe challenges the view that the era of the cold war was fertile for peace and stability. He also points out clearly that for Africa, the tilt toward a particular ideological persuasion meant active hostility to other opposing ideological camps. The intensity of social strife, civil conflicts, and ideological labeling had adverse effects on national reconstruction, development, and reconciliation. Gebe provides a detailed account to support this view. The end of the cold war thus provides opportunity for Africa. However, if African countries truly desire to solve their economic problems, Gebe argues that they have to return to themselves and take a closer look at themselves. National reconstruction in Africa will require reconciliation and compromise. The African leadership must have to recognize and/or acknowledge the fact that those who lead nations must be selfless, accountable, responsible, pragmatic, rational, and so on. Until these are achieved, development may not be forthcoming on the continent.

In Chapter 12, Owusu provides a detailed discussion and analysis of the structural adjustment program in Ghana. Owusu argues that contrary to the claims of the program's success by the IMF and the World Bank, the developmental role of the structural adjustment program is rather mythical. Using Ghana's formal wood-processing sector as a case study Owusu shows that in terms of generating foreign exchange for the country the program was a big success for its sponsors and the Ghana government. The foreign exchange generated at the end of 1988 was enough to absorb the nation's annual debt interest payment. However, in terms of intra-sectoral linkages, the program was a failure. Thus, the traditional linkage between sawmills and domestic wood processors was broken and replaced by subcontracting for foreign firms. Linkage with the informal sector became intensified, while further spatial integration was precluded. The program also reinforced the exploitative role of international capital and thwarted self-reliant technological progress. Owusu concludes that the program is essentially a neocolonial one and its adoption in Ghana was essentially metonymical. It was adopted by the government to perpetuate itself in power and accommodate international capital. The program is thus, a wrong choice for African countries.

In Chapter 13, Essuman provides further support to the conclusion that the economic recovery program in Ghana may not necessarily be a blueprint for other African countries to follow. He argues that in spite of the up-beat commentary on Ghana's reform effort by the World Bank and the IMF, the impact of the Economic Reform Program (ERP) on the human condition in Ghana is negligible. Thus, in agriculture for example, Ghana registered a modest 2% annual growth. Budget deficits have reemerged and inflation continues to be a major problem. Hasty implementation of a Value Added Tax (VAT system led to price hikes of between 300% and 400% that led to series of demonstration by the general public and the eventual repeal of the tax). Massive devaluation of the cedi, levying of user fees, curtailment of subsidies and retrenchment in public sector all combined to reduce access of vulnerable groups to education and health care and exposing many to unemployment, malnutrition and other socio-economic quagmire. Essuman cautions that, for these reasons and also because of differences in the economic, political, physical, and institutional circumstances among countries, even the so-called successes of Ghana's structural adjustment program may not be realized in other African countries.

CONCLUSION

African countries have lain in the doldrums of economic development for far too long. One of the basic reasons for this phenomenon is the building of Africa's development program on myths and theoretical formulations that have no relevance to Africa. In this book, the contributors together have argued and concluded that unless African countries recognize these myths and deal with them successfully, all development plans, policies, programs and projects will continue to fail in every country. Our call to the whole of Africa is, therefore, to see beyond the veil, perceive the misconceptions actively at work and deal with them effectively. We are convinced that when these tasks are successfully accomplished, African countries will pave the way for themselves to achieve development in the coming century.

PART II

SOCIAL ISSUES

2

POPULATION AS A CAUSE OF AFRICA'S ECONOMIC UNDERDEVELOPMENT: MYTH OR REALITY?

Benjamin Ofori-Amoah
Department of Geography & Geology
University of Wisconsin-Stevens-Point

And

Senyo B-S. K. Adjibolosoo
Faculty of Business & Economics
Trinity Western University

INTRODUCTION

The relationship between Africa's population and its economic under-development has been a source of controversy among economic development experts, demographers and governments for some time now. This controversy that reflects a much broader debate at the global level centers on two views. On the one hand there is the belief that large population size as well as rapid population growth rates divert resources that could go into productive investments into feeding a growing population. In addition, rapid population growth rates create unfavorable balance in the age structure and distribution of the population, thereby increasing the dependency burden. The pressure of feeding and taking care of the basic needs of the growing population also makes it difficult for governments to provide essential education thus leading to poor quality of population. Finally, the rapid population growth also causes environmental degradation (Coale, 1963; Hauser, 1967; Hardin, 1968; UN Population Fund, 1991, Ehrlich, 1968; Ehrlich and Ehlrich, 1972; 1990; Sai, 1986; Brown, 1974; Economic Commission For Africa, 1994). The proponents of this view therefore insist that Africa cannot develop without a reduction in its high population growth rate.

In contrast, is the view that population size and its rapid growth are not the real issue. In fact, it is argued that these population characteristics are rather important to economic development as they create needed human resources and also opportunities for change (Clark, 1969; Boserup, 1965, 1981; Simon, 1981; Simon and Khan, 1984; Erbstadt, 1986). The real problem is poverty itself, and the unfavorable international political and economic systems that make it difficult for African countries to generate enough revenues for their needs. In recent years it has been claimed by some experts on the issue that a consensus has been reached between the two sides of the issue (Wirth, 1994; Mazur, 1994). However, the view that large population size and rapid population growth are causes of underdevelopment appears to be popular among organizations that deal with population issues, and policy makers in both developed and developing countries. Thus, in a recent report, the Economic Commission For Africa (ECA) identified explosive population growth rate as the leading cause of poor agricultural performance and environmental degradation in Africa (Economic Commission For Africa, 1994). Similarly, there has been attempts by policy makers in the US and other developed countries to link the recent tribal conflicts in Rwanda and Burundi to population pressure (MacFarquhar, 1994). Furthermore, in a recent survey of American public, Camp (1994) reports that 85 to 90% of the people surveyed believe that population growth contributes to world hunger and poverty, environmental degradation, political instability and other problems. Indeed so strong is this view that family planning appears to have become tied to certain forms of aid being given to African countries (Baobab Press, 1991, 1994).

We are not opposed to reduction in population growth rates by family planning, per se. What we are opposed to is the tendency to wrongly diagnose the causes Africa's economic underdevelopment. We are opposed to this because we strongly believe that wrong diagnosis breeds wrong prognosis, which if accepted can either lead to a false start or a lost opportunity (Ofori-Amoah, 1998). In this chapter, we re-examine the contention that large population size and rapid population growth rate are the causes of Africa's economic underdevelopment. Drawing on historical and current evidence from both developed countries and Africa, we show that the emphasis on rapid population growth as a cause of economic underdevelopment is a misplaced priority. Consequently, we revive the argument that development is the best contraceptive. More importantly, we redirect the attention of African countries to focus on what we consider to be the real problem, namely, human factor decay and/or underdevelopment (Adjibolosoo, 1994, 1995).

The chapter is divided into three sections. In the next section, we outline the historical evolution of the population-development controversy to show that the controversy is an old one, while pointing out the main arguments on both sides of the issue. In the next section, we examine critically the main arguments of the debate, with respect to Africa. In the last section, we offer some lessons from the study and recommend the need for African countries to examine critically all development-related concepts, and strategies and their associated projects and plans before implementing them.

POPULATION AND ECONOMIC DEVELOPMENT: A HISTORY OF CONTROVERSY

The controversy over the relationship between population and economic development is not new. It goes back to antiquity (Stangeland, 1966; Hutchinson, 1967). For the purposes of discussion, we will divide this long period into four eras. The first is from antiquity to the end of the Middle Ages. The second is from the end of the Middle Ages to the Late 18th Century. The third is the late 18th century and the 19th century and the fourth is the Twentieth Century. For obvious reasons we pay most attention to the last period. In addition, we will divide the views during all these periods into two. The first is the population pessimists, who generally see population size and its growth as detrimental to economic development. The second is the population optimists, who see population size and its growth as useful for economic development.

From Antiquity to the End of the Middle Ages

According to Hutchinson (1967) the population-development controversy goes back to the Greek and Roman times. The Greeks were pessimists. They believed in the concept of optimum population, after which fertility was restrained. In contrast, the Romans were optimists. They saw population size as a symbol of power and explicitly promoted it. Between the fall of the Roman Empire and the end of the Middle Ages, these views were extended by Ibn Khaldun, Machiavelli, Von Hutten, Von Ward and Bodin. In his grand theory of the rise and fall of empires, Ibn Khaldun saw the growth of population as generally favorable to the maintenance and increase in imperial power. In contrast, Machiavelli indicated that poverty and disease would reduce overabundant population. However, Bodin, maintained that increased number of population was not in itself a cause of poverty. Instead, large population size gave political stability (Hutchinson, 1967).

From the End of the Middle Ages to the Late 18th Century

The rise of mercantilist ideas at the end of the Middle Ages through the 17th century continued the optimistic view of population and its growth. Mercantilists argued that a nation's population was a source of wealth. Thus, a larger population meant larger source of labor, larger market and larger armies for defense. Sympathizers to the mercantilist view however added that population growth alone was not enough. In addition it was important to have good use of land and inhabitants (Montchretein), industrious people (Seckendorf and

Petty) the quality of the people (Bereau) and good government (Petty and Coke) (Hutchinson, 1967).

On the pessimistic side, however, Raleigh, Gray, Malyners, Cook and Hale all saw population growth as an inevitable trend towards famine, disease or war, unless it was checked (Hutchinson, 1967). Thus, by the end of the 17th century, the foundations of the two sides of the population-development debate had been laid. During the 18th century, this foundation was further strengthened on the pessimists' side by the physiocrats, who saw land instead of population growth as the main source of economic growth. When at the close of the century, Malthus (1798) synthesized the pessimistic view on population and development into his famous essay on population, the old controversy between the optimist and the pessimist was revived and destined to survive the 19th century and beyond.

The Late 18th Century and the 19th Century Controversy

Malthus (1798) began his argument with two postulates. First, food is necessary to the existence of people. Second, the passion between the sexes was necessary. Given this, however, Malthus argued that the power of population was indefinitely greater than the power in the earth to produce subsistence for humans. Population when unchecked increases in a geometric progression, while subsistence increases only at an arithmetic rate. Consequently, unless there were preventive checks, through moral restraint, food production would be outstripped by population growth. This will bring in positive checks such as famine, pestilence, and misery, which will suppress population growth. Malthus received initial support from some of his contemporaries, including Ricardo, Mill and Torrens. Ricardo argued that population growth can extend the margins of cultivation into either farther afield or poorer land and thereby reducing the rent. Similarly, Torrens argued that an increase in population can lead to diminishing returns in agriculture and also increasing rent as poorer land might be brought under cultivation. Mill also showed that capital grew less rapidly than population. Consequently population growth can lead to economic ills for society (Hutchinson, 1967).

However, the optimists were also ready (Hutchinson, 1967). Gray believed that the growth in population numbers led to greater production and wealth. Convinced that every worker in the civilized world can produce more than he consumes, Godwin argued that poverty exists not because of overpopulation but maldistribution or unavoidable underproduction. Ravenstone showed that there were no diminishing returns to labor as a result of division of labor. Sadler argued that it was subsistence that depended on population, and not population on subsistence, and that food production increased more rapidly than population growth. Chalmers argued that population growth in fact might have stimulated improvement in food production methods. Edmonds also noted that population growth could not be harmful to economic growth because of the unlimited powers of labor and inexhaustible possibilities of invention. Burns also pointed out that Malthus' ideas were not consistent with England's experience that showed that food production can grow faster than population. List also maintained that each economic order had its own characteristic population capacity that increased with the level of economic development. He disagreed with Malthus that population increased faster than the means of subsistence, and pointed out that large tracts of land remained unexploited and productivity of agriculture on the land was expanding. Engles argued that not only did the Malthusian theory show the inhumane nature of capitalism, by condemning the poor to starve to death, but it also ignored the power of labor to be employed for increased production. Above all it also ignored the power of science and technological progress. Even Mill, who had made a strong defense of Malthus earlier on, modified his position in a later writing. Thus, while recognizing that returns tend to decrease with cultivation of poorer land, he also admitted improved methods provided an antidote to decreasing yield. Consequently, whether agricultural production increased or not it depended on the conflict between population and improvement in agricultural production skills. Bastiat believed that Malthus had overlooked an important factor and that was greater productive efficiency of a denser population. Marx pointed out that it was only under capitalism that Malthus' concern about resource limits arose. Throughout the last half of the 19th century, this optimism continued as evidenced in the works of Greg, Kautsky, Leroy-Beaulieu; Dumont and Nitti (Hutchinson, 1967).

The Twentieth Century

If the population-development controversy preceding the 20th century was limited to academic circles and within specific countries, the 20th century would take the controversy to the international scene and to a level demanding more involvement from governments, intergovernmental and nongovernmental organizations. It would begin with legislative action by individual governments in their respective countries during the first half of the century and end with a world action, under the auspices of the United Nations. We consider these developments under the following periods: from 1900 to 1945; 1945 to the 1950s; the 1960s; the 1970s, the 1980s, and the 1990s.

From 1900 To 1945

Soon after World War I, France passed a law prohibiting dissemination of contraceptive knowledge. In 1923, it passed further measures against abortion. In 1927, the League of Nations officially boycotted a world population conference held in Geneva, on the grounds that the League was not prepared to be involved with matters that aroused strong national feelings and of delicate character. In 1935, Sweden set up a commission to find a way to boost up its population. Belgium, Italy and Germany all had similar policies. In the former USSR, Marxist skepticism about neo-Malthusian pronouncements prevailed while abortion was only allowed in event of endangered pregnancy.

From 1945-1950s

However, it was under the auspices of the United Nations that the controversy would come to its full stature. In 1946 the Economic and Social Council (ECOSOC), a United Nations agency, created the Population Commission. The Commission was established to advise ECOSOC on issues related to population size and structure, the interplay between demographic factors and economic and social development, policies designed to influence the size and structure of population and any other relevant demographic questions. At the first meeting of the commission in 1948, controversy arose. The Soviet delegate objected to the use of the term optimum population. The Chinese member called for a study of areas where population pressure exerted an obstacle to development. The delegate from Ukraine saw activities of birth control as contrary to the UN's humanitarian mission (Johnson, 1987)

As the 1950s rolled in, the controversy intensified, this time embroiling all the other agencies of the United Nations. The most intense controversy occurred at the World Health Organization (WHO). The Director-General, Dr. Brock Chisholm, and his supporters, insisted that population growth was beyond WHO's mandate of 'mental and physical well-being,' and that WHO should become involved in population control matters only if a country requested it to do so. In opposition was the WHO's Regional Committee for South-East Asia and its supporters from Norway who urged WHO to obtain all possible demographic data from member countries and set up an international expert committee to study the health aspects of population. In the end both sides lost their resolution. By 1953, the agency had adopted a policy not to help countries that would apply for help in the area of population on the grounds that it was beyond its mandate (Johnson, 1987).

However, elsewhere among the other UN agencies, consensus was building towards the neo-Malthusian[1] stand. In 1948, Julian Huxley, the Director General of UNESCO emphasized that overpopulation could drastically affect the type of civilization possible and its rate of advance. In 1950, Dr. David Moore, International Labor Organization (ILO)'s Director - General noted that Asian countries would be able to obtain substantial and lasting form of development only if their population growth could be checked. In 1951, the sixth session of the FAO expressed concern that food production was not keeping up with population growth.

The First World Population Conference held in 1954 gave further opportunity for discussion of these issues and by end of the 1950's the consensus was building that the UN could no longer confine itself to research and studies. In 1959, the Population Commission, urged governments to study the relationship between population growth and economic development (Johnson, 1987).

The 1960s

The 1960s were a period for the population pessimist. In 1961, following the UN's declaration of the 1960s as the Development Decade, representatives from Norway and Sweden made a formal request that population growth and economic development be placed on the agenda of the UN General Assembly. After some amendments and discussion of the request, however, the issue could not pass the Assembly floor due to a split vote.[2] Hardin (1968) argued that population was the main cause of poverty and that population control cannot be curbed by appeals to conscience but by mutual coercion. The Second World Population Conference that convened in 1965, in Belgrade, Yugoslavia, concluded among other themes that attempts to achieve economic development were being offset by rapid population growth. The conference also recognized oral contraceptives and intra-uterine device as the two most potentially useful methods of birth control, even though it also recognized that as countries progressed economically people with better education and higher income might have fewer children. (Johnson, 1987).

In 1965, President Johnson of the US pledged to seek ways and use all knowledge to deal with population and problem of scarcity in world resources. A US population committee recommended to the US government to provide an amount of $100 million a year over the next three years to help countries implement family planning and strengthen national health and social services. Family planning was incorporated into development assistance activities of the US Agency for International Development (USAID. Convinced that rapid population growth was an urgent problem in developing countries, USAID believed that large scale government-sponsored programs through contraceptive use held the solution to the problem. Over the next two decades, it would contribute about $3.9 billion to population and family planning assistance throughout developing countries (Donaldson and Tsui, 1994). In 1968 the UN Population Trust Fund was established to promote awareness of population problems and their relationship to social and economic development, the implementation of population policies and the spread of family planning.

These efforts were further bolstered by the publication of a number of research reports that saw population growth as a negative influence on economic development. Ehrlich (1968) argued that population growth was the direct cause of environmental deterioration. The appearance of Ehlrich on public television shows rallied public opinion about the effects of rapid population growth. This spurned tremendous activity including a mushrooming of population organizations such as Zero Population Growth, Population Crisis Committee and the Population Institute (Donaldson and Tsui, 1994). The United Nations Association of the USA (1968) also concluded that high fertility affects individual rights. It also saw high rates of population growth as an obstacle to national goals and a threat to international stability, and conferred on the UN a legitimacy to deal with these threats.

In his first address to the Board of Governors in 1968, the newly appointed president of the World Bank, Mr. Robert S. McNamara, also identified population explosion as the most single factor that is widening the gap between the rich and poor. He declared that the claim that some countries need more population to accelerate their economic growth was a false one. Consequently, it was important to let developing countries know the extent to which rapid population growth slows down their potential development; to opportunities to finance facilities for family planning and join others to research into the most effective means for implementing and administering family planning and population control programs. He announced a new program that would increase lending to Africa and Latin America in the area of education, agriculture and control of population growth (Johnson, 1987).

The Commission on International Pearson Commission) (1969) also identified the staggering growth of population as the most important hindrance to international development, and for that reason the major cause of the large discrepancy between rich and poor nations. The Commission recommended to developing countries to identify their own population problems, if they had not done so, and draw up action plans to solve them. It also recommended to international aid givers to press for adequate analysis of population problems and their impact on development programs.

The 1970s

The pessimists' fervor that had gathered momentum towards the end of the 1960s could not, however, sustain itself during the 1970s, as developing countries began to question population programs within the context of broad economic and political framework. Some viewed the emphasis on population as an escapist route from the real problems of economic underdevelopment, by developed countries. Others viewed it as a form of cultural imperialism (Mazur, 1994). The day of reckoning came at the First International Population Conference that met in Bucharest, in 1974, when the newly formed Group of 77 non-aligned countries faced off with the pessimists of Western developed countries.

The conference opened on an optimist note by the UN Secretary-General, Dr. Kurt Waldheim, who saw it as a sign of a common understanding of the effects on population change on human life. However this optimism was dashed, when President Nicolai Ceausescu, of Romania, called for a New International Economic Order (NIEO) in his welcoming address to participants (NIEO). Ceausescu emphasized that it was only NIEO that could provide the appropriate framework for discussing the population issue (Johnson 1987). The fate of the conference was further jeopardized when China accused the two superpowers of the world for making the population issue a scapegoat. To China, the real causes of the poverty were not population as the superpowers wanted the world to believe. It was the amount of natural resources the superpowers had plundered, the social wealth they had grabbed, and the super-profits they had extorted from Asia, Africa and Latin America. Using itself as an example, China showed how wrong the superpowers were and how the population issue could be resolved. It argued:

> In the twenty years since the founding of the People's Republic, China's population has increased nearly 60% from about five hundred million to nearly eight hundred million. Yet in the same period, annual grain output has more than doubled, rising from 110 million to 250 million tons. At present the living standards of our people are still rather low, yet everyone is assured of employment, food and clothing and the livelihood of people is still improving. Facts of China's history have completely exploded the various fallacies spread by the Superpowers with regard to population and fully borne out the truth that revolution plus production can solve the problem of feeding the population (Johnson, 1987 p. 98).

China went on to emphasize the fact that any population matters must be strictly voluntary and that it was firmly opposed to the Superpowers intervention on the pretext of population explosion. Argentina, with support of Brazil, the former Soviet Union and Peru, also argued that its problem stemmed rather from a low population in relation to resources instead of rapid population growth. It questioned whether it was population growth or the lack of proper utilization of resources that constituted a problem for developing countries, and called for a suppression of the efforts of international family planning organizations. In contrast, the US, and its developed countries' allies held the view that rapid population growth was a serious impediment to development. As a result they vowed to carry out the World Population Plan and help other countries do so by providing aid for development of health care system. In the end, the newly formed G77 non-aligned nations of developing countries, led by India, and with the support of the Vatican argued that the best contraceptive is development. Thus, the World Population Action that was adopted in August 1974 gave greater emphasis to social and economic development while it was stripped of all references that made population growth as an influence on development (Johnson, 1987).

However, events after the conference did not show any let up on the part of those who believed that population has a detrimental effect on economic development. Thus, a number of countries instituted family planning programs and received funding from the UN. In addition, the Colombo Conference of Parliamentarians of August 1979 made a link between population, development and pressure on resources. Various aspects of the population development relationship along similar lines became the subject of conferences, reports and declarations during the early part of the 1980s.

The 1980s

The 1980s were a period of mixed victory for pessimists and optimists alike. For the pessimists, it was a period during which developing countries showed increasing commitment to family planning. However, it was also a period in which they lost their most important ally, the US government. For the optimists, it was a period in which they lost many of their old allies, namely developing countries, while gaining an important ally, the US government.

The early part of the 1980s saw a number of attempts to recapture the lost ground in the 1970s by the pessimists by way of various conferences and declarations. The International Conference on Population and Urban Futures held in Rome, 1980, focused on effects of population growth on unplanned urbanization. It declared that the process of urbanization can only be managed when demographic factors contributing to the process are controlled by economic, social, political and cultural factors.

The Independent Commission on International Development Issues (The Brandt Report) (1980) also noted the consequences of the rapid growth rates of population. It pointed out the population growth in certain Third World countries was a source of alarm and the need for environmental management. The Global 2000 Study (1980) also concluded that population in sub-Saharan African countries, among other regions, already exceeded the carrying capacity, and expressed some hope that policies such as family planning would begin to make a change. The International Union for the Conservation of Nature and Natural Resources (1981) in cooperation with the United Nations Environment Program (UNEP) also made a link between population, development and conservation. It argued that population growth and inequities were causing habitat destruction, and over-exploitation of resources. Other connections were made between population growth, peace and gender.

However, this was not a smooth ride for the pessimists at all. Simon (1981) argued that as much as an additional person to existing number of people will become an economic burden on society in the growing years of the person, that same person will also be a boon. The person will pay taxes, contribute energy and resources to the community. He or she will produce goods and services for consumption of others. More important the person will contribute to increasing efficiency of production through new ideas and improved methods. He went on to refute all the pessimistic notions about population including the effects on rapid population growth on land, natural resources, energy, pollution and standard of living. Similarly, Simon and Khan (1984) criticized the Global 2000 Report for painting an overall picture of a global trend that was fundamentally wrong. Among other things, they countered that even though there would be more people in the world by the year 2000, the world's people will be enjoying a higher standard of living than before. In addition, they will be living in a cleaner environment than before; and raw materials will be less scarce relative to human work-time.

Then came the Second International Conference on Population in Mexico City, in August 1984. In direct contrast to its position in Bucharest, the US asserted at this conference that the 1960s and 1970s were periods of demographic overreaction with too many governments undertaking population policy without sound economic policies that would raise the living standards of their people. The US went on to state that it would not support abortion, as a birth control measure and would not fund any organization that supported abortion as method of family planning (Johnson, 1987).[3] The Vatican also opposed abortion and the practice of sterilization. Brazil rejected the practice of blaming population growth as a cause of all the ills of developing countries and emphasized universal health care instead. However, many countries defended the need for population control and family planning. Among these were China, India, Indonesia, Kenya, Nigeria and then the World Bank. On August 14 1984, the Mexico City Declaration on Population and Development was adopted. The Declaration affirmed commitment of countries to the World Population Plan.

The 1990s

The 1990s have seen a rising interest in population issues once again, with an additional focus of controversy, namely the impact of population growth on the environment. Once again this has brought up new controversies. From September 5 to 13, 1994 the International Conference on Population and Development (ICPD) met in Cairo, under the auspices of the United Nations. To identify objectives, themes and produce a draft program of action, the conference was preceded by three preparatory committee meetings held between March, 1991 and April, 1994; a general discussion at the 48th UN General Assembly on November 4-5, 1993 and pre-conference consultations on September 3-4, 1994. However, the focus on population and development was once again hijacked by severe disagreements over definition and implications of such concepts as reproductive rights and reproductive health, fertility regulation and family units. In particular, the disagreement brought the Holy See, some Catholic and Islamic states on a collision course with advocates of sexual and reproductive health programs that include family planning by way of abortion and contraception.

Most Islamic states saw the conference as an attempt to destroy Islam, while some developing countries saw it as an attempt to impose western values on developing nations. As reported by MacFarquhar (1994) these disagreements led Saudi Arabia, Sudan and Lebanon to withdraw their delegates. In addition, three of the women rulers of Muslim States, Khaleda Zia of Bangladesh, Tansu Ciler of Turkey, and Queen Noor of Jordan dropped out, while the world center of Islamic scholarship, Cairo's Al-Azhar University, denounced the conference as un-Islamic. In the end, abortion was rejected as a method of family planning and most of the disagreements were resolved. Even so, many countries indicated that they would interpret the adoption and implementation of the various action programs within the context of their national and religious laws. In a summary analysis of the conference, the Conference Secretariat noted:

> Although delegates agree that the Cairo Conference was a success, the Conference did not succeed in meeting all of its objectives. As the title to the Conference indicates, this was supposed to be a conference on population and development. Yet, if a conference is judged by media attention and the number of minutes spent discussing certain issues, the Cairo Conference could have been called the Abortion Conference. So many hours were spent on paragraph 8.25, that it became almost synonymous with abortion. Many delegates from developing countries commented that the Conference's lack of an emphasis on development will hurt them in the long run.

This broad historical outline shows that after several centuries of debate, the population-development controversy is far from over. Today the debate continues to rage around the same old issues of the relationship among population size, rapid population growth and economic development. On the one hand is the belief that large population size and rapid population growth rates are a prescription for disaster and need to be checked in order for development to take place. On the other hand is the view that large population size and rapid economic growth are not the issues. The issue is development itself. Even though to some observers, there seems to be an emerging consensus that the population and development are interdependent, the balance seems to be tipping in favor of those who believe that population growth is a cause of underdevelopment. In the next section, we examine these issues in a more contemporary context. We look at population size first and then rapid population growth.

POPULATION SIZE AND ECONOMIC DEVELOPMENT

The tendency to equate population growth and economic development has created the erroneous impression that Africa, as a whole, is underdeveloped because of its large population size. This view is not only false, but also a clear showing of ignorance. To illustrate this, we compare the population statistics of African countries as of 1996 (Table 2.1) with the population statistics of a selected number of metropolitan areas in the economically developed world (Tables 2.2 and 2.3).

This comparison shows that 47 out of the 54 African countries had fewer people than Tokyo-Yokohama, the most populous metropolitan area in the developed world, in 1995. At the same time each of the remaining 48 countries had fewer. If we take Nagoya, Japan, the least of the top ten cities of the developed world (Table 2.2) and compare its population with African countries, we find that 31 African countries had more, while the remaining 23 had less. Furthermore, Table 2.3 shows as many as 43 African countries had fewer people than the New York Metropolitan Area, the largest metro area in the US, by population. More revealing, 41 African countries had fewer people than the Los Angeles metropolitan area, the largest metropolitan city by land area, in the US. Compared to Houston, the least of the top ten US metropolitan areas, 20 African countries had less population. Thus, we have a situation here in which there are many more people living in single metropolitan cities than in individual African countries. Yet none of these cities have raised the concern of population experts and the prophets of doom and gloom as African countries have.

On the basis of population size, we are persuaded to conclude that, the current concern about Africa's population is not so much because of its large size. As we have already seen, one could in fact argue that Africa's population is too small for its development. Instead, the real reason why there is so much concern about Africa's population is because of its low level of economic development. If this is the case, it is ironic then to move away from what is making population size an issue and focus on what is really the result of the issue. We can see population pessimists responding that it is not so much of population size but the rapid population growth rate of Africa that calls for concern. However, that too will not cut it because in addition to a basic mathematical problem inherent with all growth rates, the conventional arguments advanced to support this concern seem to be misplaced. Let us now focus on these.

TABLE 2.1
POPULATION OF AFRICAN COUNTRIES (1996 ESTIMATES)

Country	Area (Sq. Km)	Population	Density Sq/Km.	Growth Rates
Algeria	2,381,740	29,183,032	12	2.21
Angola	1,246,700	10,342,899	8	2.68
Benin	112,620	5,709,529	51	3.32
Botswana	600,370	1,477,630	2	1.63
Burkina Faso	274,200	10,623,323	39	2.53
Burundi	27,830	5,943,057	214	1.54
Cameroon	475,440	14,261,557	30	2.89
Cape Verde	4,030	449,006	111	2.93
Central African Republic	622,980	3,274,426	5	2.08
Chad	1,284,000	6,976,845	5	2.68
Comoros	2,170	569,237	262	3.55
Congo Republic	342,000	2,527,841	7	2.19
Congo, Dem. Rep.	2,345,410	46,488,539	20	1.67
Cote d'Ivoire	322,460	14,762,445	46	2.92
Djibouti	22,000	427,642	19	1.50
Egypt	1,001,450	63,575,107	63	1.91
Eqt. Guinea	28,050	431,282	15	2.58
Eritrea	121,320	3,427,883	28	2.79
Ethiopia	1,127,127	57,171,662	51	2.72
Gabon	267,670	1,172,798	4	1.47
Gambia	11,300	1,204,984	107	3.55
Ghana	238,540	17,698,271	74	2.29
Guinea	245,860	7,411,981	30	1.85
Guinea-Bissau	36,120	1,151,300	32	2.35
Kenya	582,650	28,176,686	48	2.27
Lesotho	30,350	1,970,781	65	1.90
Liberia	111,370	2,107,789	19	2.13
Libya	1,759,540	5,445,436	3	3.67
Madagascar	587,000	13,670,507	23	2.80
Malawi	118,480	9,504,679	80	1.70
Mali	1,024,000	9,653,261	9	2.95
Mauritania	1,030,700	2,336,048	2	3.17
Mauritius	1,860	1,140,256	613	1.23
Morocco	446,550	29,779,156	67	2.05
Mozambique	801,590	17,877,927	22	2.65

TABLE 2. 1 CONTINUED

Country	Area (Sq. Km)	Population	Density Sq/Km.	Growth Rates
Namibia	825,418	1,570,163	2	2.94
Niger	1,267,000	9,113,001	7	2.98
Nigeria	923,770	104,094,527	113	3.50
Rwanda	26,340	6,272,857	238	2.50
Sao Tome & Principe	960	141,217	147	3.10
Senegal	196,190	9,092,749	46	3.30
Seychelles	455	77,544	170	0.70
Sierra Leone	71,740	4,793,121	67	4.14
Somalia	637,660	9,639,151	15	3.10
South Africa	1,219,912	41,743,459	34	1.76
Sudan	2,505,810	31,547,543	13	3.48
Swaziland	17,360	998,730	58	3.24
Tanzania	945,090	29,058,470	31	1.15
Togo	56,790	4,570,530	80	3.56
Tunisia	163,610	9,099,687	56	1.81
Uganda	236,040	20,158,176	85	2.24
Western Sahara	266,000	222,631	1	2.46
Zambia	752,610	9,159,072	12	2.11
Zimbabwe	390,580	11,271,354	29	1.41

Source: US Census Bureau International Statistics

TABLE 2.2
TOP TEN CITIES IN DEVELOPED COUNTRIES (1995 POPULATION ESTIMATES)

City	Population	Area (Sq. Mi.)	Density (Sq./Mile)
1. Tokyo-Yokohama, Japan	27,540,000	1,089	25,019
2. New York, USA	14,638,000	1,274	11,480
3. Osaka-Kobe-Kyoto, Japan	14,060,000	495	28,025
4. Moscow, Russia	10,769,000	1,274	27,562
5. Los Angeles, USA	10,414,000	1,110	9,126
6. London, UK	8,897,000	874	10,429
7. Paris, France	8,764,000	432	20,185
8. Essen, Germany	7,506,000	704	10,585
9. Chicago, USA	6,493,000	762	8,568
10. Nagoya, Japan	4,909,000	344	13,806

Source: World Almanac, 1995

TABLE 2.3
TOP TEN METRPOLITAN AREAS IN THE UNITED STATES (1994)

Metropolitan Area[+]	Population	Area (Sq. Km)	Density (Sq. Km)
1. New York CMSA	19,705,000	7,627	2,583
2. Los Angeles CMSA	15,302,000	33,965	450
3. Chicago CMSA	8,526,000	5,618	1,517
4. Washington, DC MSA	7,051,000	3,966	1,777
5. San Francisco CMSA	6,513,000	7,368	883
6. Philadelphia CMSA	5,959,000	5,345	1,114
7. Boston MA	5,730,000	2,440	2,348
8. Detroit, MA	5,255,000	5,175	1,015
9. Dallas, TX CMSA	4,362,000	6,967	626
10. Houston, CMSA	4,098,000	7,107	577

Source: US Census Bureau

[+] A metropolitan area (MA) has a nucleus of at least 50,000 people. A primary metropolitan statistical area (PMSA) is an MA of one million or more. A consolidated metropolitan statistical area (CMSA) is the largest metro area with a PMSA (Source: 1996 US County and City Extra Appendix A).

RAPID POPULATION GROWTH RATES AND ECONOMIC DEVELOPMENT

By all standards the single most important element in the population-development controversy is that of rapid population growth rate. About four main arguments have been advanced to show that rapid population growth rates are detrimental to development. First, there is the belief that rapid population growth rates divert resources that could go into productive investments into feeding a growing population. Second, rapid population growth rates create unfavorable balance in the age structure and distribution of the population, thereby increasing the dependency burden. Third, the pressure of feeding and taking care of the basic needs of a growing population also make it difficult for governments to provide essential services, especially education, thus leading to poor quality of population. Finally, rapid population growth also causes environmental degradation (Coale 1963; Hauser 1967; Hardin, 1968; UN Population Fund, 1991, Ehrlich 1968; Ehrlich and Ehrlich, 1972; 1990; Brown, 1974; ECA, 1994).

Before we scrutinize these arguments, however, let us examine an inherent problem with growth rates in general, which is the problem of small and large base effects. To do this we examine Table 2.4, which shows the population statistics of a selected number of countries for 1970 and 1980. If we were to pick three countries with rapid population growth rates, these would be Western Sahara, Angola, and Algeria. The countries with the low population growth rates are the US, China and India. In fact one can raise a tumultuous concern about Western Sahara's growth rate of 10.4% compared to China's 2.0% and can easily deduce that such a high population growth rate underlies the poor living conditions in Western Sahara. This picture, however, changes when we begin to look at other statistics in the Table 2.4.

Thus, if we look at the increment we find that the US had an increment of 22,843,000 people vis-à-vis Western Sahara's 7,900; yet the US recorded a growth rate of only 1.1%, while Western Sahara had 10.4%. The situation gets even more puzzling, when we compare Western Sahara's increment with those of China and India. Yet both China and India recorded much lower growth rates. This then is the problem of small and large base effects. The growth rate of Western Sahara is 10.4% because the population of the base year (1970) was much smaller than the base year populations of the US, China and India. As a result of its small base, Western Sahara's population growth becomes more distorted than the countries that had larger base year populations. Mathematically, one can argue that in relation to its population size, Western Sahara added more people to its population than the US, India and China respectively did.

TABLE 2.4
POPULATION STATISTICS OF SOME SELECTED COUNTRIES

Country	Population		Increment	Annual Growth Rate
	1970	**1980**		
Afghanistan	12,431,000	16,063,000	3,632,000	2.9
Algeria	14,330,000	18,666,000	4,336,000	3.0
Angola	5,588,000	7,722,000	2,134,000	3.8
Cameroon	6,610,000	8,653,000	2,043,000	3.1
Costa Rica	1,731,000	2,246,000	515,000	3.0
China	818,316,000	981,242,000	162,926,000	2.0
India	554,911,000	688,856,000	133,945,000	2.4
USA	204,879,000	227,722,000	22,843,000	1.1
Western Sahara	76,000	155,000	79,000	10.4

Source: Brittanica World Data, 1983.

However, that is precisely the point, that growth rates are only relevant in relation to the base year population of that country. This obviously creates a problem of what constitutes a rapid growth rate and when comparing countries that do not have the same population base. The indiscriminate use of population growth rates without any consideration of the base, therefore is a mistake. Let us now examine the four arguments.

Rapid Population Growth and Diversion of Resources

The argument that rapid population growth diverts resources away from productive investments into feeding a growing population leaves one to question what kind of productive investments are being considered. First, the argument assumes the old Malthusian trap of food production not being able to match population growth. Thus, it also assumes that food production in African countries cannot be improved and that the only other alternative is food imports. Consequently, it also assumes that investment in agricultural production is not productive, thus it is not economical. As a result, the only alternative left for African countries is to curb their rapid population growth. However, all evidence on the subject now shows clearly that none of these assumptions holds, because as the history of developed countries has shown, food production could indeed grow faster than population growth. This did not occur after controlling population. In addition, African countries are predominantly agricultural and common sense will show that any attempt to lift African countries on to the path of development must involve, in addition to developing the appropriate human resources, making their agriculture more efficient than what it is now. This means that if there are to be any productive investments, these must begin with agriculture (i.e., the production of food, raw materials, etc.). Thus, as Boserup (1981) has argued, rapid population growth must rather provide a pretext of more investment in Africa's agriculture and not food imports. The problem of diversion of resources therefore exists not because of rapid population growth rates, but because African countries are trying to solve the problem with the wrong method.

Rapid Population Growth, Dependency Ratio and Population Distribution

The argument that rapid population growth leads to high dependency ratio seems to be plausible at the first sight. After all, rapid population growth brings in too many young people into the population, who then have to be supported by a smaller proportion of the population. However, as Simon (1981) has argued, every new member that is added to the population eventually grows to be a contributor to the household and the family economy. In Africa, this role even begins earlier than usual. Thus, children begin to contribute to the household income in a number of ways including fetching water, selling products, and providing farm, field and other domestic labor.

The main issue with the dependency ratio then as Simon (1981) has argued is how to take care of the children till they are fully independent. We submit that whether this will be done or not is a function of the capacity and ability of those who have to provide the support. In turn this capacity or ability to provide the support depends on the resources and opportunities that are available to the supporters rather than the numbers. Thus, just as in developed countries only 3% of the population are farmers and yet are able to provide enough food for the remaining 97% of the population, it should not be difficult for Africans to support a growing population if they had the same abilities. In effect, what we are arguing here is that a high dependency ratio is by itself a mere statistic. As such, its real impact on the well-being of people is relative to the productive capacity and abilities that are present in the population. The argument that rapid population growth leads to a high dependency ratio therefore tends to ignore the main reason why a high dependency ratio constitutes a problem. We submit that a high dependency ratio of the kind that results from rapid population growth becomes a problem only because of a weak economic development base.

With respect to the relationship between rapid population growth rates and imbalance in population distribution, we beg to differ. The argument here is that rapid population growth rates lead to excessive urbanization that creates population imbalance and other pressures of the urban areas. In the first place we do not think that Africa is excessively urbanized. In spite of all the fun fare that has accompanied the so-called rapid urbanization, Africa is predominantly a continent of rural settlements. Except for Nigeria, the Lower Nile Valley and the Witwatersrand region of South Africa, the huge conurbation and sprawling megalopolis that are found in developed countries are completely non-existent on the continent of Africa. Apart from this, population distribution is generally unbalanced. There is nowhere that population distribution is even and the causes of such imbalance are more than just rapid population growth. In Africa, the fundamental reason why people move into the urban areas is limited opportunities that are available to rural dwellers, in terms of jobs, and amenities for social advancement. This state of limited opportunities has been created by past development efforts that have bypassed the rural areas. The result is that the only source of livelihood in most rural Africa is farming, which as a result of long neglect, does not seem to have any prospects for the youth. Under these circumstances, rural-urban migration will occur even without rapid population growth. To argue that rapid population growth leads to imbalance in population distribution is therefore inaccurate.

Rapid Population and Provision of Essential Services and Quality of Population

It is also argued that rapid population growth makes it difficult to provide essential services such as education, health care and other infrastructural facilities that are needed by the population. The result is that the quality of population also deteriorates. We argue that rapid population growth may stretch existing services, especially when nothing is being done to extend their capacities or maintain the existing ones. However, we believe also that the inability of existing facilities to meet the demand of a growing population is not always due to rapid growth rates of the population. Even if the population is not growing, existing facilities everywhere have a lifetime that can only be extended by continuous maintenance. As Adjibolosoo (1995) has rightly pointed out, the practice of maintenance management in African countries leaves much to be desired. The particular notion of the government held by many people leads to a carefree attitude towards facilities that are government-owned. In addition, there are numerous cases of mismanagement and misappropriation of funds that are budgeted for maintenance of existing facilities.

Apart from these, there is also a problem of attitudinal change when it comes to certain established ways of doing things. Thus, some of the service facilities that have become outstretched do not have to be if only their management and administration could be changed. An example of this is the residential system of high schools and college education that is found in many African countries. This system requires every student to stay on the school or college campus instead of living off campus. This has naturally brought pressure on existing facilities. The pressure could, however, be eased in part by reverting to a mixture of residential and non-residential systems and effective maintenance of existing facilities.

As regards the impact of rapid population growth on essential education and for that matter the quality of population, we find that the provision of essential education is qualitative more than quantitative. As the works of Adjibolosoo and the members of the International Institute for Human Factor Development (IIHFD) have clearly shown the provision of quality education relates more to the content of the education process than the number of education facilities made available (Adjibolosoo 1993; 1994; 1995; 1996). In particular, it is one thing having schools in every nook and corner of a country and another imparting the appropriate human factor characteristics that are relevant to a nation's development program. Africa's most important need is people with the appropriate human factor characteristics, which we define as "the spectrum of personality characteristics and dimensions of human performance that enable social, economic, and political institutions to function and remain functional over time." (Adjibolosoo, 1995). Within the context of Africa, essential education will have to incorporate this and this does not have to be necessarily hindered by rapid population growth.

Rapid Population Growth and Environmental Degradation

Rapid population growth has also been identified as a source of environmental degradation. Our view on this argument is once again on the contrary because as Commoner (1994) has also argued, it is not so much of the population numbers but the technology of production of goods and services that degrades the environment. Thus, rapid population growth does not have to call for more land for both agriculture, and more wood for fuel, if Africans did not have to farm by rotational bush fallow technique and rely on wood for fuel. It is therefore the existence of a weak and outmoded technological base, which in itself results from lack of economic development, that is the root of the problem. This limits the choices that are available to Africans. Thus, lack of adequate electricity for fuel and energy leads to the use of wood and subsequently the degradation of forest cover. Lack of better farming techniques leaves the African no choice but to resort to shifting cultivation technique of farming that leads to frequent clearing of forests, and grasslands and subsequent soil erosion (Ofori-Amoah, 1998). It is therefore not the population growth rate per se but the technology for the production of goods and services that degrades the African environment.

CONTROLLING POPULATION GROWTH TO ACHIEVE ECONOMIC DEVELOPMENT

So far every aspect of our survey of the relationship between population size, rapid population growth rate and economic development seems to raise the question of whether controlling population growth as a means of economic development is a viable strategy. In this section, we examine this issue in more detail. We argue that while population control is a good thing, it cannot bring about economic development. There is nothing inherent in it that can bring about a positive change in the living conditions of people unless a conscious effort is made to increase the productive capacities and abilities of people.

The basis of our argument rests on our belief that the factors that generate economic development are too complex for one factor to be singled out as the sole cause. Besides, there is more evidence to support the controlling influence of economic development on population size and growth than there is for the controlling influence on population size and growth on economic development. To further explain this, let us begin with a look at the population statistics of the US shown in Table 2. 5. The growth rates show a clear decline over the years. What are the reasons for this trend?

Over the several years that the senior author of this chapter has asked his American students to analyze this trend together with their own family tree histories, the students have come out with two main sets of reasons. The first set is the possible influence of small and large base effect. Thus, while the growth rates have fallen from a high of 3.61% in 1810 to a low of 0.98% in 1990, at the same time both the ten-year and the average annual population increments have increased over the years. The result is that the increasing sizes of the base year populations have partly contributed to the lowering magnitude of the growth rates.

The second sets of reasons relate to the possible effect of increased level of economic development achieved. Thus, the predominantly agricultural economy of the country back in the 1800s required more hands on the farm. Large families were therefore the order of the day. However, as agriculture became more and more efficient through the application of capital and technology, this need began to disappear. In addition, the need for more people to open up the frontier and develop the new country was in part met by encouraging large-scale immigration. Again increased level of economic development made available more educational resources, improvement in health care including family planning methods as well as changing roles of the sexes, with women working more and more outside the home. Finally, it has made it more expensive to raise children and maintain household living standards.

TABLE 2.5
POPULATION STATISTICS OF THE US 1790-1990

Year	Population	Increment	Annual Growth Rate
1790	3,929,214		
1800	5,308,483	1,379,269	3.51
1810	7,239,881	1,931,378	3.61
1820	9,638,453	2,398,572	3.31
1830	12,866,020	3,227,567	3.35
1840	17,069,453	4,204,433	3.27
1850	23,191,876	6,122,423	3.59
1860	31,443,321	8,251,445	3.56
1870	39,818,449	8,375,128	2.66
1880	50,155,783	10,337,334	2.60
1890	62,947,714	12,791,931	2.55
1900	75,994,575	13,046,861	2.07
1910	91,972,266	15,997,691	2.10
1920	105,710,620	13,738,354	1.49
1930	122,775,046	17,664,426	1.61
1940	131,669,275	8,894,229	0.72
1950	150,697,361	19,028,086	1.45
1960	179,323,175	28,625,814	1.90
1970	203,235,298	23,912,123	1.33
1980	226,545,805	23,243,774	1.14
1990	249,709,873	22,164,068	0.98

Source: Historical Statistics of the US Census Bureau

The conditions in African countries today are not very different from the conditions described above. Apart from the role of children as social security, the need for children in other areas of life is dictated by other economic and social conditions. Unlike western developed countries, the use of child labor is still very prominent in African countries mainly because of the production and distribution technologies of goods and services. In spite of the fact that health care services have improved far beyond early post-independence periods, there is still a number of debilitating diseases that cause relatively higher rates of infant mortality in African countries. The need to have more children to safeguard future security is therefore still strong and so is the value perception of the genders in many African cultures. All these factors that exert influences on fertility and mortality rates and for that matter rapid population growth are inversely related to the rising level of economic development.

Indeed the whole history of developed countries testifies to this fact that it is economic development that leads to reduction in population growth rates. Europe did not escape Malthus' prediction by reducing its population growth rates. Instead, it was the result of the industrial revolution that made food production grow faster than population growth. Yet, everything that is being thrown at Africa today regarding the population question seems to say the contrary. The demographic transition model, a model that shows a decline in birth and death rates as economies developed, it is now asserted, cannot be emulated by developing countries because it is European. Meanwhile, African countries can emulate other European cultural elements, among which are education systems, democratic systems of government, birth control and other family planning practice methods. Thus, instead of helping African countries to create another industrial revolution, they are being told to basically reduce their birth rates because they are poor and cannot afford to have many children. This is a vicious myth that all African countries must stand against together and reject it outrightly.

CONCLUSION

The problems facing Africa in its search for economic development are now very complex and have therefore been analyzed in many different ways. As part of this, there has been the tendency for researchers to wrongly diagnose a problem and offer prescriptions that eventually result in false starts or missed opportunities. It is therefore important to critically examine these practices before accepting them.

In this chapter, we have investigated specifically this need within the context of population growth as a cause of Africa's economic underdevelopment. Our investigation so far has led us to the familiar but now less accepted conclusion that the best contraceptive to the population problem is development itself. African countries cannot develop their economies by assigning top priority to population control programs. Given that the whole population-development controversy rests on the judicious use of scarce resources, what African countries need to pay most attention to is to seek ways to develop their existing human resources in the qualities that will make the use of their scarce resources possible. What Africa needs is to emphasize on the development of the appropriate human factor without which no planning will be successful. Among these human factor characteristics are integrity, dedication, accountability, trustworthiness, responsibility, and creativity. Africa's educational and training programs must see to it that these human qualities are developed in the people.

NOTES

1. Neo-Malthusians believe that poverty is the direct outcome of rapid population growth. To alleviate poverty, therefore, population growth must be curbed through birth control and other family planning methods.

2. The vote was 34 for 34 against and 32 abstentions.

3. In 1985, the US government withheld $10 million of the $46 million it had designated to the UNFPA. I986 it discontinued all support to the UNFPA.

REFERENCES

Adjibolosoo, S. ed. 1996. Human Factor Engineering and the Political Economy of African Development. Westport , CT: Praeger.

Adjibolosoo, S. 1995. *The Human Factor In Developing Africa.* Westport, CT: Praeger.

Adjibolosoo, S. 1994. "The Human Factor and the Failure of Economic Development Policies in Africa." In F. Ezeala-Harrison and S. Adjibolosoo, eds. *Perspectives on Economic Development in Africa.* Westport CT: Praeger.

Adjibolosoo, S. 993. "The Human Factor In Development." *The Scandinavian Journal of Development Alternatives* XII (4): 139-149.

Baobab Press. 1991. "It's not Safe to be a Woman in Kenya" *Baobab Press* 1 (3)

Baobab Press. 1994, "Western Policy and Political Reality: Some Things Never Get Said in Public." *Baobab Press* 4 (11).

Boserup, E. 1965 The *Conditions of Agricultural Growth*. London: Allen and Unwin.

Boserup, E. 1975. "The Impact of Population Growth on Agricultural Output." *Quarterly Journal of Economic*, 89.

Boserup, E. 1981. *Population and Technological Change: A Study of Long Term Trends*. Chicago: The University of Chicago Press.

Brown, L. 1974. *In the Human Interest: A Strategy to Stabilize World Population*. New York: Norton.

Camp, S. L. 1994. "The Politics of U. S. Population Assistance." In A. L. Mazur ed. *Beyond the Numbers: A Reader on Population, Consumption and the Environment*. Washington, DC: Island Press.

Clark, C. 1969. "The 'Population Explosion' Myth." *Bulletin of the Institute of Development Studies*.

Coale, A. J. 1963. "Population and Economic Development" In P. Hauser, ed. *The Population Dilemma*. Englewood Cliffs, NJ: Prentice-Hall.

The Commission on International Development (The Pearson Commission 1969. *Partners In Development. Report of the Commission on*

International Development. New York: Praeger.
Donaldson, P. J. and Tsui, A. O. 1994. "The International Family Planning Movement." In A. L. Mazur, ed. *Beyond the Numbers: A Reader on Population, Consumption and the Environment*. Washington, DC: Island Press.
Economic Commission of Africa 1994. "Major Population and Environment Problems in Africa." In United Nations (ed.) *Population, Environment and Development*. New York: United Nations.
Ehrlich, P. R. 1968. *The Population Bomb*. New York: Ballantine.
Ehrlich, P. R. and Ehrlich, A. H. 1972. *Population, Resources and Environment: Issues in Human Ecology*. 2nd Edition. San Francisco: Freeman.
Ehrlich, P. R. and Ehrlich, A. H. 1990. *The Population Explosion*. New York: Simon & Schuster.
Eberstadt, N. 1986. "Population and Economic Growth." *Wilson Quarterly* (Winter): 95-129.
Global 2000 Study (US). 1980. *The Global 2000 Report to the President: Entering the Twenty-First Century*. Prepared by the Council on Environmental Quality and the State Department. Washington, DC: US Government Printing Office.
Hardin, G. 1968. "The Tragedy of the Commons." *Science* 162: 1243-1248.
Hauser, P. M. 1967. "Population and Labor Force Resources As Factors in Economic Development." In R. J. Ward, ed. *The Challenge of Development: Theory and Practice*. Chicago: ALDINE Publishing Company.
Hutchinson, E. P. 1967. *The Population Debate: The Development of Conflicting Theories up to 1960*. Boston: Houghton Mifflin.
The Independent Commission on International Development Issues. 1980. *North-South, A Programme For Survival: Report of the Independent Commission on International Development Issues*. Cambridge, MA: MIT Press.
Johnson, S. P. 1987. *World Population and the United Nations: Challenge and Response*. Cambridge: Cambridge University Press.
Malthus, T. R. 1798 *An Essay on the Principle of Population As it Affects the Future Improvement of Society, with Remarks on the Speculations of Mr. Godwin, M. Condorcet and Other Writers*. London: Printed for J. Johnson in St. Paul's Churchyard.
MacFarquhar, E, 1994. Population Wars *US News & World Report*. September 12, 117 (10): 54-56.
Mazur, L. A. 1994. "Beyond the Numbers: An Introduction and Overview." In L. A. Mazur (ed.) *Beyond the Numbers: A Reader on Population, Consumption and the Environment*. Washington, DC: Island Press.
Ofori-Amoah, B. 1998. "Environment and Gender-Based Development Strategies: New Development Directions or Another Set of False Starts." In B. Ofori-Amoah and S. Adjibolosoo, eds. *Seeing Beyond the Veil: Some*

Misconceptions about Africa's Economic Development New York: The Edwin Mellen Press.

Sai, F. T. 1986. "Population and Health: Africa's Most Basic Resource Development Problem." In R. J. Berg and J. Seymour Whitaker, eds. *Strategies for African Development. A Study for the Committee on African Development Strategies*. Berkeley: University of California Press.

Simon, J. L. 1981. *The Ultimate Resource*. Princeton, NJ: Princeton University Press.

Simon, J. L. and Khan, H. 1984. Eds. *The Resourceful Earth: A Response to Global 2000.* London and New York: Basil Blackwell Inc.

Stangeland, C. E. 1966. *Pre-Malthusian Doctrines of Population: A Study in the History of Economic Theory*. New York: A. M. Kelley.

United Nations Population Fund. 1991. *Population, Resources and the Environment: The Critical Challenges*. London: Banson Publication.

Wirth, T. E. 1994. "Foreword." In L. A. Mazur, ed. *Beyond the Numbers: A Reader on Population, Consumption and the Environment*. Washington, DC: Island Press.

3

SOCIAL INEQUALITY AND AFRICA'S UNDERDEVELOPMENT: A CRITICAL ASSESSMENT

Francis Adu-Febiri
Department of Social Sciences
Camosun College

INTRODUCTION

Many developing countries, unlike the developed ones, have started their development programs with a clear emphasis on creating equality (Myrdal, 1970). Sub-Saharan African countries are typical. Notwithstanding the differences in the ideological professions and the governing styles of the various governments, which have come to power in sub-Saharan Africa, they have all claimed to aspire to establish a solid basis for equitable distribution of incomes. For example, in the 1960s and 1970s sub-Saharan African countries, in the Organization of African Unity (OAU) summits, declared the reduction of inequality as a major development objective. This objective was re-affirmed in the 1980s as evident in the Lagos Plan of Action (Adedeji, 1985, p. 15).

The main reason for adopting this development objective seems to be that income equality leads to greater economic growth. The Eastern countries, for example, were thought to enjoy rapid economic growth mainly because of their socialist programs, which placed a premium on income equity. Also, it is believed that the dramatic economic development of Japan is related not only to the effective cooperation and group-oriented national culture, but also to its relatively egalitarian income distribution (Chirot, 1986; Laxer, 1987; Mizruchi and Schwartz, 1987). Another example is that the economies of the Western countries have grown a great deal since their adoption of equality as a crucial development strategy (Myrdal, 1970).

A logical conclusion to the above is that sub-Saharan African countries have serious income inequality which is impeding their economic development. This chapter attempts to counter that notion. It argues that the emphasis on income inequality in the analysis of sub-Saharan Africa's economic underdevelopment is misplaced. This is because (1) in most of the economically developed Western countries income inequality persists, and (2) in sub-Saharan African countries, real income inequality is low due to the prevalence of the collectivistic ethic[1] which generates a complex process of informal income redistribution in favor of underprivileged groups (Adu-Febiri, 1994). The real issue is that there is just not enough to go round due to low productivity. This disparity between basic needs and available goods and services is attributable to other factors besides income inequality. These other factors may be related to sub-Saharan Africa's entrenched commercial capitalist economy (see Febiri, 1991; Ninsin, 1991). In turn this is being perpetuated by human factor (HF) weaknesses such as the lack of integrity, responsibility, accountability and loyalty to the state; and disunity, particularly on the part of the political leadership (see Adjibolosoo, 1995, pp. 25-27).

Against this backdrop, the chapter analyzes the problem of using income inequality to account for Africa's poverty and underdevelopment. The first section deals with inequality and underdevelopment in sub-Saharan Africa. It highlights the mitigation of income inequality by the collectivistic ethic, a culture which commercial capitalism[2] preserves while underdeveloping the sub-Saharan African economy. Section two addresses the issue of dealing with poverty, a significant aspect of underdevelopment. It suggests the need to create the relevant HF as the most viable alternative to transform commercial capitalism, which is one of the major immediate sources of underdevelopment in sub-Saharan Africa. It is in this connection that the concluding section asserts that the elimination of income inequality may not play any significant role in dislodging underdevelopment from sub-Saharan African societies.

INEQUALITY AND UNDERDEVELOPMENT IN SUB-SAHARAN AFRICA

Gender, class and ethnic inequalities have been associated with income distribution in sub-Saharan African countries (United Nations, 1978; Nafziger, 1988; Onimode, 1988). The United Nations (1978) in its extensive study of the income distribution situation of developing countries concluded that African women provide from 60 to 80 percent of all agricultural labor, yet receive virtually none of the agricultural income. Recent research arrives at a similar conclusion. For example, according to Matlon (1981), in the rural areas of Northern Nigeria, the average female earns 23% of that of males. The greater majority of women in Africa are employed in the low-paying, low-mobility informal economic sector (Febiri, 1991). In Botswana and Tanzania, for example, about 80% and 53% respectively of the female labor force work in the informal sector of the economy (Sundar, n.d.; Shields, 1980).

Income inequality among the various socio-economic categories in Africa has also been noted by authors such as Onimode (1988) and Nafziger (1988). As the data In Table 3.1 show there seems to be a wide income disparity between top civil servants and workers of some sub-Saharan African countries.

Apart from Ghana, which has a low gini coefficient (0.3), other sub-Saharan African countries show high income gaps. For example, in Zambia, "earning disparities between non-Zambian and Zambian employees, public-parastatal and private sectors, highest and lowest wage earners, and urban and rural workers are wide." (Nafziger, 1988, p. 98). The Congolese (Zairian) situation is no different. In the 1970s, 6.6% of those in high managerial positions in the public sector of the Democratic Republic of Congo (Zaire) earned 29.2% of all government wages and salaries (Nafziger, 1988, p. 99). Likewise in the private sector, the 2.8% of high level managers received 30.8% of the total wages (Nafziger, 1988, p. 99).

TABLE 3.1
INCOME RATIO OF TANZANIA, KENYA, UGANDA AND NIGERIA

Country	Income Disparity Ratio	
Tanzania	33:1 (1967); 15.1 (1974)	5:1 (1981)
Kenya	30:1 (1986)	N/A
Uganda	42:1 (1970s) *	N/A
Nigeria	17.6:1 (1975)	N/A

* This represents the income distribution of the military.
Source: Compiled from Nafziger (1988, pp. 92-101)

What is the ethnic composition of the 73.7% poor Liberians, 62.8% poor Nigerians, 52% poor Ghanaians and 51% poor Sierra Leoneans that Onimode (1988) identifies? Expressed differently, what ethnic groups constitute the 3.6%,

1.1%, 6.1% and 1.8% rich Liberians, Nigerians, Ghanaians and Sierra Leoneans respectively? Nafziger (1988) attempts to provide an answer to this question by analyzing the income distribution of selected African countries from an ethnic perspective. He concludes that in Uganda, Nigeria and Kenya, ethnic/regional disparity in income is glaring. According to him, this is evident in the Bagandan dominance in business, government and education in Uganda. It is also evident in the Nigerian government expenditure per capita which is skewed four to five times in favor of Lagos State and Kwara State; and the predominance of the Kikuyu in the bourgeois class of Kenya. Other sub-Saharan African countries may exhibit similar income inequality among the various ethnic groups.

What these studies on income inequality in sub-Saharan Africa fail to consider, however, is that this high-income inequality may be an apparent one existing only in the realm of official statistics. In the collectivistic culture of sub-Saharan African countries, income inequality is mitigated by informal redistribution. The commercial capitalist economy is unable to transform the basic elements of the traditional African social formation, which nourishes the collectivistic ethic.

The penetration of the capitalist mode of production into the pre-existing social formation of sub-Saharan Africa set into motion an interaction between non-capitalist and capitalist modes of production, a process which created a commercial capitalist rather than an industrial capitalist social formation (see de Silva, 1982; Febiri, 1991).

Commercial capitalism is a social formation dominated by petty economic activities such as petty commodity production and petty trading (Mamdani, 1975 and 1976; Mathews, 1987; Onimode, 1988; Ninsin, 1991). Petty commodity production comprises traditional agricultural activities, extraction of primary products (minerals, lumber, etc.) and what Ninsin (1991, p. 43) terms "precarious industrialization." The predominance of petty economic activities, the *raison d'etre* of commercial capitalism, in sub-Saharan Africa is evident in three main features of the African economy. First, small farmers produce over 90% of all export and food crops using traditional agricultural methods and implements (Onimode, 1988). Second, a large informal sector of "precarious industrialization" produces indigenous detergents/soaps, simple farm implements and weapons, cooking utensil, furniture, and bolts and nuts for the local market (Mathews, 1987; Ninsin, 1991). Third, the existence of a large number of petty traders (Febiri, 1991; Ninsin, 1991).

Traditional agriculture and precarious industrialization promoted by commercial capitalism through the informal economic sector are incapable of creating many viable or substantive employment avenues. Thus they push most of the active labor force into petty trading, the most dominant aspect and the least productive element of commercial capitalism. Petty trading has had these characteristics since colonial times. For example, alarmed by the widespread commodity peddling in the Gold Coast (now Ghana) in the 1850s, Cruickshank (1853, pp. 32-54) observed that:

> there was not a nook or corner of the land to which the enterprise of some sanguine trader had not led him. . . . Every village had its festoons of Manchester cotton and China silk, hung up upon the walls of the houses, or around the trees in the market place, to attract the attention and excite the cupidity of the villagers. . . . All that made the observer wonder whether there is any room for buyers among such a nation of peddlers. . .

A cursory observation in the cities and villages of contemporary sub-Saharan Africa reveals a similar, if not worse, picture. From Dakar, Abidjan, Accra, Lome and Lagos in West Africa, through Kinshasa and Bujumbura in Central Africa, to Addis Ababa, Nairobi and Dar es Salaam in East Africa, one encounters a horde of petty traders everywhere. They sell mostly imported commodities ranging from apples, rice and turkey tails through toiletries, handkerchiefs and belts to dog chains, car dusters and car parts. As Ninsin (1991, p. 36) rightly observes, this is a socio-economic malady. At best, it hides unemployment or underemployment and harbors political instability; at worst, it perpetuates economic underdevelopment by servicing an external economy and encouraging low value-added production.

To summarize, commercial capitalism performs management and mediation functions for petty commodity production, petty trading and an external economy. In the process it stunts the development of an industrial capital base which could create sustained economic development in sub-Saharan Africa. It is important to note, however, that although the socio-cultural, economic, political and ideological dynamics of the commercial capitalist social formation retard economic growth, they do not exacerbate income disparity among the social classes and between the genders. The predominance of commercial capitalism in sub-Saharan Africa, coupled with the existence of strong collectivistic culture, tend to impede the formation of a class system--in the Marxist or Western sense--in these societies. The structure and dynamics of the class system in sub-Saharan African societies are quite different from those in industrial capitalist countries. The existing Eurocentric class theory is therefore inadequate to explain income inequality in sub-Saharan Africa.

Certainly, classes as economic categories exist in sub-Saharan Africa with different income levels. For example, the commercial capitalist social formation has created socio-economic categories such as higher, middle, and lower income groups; as well as occupational categories like professionals, business people, the military and police, peasants, wage laborers, etc. The social dynamics that shape these economic categories are, however, different from those in industrial capitalist societies. Classes in sub-Saharan Africa are deeply incised by, or intricately interwoven with, kinship, ethnicity and gender. They, therefore, do not constitute uni-dimensional divisions.

In the structure of sub-Saharan African societies, nuclear families are linked to extended families; extended families to lineages; lineages to clans; and clans to ethnic groups. In these societies, it is rare to find an extended family, lineage, clan or ethnic group whose members are all relatively rich or highly educated constituting an upper or middle class. The strong influence of the collectivistic ethic compels the rich and educated to relate more closely to their poor or uneducated extended family and ethnic members than to their colleagues. They help these underprivileged members by giving them monetary and other material assistance, contributing to their education, housing them, employing them in their private ventures, or helping them to obtain employment in the formal sector of the economy. Also, there are many instances where rich and highly educated men marry poor women with little education. In fact, class does not seem to play any significant role in the organization of sub-Saharan African societies.

In effect, kinship, ethnicity and gender appear to be more central in peoples' consciousness and allegiances than is class. In such socio-cultural situations income inequality among the various income categories is lower than official statistics show. Unlike the case in the industrial capitalist countries, therefore, the gap between higher-income and lower-income earners in sub-Saharan African countries may not be as wide as official income statistics (gini coefficient of more than 0.5; see Nafziger, 1988) show. This is because of the redistribution of income in favor of the lower-income categories through the kinship system. In this light, for example, Ghana's gini coefficient of income inequality is likely to be even lower than the exceptionally low 0.3471 representing the inequality of household expenditures reported by Glewwe and Twum-Baah (1991, Table 13).

Despite this sharing of the income of the rich with the poor in sub-Saharan Africa, however, the lower-income groups, unlike their counterparts in the industrial capitalist society, may experience "absolute poverty." This is because the commercial capitalist nature of the sub-Saharan African social formation tends to inhibit the growth of the forces of production, thus rendering production levels and capacity abysmally low. In such an economy, equitable distribution does not eradicate poverty, but rather democratizes it.

Both commercial capitalist and industrial capitalist social formations create class, gender and ethnic/racial inequalities. However, the structure of these forms of social inequality, their relationships and the processes of their formation and reproduction in each of the social formations, may be very different in two respects. Thus, there are differences in the levels of development in their forces of production; differences in cultures, particularly the gender ideological forms and the centrality (or otherwise) of kinship and ethnicity in the organization of society.

In sum, commercial capitalism, like industrial capitalism, creates interconnections among class, gender and ethnic/racial inequalities, which make the privileged of society simultaneously upper and middle classes, male, and people of specific ethnic/racial backgrounds. However, the dynamics of culture may mitigate or accentuate the intensity of these forms of social inequality and poverty.

DEALING WITH POVERTY: AN ALTERNATIVE SUGGESTION

Economic development does not necessarily promote income equality or vice versa. However, in many societies there is a dynamic relationship between the two. On the one hand, income equality may create relative satisfaction and stability in society, and thus a conducive atmosphere for economic innovation. On the other hand, economic development may establish a strong resource base for the achievement of "relative equality," that is, a situation in which both the privileged and the majority of the underprivileged live above the poverty line. In commercial capitalist societies such as those of the sub-Saharan African countries, whose economies are caught in a low productivity syndrome, the great majority of the population lives in abject poverty. Such societies could be perceived as characterized by "absolute inequality," especially in the ethnic/racial arena. It is in this light that I agree with the view of Heilbroner (1989, p. 83) that:

> if we are to enjoy a greater material well-being, generally speaking, we must produce more. This is particularly true when we begin at the stage of scarcely-better-than-subsistence that characterized so much of Europe before the Industrial Revolution. For such a society to raise the standard of living of its masses, the first necessity is unquestionably higher production. Despite all the inequities of distribution that attended the society of serf and lord, capitalist and child-employee, underlying the meanness of the times was one overriding reality: the sheer inadequacy of output. There was simply not enough to go round, and if somewhat lopsided distributive arrangements might have lessened the moral dignity of the times, they would not have contributed much to a massive improvement in basic economic well-being. Even assuming that the wage of the city laborer and the income of the peasant could have been doubled had the rich been deprived of their share--and this is a wildly extravagant assumption--still, the prime characteristic of rural and urban life would have been its poverty

In societies like those found in sub-Saharan Africa where most people are absolutely poor, no amount of redistribution of income would eliminate poverty. These countries need to produce more, and income equity may play only a minor role in the process. As Rimmer (1992, p. 11) rightly noted in the case of Ghana, the scope of equity policies in Third World countries is always very limited. The reasons may include the following. (1). The poorest of the poor could not be easily identified because of the collectivistic ethic. (2) Even if they could be readily identified, they could not be reached with the crude policy instruments available, and (3) The blunt nature of the available instruments would rather increase income inequality and/or have disincentive effect on productivity. The relevant HF should be effectively applied in order to resolve these difficulties, and for increased and sustained productivity.

According to Kay (1975), in order to expand the forces of production or raise the level of labor productivity, commercial capital has to be subordinated to industrial capital within a country. How could this be achieved? According to him, in the capitalist European countries, this was attained through state intervention. For example, in Britain, the power of commercial capital was weakened by the parliamentary reforms of the 1830s, and its independence was finally smashed by the repeal of the Corn Laws in the 1840s (Kay, 1975). These success stories of Britain, Japan and the South-East Asian Newly Industrializing Countries in recent times show how crucial state intervention may be in preventing commercial capital from retaining its dominant position in contemporary sub-Saharan Africa (Dore, 1973; Deyo et al, 1987; Evans, 1987; Winckler and Greenhalgh, 1988). What these authors do not point out, however, is that the effectiveness of state intervention in the economy depends on the quality of the available HF.

In sub-Saharan Africa, so far, increasing state involvement in the economy has not resulted in the demise of commercial capitalism, nor has it created rapid economic growth. This is largely because of the weak nature of the state resulting from sub-Saharan Africa's dismal HF situation. The sub-Saharan African countries operate "soft" or "weak" states (Myrdal, 1970, p. 208; Price, 1984, p. 188). These scholars attribute this weakness to the excessive permeation of the state by personal, kinship and ethnic interests. What they fail to realize, however, is that such permeation creates problem for Africa's development mainly because there is a virtual lack of human qualities such as accountability, responsibility, honesty and loyalty to the state.

The processes of modern state formation in sub-Saharan Africa have failed to foster the development of the appropriate HF characteristics. In particular, the processes have failed to extend the traditional kin/ethnic loyalty to the modern state. Sub-Saharan African nationals are, therefore, scarcely committed to promoting the interest of the larger society. There are constant struggles among factions of the various elite groups--professionals, business people, intellectuals, military and police officers--to capture the state apparatus. Their basic objective is to advance their private economic interests and the interests of their kin groups and ethnic entities rather than integrating the various social groups to harness available resources for national socio-economic development. This unpatriotic agenda of sub-Saharan African elite largely contributes to the chronic political instability, which apart from exacerbating the weakness of sub-Saharan African states, diminishes the prospects of economic development.

In effect, the main weakness of contemporary states is not that they are plagued by kinship and ethnic inequalities, but rather that they lack the relevant HF. No matter how deeply the state is incised by kinship, ethnicity/race, gender and class, if the state functionaries possess the human qualities of responsibility, accountability, integrity, patriotism, and such, they are likely to build a strong state capable of collaborating with the private sector to create sustained economic development.

Sub-Saharan African countries may eliminate all cleavages in their states by creating absolute equality among the various kin groups, ethnic/racial entities, gender and classes. But if they neglect the development of the relevant HF they are not likely to succeed in uprooting underdevelopment. Irresponsible, unaccountable, dishonest and unpatriotic Africans will always embezzle state funds, misuse state property, steal state money and deposit it in their foreign accounts, receive and give bribes, use official work time to do their personal business, stage *coups d' etat*, and abuse the traditional cultural welfare system. It is in this regard that African governments' objective to deal with the problem of poverty via equality is futile.

The real solution to sub-Saharan Africa's development puzzle is the promotion of the relevant HF. African governments should therefore marshal all available resources to provide their populace with the fundamental human qualities of responsibility, accountability, integrity, patriotism, commitment, self-discipline, and the like. With these qualities, sub-Saharan African countries would be able to create strong states and the right labor force to dismantle commercial capitalism, a major immediate cause of absolute poverty. Africa can cultivate the relevant HF through childhood socialization in the family, informal education in local communities, the formal school system, seminars and the mass media. These educational processes must be reinforced by concrete incentives such as free travel to places where the HF is actively at work, cash and material prizes, and community and national recognition of people who demonstrate the necessary HF in their every day lives. The mass media should take care of the publicity aspect of this HF promotion.

CONCLUSION

Absolute poverty is the real consequence of underdevelopment, and this is not necessarily created by income inequality. In the case of sub-Saharan Africa, underdevelopment is directly related to the persistence of commercial capitalism. The low productivity syndrome of commercial capitalism can only be transformed by systematic cooperation between government and industry. To be successful in this direction, the state must be operated by leaders and supported by a people with the vital human qualities such as integrity, responsibility, accountability, sacrifice, commitment and patriotism. Reduction or eradication of income inequality may not play any significant role in this process. This is mainly because in the context of contemporary sub-Saharan African societies, income inequality is rendered insignificant by the informal redistribution of income made possible by the collectivistic ethic. Thus the solution to the weakness of sub-Saharan African states and the low productivity syndrome of commercial capitalism, which are major roots of poverty and underdevelopment, lies more in the cultivation of relevant HF than the creation of equality.

NOTES

1. By collectivistic ethic I mean the "normative system of interpersonal relations based upon the principle of corporatism and the rule of mutual obligation" (Adu-Febiri, 1995, p. 5). In sub-Saharan African societies the extended family and the ethnic entity constitute the pivot around which this cultural welfare system revolves.

2. Commercial capitalism, strictly speaking, is an economic system prevalent in contemporary developing countries. It concentrates on traditional agriculture, extraction of raw materials such as minerals and timber, substandard industrialization and petty trading.

REFERENCES

Adedeji, A. 1985. "The Monrovia Strategy and the Lagos Plan of Action: Five Years After." In Adedeji and T. M. Shaw, eds. *Economic Crisis in Africa: African Perspectives on Development Problems and Potentials.* Boulder: Lynne Rienner Publishers Inc.

Adjibolosoo, S.1995. *The Human Factor in Developing Africa*. Westport, CT.: Praeger.

Adu-Febiri, F. 1994. "Tourism and Ghana's Development Process: Problems of and Prospects for Creating a Viable 'Post-Industrial' Service Industry in a Non-Industrial Society." Unpublished Ph. D. Dissertation. Department of Anthropology and Sociology, The University of British Columbia, Vancouver, Canada.

Adu-Febiri, F. 1995. "Is Africa's Development a Basket Case?" *Review of Human Factor Studies*, 1 (1): 45-60.

Chirot, D. 1986. *Social Change in the Modern Era.* Toronto: Harcort Brace Jovanovich Canada.

de Silva, S. B. D. 1982. *The Political Economy of Underdevelopment*. London: Routledge and Kegan Paul.

Cruickshank, B. 1853. *Eighteen Years on the Gold Coast of Africa.* London: Hurst and Blackett.

Deyo, F. C. ed. 1987. *The Political Economy of the New Asian Industrialism.* Ithaca: Cornell University Press.

Dore, R. P. 1973. "The Late Development Effect." In Hans-Dieter, ed. *Modernization of South East Asia.* London: Oxford University Press.

Evans, P. B. 1987. "Class, State and Dependence in East Asia: Lessons for

Latin America." In F. C. Deyo, ed. *The Political Economy of the New Asian Industrialism*. Ithaca: Cornell University Press.

Febiri, F. A. 1991. "Marxism, Social Class, Ethnic and Gender Inequalities in Contemporary African Societies." *The African Review*, 18 (1 & 2): 39-56.

Glewwe, P. and Twum-Baah, K. A. 1991. *The Distribution of Welfare in Ghana 1987-88*. Washington, D.C.: World Bank, Living Standards Measurement Study Working Paper No. 75.

Heilbroner, R. L. 1989. *The Making of Economic Society*. Englewood Cliffs, NJ.: Prentice Hall.

Kay, G. B.1975. *Development and Underdevelopment: Marxist Analysis*. New York: The Macmillan Press Ltd.

Laxer, J. 1987. *Decline of the Superpowers*. Toronto: Lorimer.

Mamdani, M. 1975. "Class Struggles in Uganda." *Review of African Political Economy*, 4: 26-61.

Mamdani, M. 1976. *Politics and Class Formation in Uganda*. New York: Monthly Review Press.

Mathews, R. 1987. "The Development of Local Machinery Industry in Kenya." *The Journal of Modern African Studies*, 25 (1): 67-93.

Matlon, P. 1981. "The Structure of Production and Rural Incomes in Northern Nigeria." In H. Bienen and V. P. Diejomaoh, eds. *The Political Economy of Income Distribution in Nigeria*. New York: Holmes and Meier.

Mizruchi, M. S. and Schwartz, M. eds. 1987. *Intercorporate Relations: The Structural Analysis of Business*. Cambridge, MA.: Cambridge University Press.

Myrdal, G. 1970. *The Challenge of World Poverty: A World Anti-Poverty Program in Outline*. New York: Vintage Books.

Nafziger, W. E. 1988. *Inequality in Africa: Political Elites, Proletariat, Peasants and the Poor*. Cambridge: Cambridge University Press.

Ninsin, K. A. 1991. *The Informal Sector in Ghana's Political Economy*. Accra: Freedom Publications.

Onimode, B. 1988. *A Political Economy of the Crisis*. New York: Zed Books Ltd.

Price, R. M. 1984. "Neo-colonialism and Ghana's Economic Decline: Critical Assessment." *Canadian Journal of African Studies*, 8 (1): 163-193.

Rimmer, D. 1992. *Staying Poor: Ghana's Political Economy 1950-1990*. Oxford: Pergamo Press.

Shields, N. 1980. *Women in the Urban Labor Markets of Africa: The Case of Tanzania*. World Bank Staff Working Paper, No. 380. Washington, D.C.: The World Bank.

Sundar, P. (Not Dated). "Credit and Finance Needs of Women Workers." Mimeo. United Nations Commission for Africa, Research Series.

United Nations. 1978. *Effective Mobilization of Women in Development*. New York: Secretary General of United Nations.

Winckler, E.A. and Greenhalgh, S. M. 1988. *Contending Approaches to the Political Economy of Taiwan*. New York: M. E. Sharpe, Inc.

4

THE FAILURE OF SOCIALIST EXPERIMENTS IN AFRICA: MISCONCEPTIONS, MYTHS AND REALITIES

Francis Adu-Febiri
Department of Social Sciences
Camosun College

INTRODUCTION

African socialist experiments are premised on the notion that traditional African societies were participatory, egalitarian and collectivist. Hence the attractiveness of Marxist-Leninist programs to these regimes which seek to achieve rapid economic development and social equality through localized collectivization, state enterprises and human capital acquisition. So far all the socialist experiments of Africa have failed to create viable economies, social equality and grassroots participatory democracies. This chapter argues, that socialist experiments in Africa have failed to achieve their claimed objectives not necessarily because of their failure to recognize that African traditional societies were essentially capitalistic nor due to their concentration on state entrepreneurship. Instead, they have failed because they fail to recognize and promote the human factor (HF) (Adjibolosoo, 1994).

Many African socialists buy the myth that the acquisition of human capital and adoption of local collectivization and state entrepreneurship are enough to create economic development and social equity. They fail to realize that (1) local collectivization and statism do not necessary produce development and (2) human capital, a small component of the HF, is a necessary but insufficient condition for development (Adjibolosoo, 1995b). Skills acquisition (human capital), collectivization and state activism in the economy unaccompanied by the cultivation of human qualities such as discipline, responsibility, accountability, hard work, loyalty to the larger society, and integrity are useless to the development process.

Although some African socialists such as Julius Nyerere, Kenneth Kaunda and Tom Mboya realize the importance of some of these HF elements in traditional African societies and their potential to facilitate the development of contemporary Africa, they fail to go beyond rhetoric. This chapter seeks to suggest to African intellectuals, politicians and planners to concentrate their efforts on reactivating the HF inherent in traditional African societies instead of the haggling over the adoption of a socialist or capitalist strategies of development. In fact, the human qualities the HF represents constitute the roots of all successful capitalist, socialist and newly industrializing societies.

This chapter addresses the above issues in three sections. The first section discusses the anatomy of African socialist experiments, while section two attempts to demonstrate that the available criticisms of African socialism are misplaced. The third and final section highlights the lack of appropriate HF as the real cause of the failure of the African socialist experiments to generate development (Adjibolosoo, 1994).

ANATOMY OF AFRICAN SOCIALIST EXPERIMENTS

Out of the 54 African countries, as many as 26 have claimed to follow socialist development strategy at one time or another (see Onimode, 1988, p. 245). There are two main reasons for this socialist experimentation in Africa. First, until recently the rapid technological and economic development of the former Soviet Union provided a model for newly independent Africa countries desirous of achieving rapid socio-economic development. Second, many African nationalist leaders were under the impression that the organization of production and consumption in traditional African societies were collectivist, and that Africa already had a strong basis for socialist-style development (Senghor, 1961; Dia, 1961; Nyerere, 1962; Mboya, 1963; Nkrumah, 1963). This latter notion, symbolized by "African Socialism," was quite central to the ideologies of first generation modern African nationalist leaders such as Kwame Nkrumah of Ghana, Leopold Senghor and Mamadou Dia of Senegal, Sekou Toure of Guinea, Nimeiry of Sudan, Julius Nyerere of Tanzania, Kenneth Kaunda of Zambia, and Tom Mboya of Kenya.

These African politicians and other African socialist advocates in other parts of the continent usually cite the pre-colonial communal African social formation and egalitarian distribution of wealth to support their proposition for becoming socialist. The articulated view of Julius Nyerere, the former president of Tanzania, sums it up in the following words:

> There was an innate feeling of brotherhood within the community, sustained by the principle of love among men (and women), and the

> right to work and to share equally the fruits of labor. These were the principles, which kept the community (indeed the whole society) together, and they must be safeguarded if the community is not to destroy itself. People appointed leaders to power democratically on the principle that all were equal and there were built-in ways within the community for restraining their leaders from abusing their powers. There was a moral distaste for private ownership of property, and although such private ownership did exist in a minor way, the dispossessed had expectations of sharing it on the principle of brotherhood (cited by Babu, 1981, pp. 55-56).

In effect, what Nyerere (1962, p. 246) is saying is that "we, in Africa, have no more need of being 'converted' to socialism than we have of being 'taught' democracy. Both are rooted in our own past--in the traditional society which produced us." Based upon these notions of traditional African societies and the apparent success of the Eastern countries, the African socialist states nationalized many of the utility services and private businesses. In addition, they created a number of state enterprises. Nkrumah (1963, p. 1) emphasizes that "the community through its government must play a major role in the economy." Tom Mboya (1964, p. 253) echoes this view when he asserts that "socialism stands for. . . . the state regulation of economic life, state control of vital means of production and distribution." As Friedland and Rosberg (1964, p. 5) aptly observed, "in stressing the role of government in 'planning,' in providing capital, and in guiding the economy, not much encouragement has been given to the growth of a class of African entrepreneurs."

It is important to note that in Africa, it is not only professed socialist governments, which promote state enterprises; a number of regimes, which claim to be capitalist also, create them. While African socialists promote state entrepreneurship mainly out of sheer socialist fanaticism, the non-socialists do so mainly because of their perception that the African private sector lacks the capital and skills required for economic enterprises. A typical representation of state enterprise economy was Nkrumah's Ghana from 1961 to 1966.

Under the Convention People's Party (CPP) of Kwame Nkrumah, the Ghanaian state not only made policies that determined the framework within which economic activities in the country were organized, but it also participated directly in the economy as an entrepreneur. The state owned and operated cocoa, coffee, palm, cotton, tobacco and food crop plantations. It had majority shares in many mining and timber ventures. In addition the state was the sole owner and a major participant in many industrial and business enterprises.

The year 1961 marked the beginning of unprecedented increase in the state's direct active participation in the Ghanaian economy. When Arthur Lewis' economic development model for Ghana failed to attract any substantial foreign financial assistance, President Nkrumah turned to the East, particularly the Soviet Union, and declared Ghana a socialist state with the attainment of command economy as its goal (Fitch and Oppenheimer, 1966, p. 83). The state became Ghana's main economic controller and entrepreneur. Attempts to dismantle this state entrepreneurship since 1967 have virtually failed.[1] Ghana also created elaborate education and training programs to help its citizens acquire the necessary human capital or skills to use state entrepreneurship successfully for sustained economic development. The CPP government put into place a policy of universal fee-free elementary education in the 1960s. It also established a number of secondary schools, technical institutes, vocational programs, agricultural research institutions, teacher training colleges, two additional universities and overseas (particularly Soviet and East European) scholarship schemes to facilitate skills acquisition. As a result of these programs and projects, Ghana produced a large number of skilled teachers, agricultural workers, technicians, engineers, doctors, artisans, soldiers, police personnel and administrators. The irony is that neither massive state enterprises nor the availability of a skilled labor force could help Ghana transform its development dreams into reality.

Toure's Guinea, Traore's Mali, Boumediene's/Chedli's Algeria, Mengistu's Ethiopia, Nimiery's Sudan, Kaunda's Zambia, Machel's/Chissano's Mozambique, Neto's Angola, Mugabe's Zimbabwe, to mention only a few, all adopted state entrepreneurship and human capital acquisition programs similar to Ghana's, especially with regard to active state participation in the economy. For example, according to Sklar (1975, p. 193), fifteen years after Zambia's independence, "The government, through 113 parastatals grouped under one enormous octopus-like holding company known as *Zimco*, controlled over 80 percent of all economic activity." It must be noted, in addition, that "right from the time of independence, the notion prevailed [in Zambia] that the economy had to be organized under the control of large parastatals and that the central government was the prime mover of change." (Ottaway, 1986, p. 43).

In addition, Guinea nationalized all French companies in the modern sector of the economy right after independence, creating state monopolies in banking, insurance, exports, imports and transportation, and establishing state farms (Ottaway, 1986, pp. 54 and 59). Although Nyerere's Tanzania emphasized grassroots collectivization in the form of villagization or *ujamaa* programs, it nevertheless operated on statist principles akin to centrally planned economies. As Ottaway (1986, p. 46) stated correctly, "the ideology of *ujamaa* translated into a series of policies: nationalization of banks and major industries to strengthen the government's control over the economy lack of encouragement of private enterprise. . . ." Expectedly, like Ghana, all these other countries have failed to transform their underdeveloped economies and societies.

The critical questions then are what prevents African socialism from creating sustained development, and what will make African societies develop? These questions are addressed in the following sections of the chapter.

CONVENTIONAL CRITIQUES OF AFRICAN SOCIALIST EXPERIMENTS

Since their political independence in the late 1950s and later years, many African countries have pursued socialism but have apparently been unsuccessful in using it as a politico-economic strategy for mobilizing resources for rapid and sustained socio-economic development. Attempts to explain this failure of socialist experiments in Africa have come from two main camps. These are the African Marxists, conservatives and/or liberals.

African Marxists like Babu (1981) and Onimode (1988) postulate that the way to go is socialist, but African socialism has failed to achieve its objectives due to a number of reasons. These reasons, according to African Marxists, include African socialists' assumption of classless African societies, the mixing of state and private ownership and enterprises, and African socialism's concentration on abstract platitudes and socialist rhetoric. The simultaneous pursuit of state and private enterprises and ownership of property is, however, projected as the most significant reason for the failure. The conservatives and liberals on their part believe that African socialism is unable to provide solutions to Africa's development crisis because of its focus on collectivization and state enterprises (see Ahiakpor, 1987). They perceive these development strategies as being at variance with the capitalistic fabric of traditional African societies (see Kitching, 1982).

The State and Private Enterprises Mix

Babu (1981) argues that African socialist experiments have failed mainly because they place their resources in the area of socialist rhetoric rather than practice. The interpretation is that instead of the state abolishing all private entrepreneurship and ownership, it unfortunately allows them to coexist with state enterprises and public ownership. Onimode (1988) also alludes to African socialist states' failure to pursue the strategy of command economy to its logical conclusion. He emphasizes that the mixture of state and private economic activities and ownership structures frustrates the attainment of economic development in socialist Africa. Ninsin (1991) seems to express similar views in his critique of Ghana's informal sector. According to him, the African private sector is mainly the informal sector which is "crowded by people forced by low income, unemployment, and by desperate poverty to engage in any kind of income-generating activity for subsistence" (Ninsin, 1991, p. 2). His main argument is that the retention of the informal sector is a capitalist ploy to perpetuate underdevelopment in developing countries. Hence his statement:

> I dispute claims by policy-makers, advisers, and consultants that the informal sector is dynamic and (especially, its manufacturing sector) is capable of generating infinite employment and reasonable levels of income towards the amelioration of unemployment and poverty in developing countries that are caught in the quagmire of development crisis (Ninsin, 1991, p. ix).

This chapter disputes the state-private sector mixture argument on two grounds. (1) The viable economies of traditional African societies combined state and private ownership of property and organization of economic activities. (2) Japan, South Korea, Singapore, Hong Kong, Taiwan, Malaysia and lately China operate a mixture of state and private entrepreneurship, yet they currently experience the fastest economic growth rates in the world. The success stories of these countries demonstrate the viability of developing co-existing state and private entrepreneurship. The African ownership and production situations are discussed below.

Traditional African socio-economic formations were a comprehensive mixture of private and public enterprises. There was the often-cited communal ownership of the basic means of production, land. Provision of capital, mobilization of labor, and planning and organization of production were done by private entrepreneurs, the community and the ethnic state. For example, in many traditional African societies there were both private and public farms and artisanal enterprises. Mining and construction of wells, roads and toilets were mainly communally organized. A similar situation prevailed in the area of property ownership. While precious minerals above a certain value/volume and big game, for example, were state-owned or owned by the ruling elite in the case of stateless societies in trust for the people, a reasonable level of private ownership of property existed. For example, private individuals and families owned houses, farms, production tools, weapons, jewelry, foundries, manufacturing and trading businesses.

In contradistinction to this traditional African organization of production, economic policies of many contemporary African socialist and capitalist experiments tend to concentrate on public sector development. In fact, the African problem is that governments make little or no conscious effort to create any dynamic indigenous entrepreneurial class. Contemporary indigenous African entrepreneurship has been largely proto-entrepreneurship developed by default mostly in the neglected informal sector of the economy. This kind of African entrepreneurship, apart from its crude and precarious nature, does not seem to possess the necessary human qualities of cooperation, trust, loyalty to the larger society, integrity, honesty, discipline and responsibility. For example, the lack of cooperative spirit among African entrepreneurs results in the proliferation of non-viable/non-sustainable economic ventures in the private sector. African entrepreneurs do not seem to trust each other enough to pull their capital and organizational resources together to create viable, dynamic businesses.[2]

Traditional African Capitalistic Social Organization

The conservative and/or liberal critics attribute the failure of African socialism to generate economic development and social equity to (1) African socialists' misconception of African traditional societies and (2) the state's direct, active participation in the economy. Contrary to the notion of African socialists, socialism as proposed by Marxists and practiced by the former Soviet Union and Eastern European countries is incompatible with the principles of socio-economic organization of traditional African societies.

The conservative and/or liberal critics may be right in pointing out that the ownership of the means of production, and the organization of production and distribution in pre-colonial, colonial and post-colonial African societies do not uphold the principles of socialism. However, like the peddlers of the ideology of African socialism, they also fail to recognize a crucial factor underlying the sustainability of traditional African societies and economies, and for that matter, all societies that have attained sustained development. In fact, what made traditional African societies viable and self-sustaining was neither the existence of proto-socialistic social and economic structures nor capitalist practices. Rather, it was the creative development and application of the appropriate human qualities such as honesty, responsibility, egalitarianism, discipline, loyalty to the larger society/state, respect for the law, mutual trust, dutifulness and hard work. These are essential human, universal and time-honored qualities for sustained development.

Another factor conservative and/or liberal critics project as a cause of the failure of African socialism to develop Africa is the command economy strategy. Ahiakpor (1987) is a strong proponent of this view. Focusing on Ghana, he argues that the main reason why Ghana has failed to attain economic development is because of its statist ideology.

It is a fact that the exclusive adherence to socialist ideology explains why African socialists want to create command or centrally planned economies. However, it is essential to note that state entrepreneurship encouraged by African socialists is not a bad thing in and of itself. The promotion of some level of public sector economic activities in Japan and the newly industrializing countries of Asia has not impeded their development. A serious shortcoming of the African socialist experiments, however, is that state entrepreneurship operates at the expense of reactivating the values of cooperation, hard work, discipline, mutual trust, integrity, honesty and loyalty to the state or larger society. These were the qualities, which sustained African civilizations before foreign intervention; these are the qualities that undergird the existing advanced capitalist, successful socialist (China) and the newly industrializing countries of Asia.

UNDERSTANDING THE FAILURE OF AFRICAN SOCIALISM TO GENERATE DEVELOPMENT

The main point stressed in this chapter is that the failure of African socialist experiments to create viable economies is attributable more to the lack of the appropriate HF than the factors the Marxist and conservative and/or liberal critics stress (See details in Adjibolosoo, 1994 and 1995b). In other words, African socialist experiments have been unable to eliminate underdevelopment and absolute inequality from contemporary African societies where they operate because they have not cultivated in their citizens the fundamental ingredients of development, the HF.

Poor HF pervades all sectors of contemporary African societies. Many African countries have produced a reasonable number of skilled and knowledgeable personnel (human capital) in many fields of human endeavor. However, the great majority of these personnel have been part of the "brain drain" statistics. The few who remain in Africa do not work hard. Moreover, they indulge in embezzlement of state funds, pilfering of state resources, disrespect for state property, mismanagement of state institutions and enterprises, dubious businesses, and conniving and condoning with unscrupulous foreign investors to cheat the state. The private also sector suffers from similar HF decay problems (see Adu-Febiri, 1995).

The underlying factor for all these behavior patterns of some Africans is their lack of the right HF characteristics, in particular strong loyalty to the larger society/modern state (Adu-Febiri, 1995). Mboya (1964, p. 254) in discussing the objectives of the East African Common Market, rightly submitted (but only in passing) that "without basic *loyalty* to Kenya and East Africa, the achievement of these objectives can be an impossible proposition." (emphasis supplied). In fact, it seems Africans from all walks of life suffer from a disloyalty-to-state syndrome. On the whole, African socialist experiments and their critics fail to address this and other crucial HF problems. This is mainly because of their preoccupation with the creation of various "ISMS" in Africa: African socialism (Nkrumah's consciencism, Senghor's Negritude, Kaunda's Humanism, Nyerere's Ujamaa); Arab socialism; scientific socialism; communism; communalism; Marxism-Leninism; and capitalism. Yet the development or reactivation of the right HF is crucial if Africa is to create a dynamic force powerful enough to attain a sustained socio-economic transformation.

CONCLUSION

The success of productive ventures in any socio-economic system, be it socialist, communist, capitalist, or other, depends largely on the caliber of people operating it. Socio-economic systems in and of themselves have no magic wand for attaining sustained development. The secret behind development is people. People who have strong loyalty to their societies/state and a sense of urgency and commitment and are also confident in their capabilities and abilities. People who are disciplined, responsible, accountable and scrupulous; and people who have enough trust in each other to engage in cooperative development efforts.

Many traditional African societies could boast of such human qualities. Unfortunately, the processes of colonialism and neocolonialism have eroded or rendered dormant these crucial human ingredients of development. No wonder public institutions and state enterprises, as well as private businesses in contemporary Africa, are replete with mismanagement, pilfering, embezzlement, fraud, corruption and underproduction. Class struggles and socialist revolutions will not resolve these issues, contrary to what Onimode and similar other African intellectuals and politicians believe. Neither will structural adjustment programs as promoted by the IMF/World Bank and their neo-classical economic advisors. The existing informal sector could not necessarily do the trick. The flow of foreign capital, expertise and development aid cannot cope with Africa's development crisis either. Africa needs to take its HF decay problems seriously, for they are the real sources of the development crises of the continent. The good news is that contemporary African societies can create and sustain the appropriate HF through society-wide HF education backed by concrete rewards to individuals who exhibit the appropriate HF characteristics in their private and public lives.

NOTES

1. Killick (1978) and Ahiakpor (1987) highlight this continuity. According to Killick (1978, p. 311), despite the National Liberation Council (NLC) and the Progress Party (PP) governments' declaration to encourage and give substantive support to private ventures these governments failed to reduce state participation in the Ghanaian economy.

The NLC, upon its ascension to political power in February 1966, declared its intention to reduce drastically state involvement in industry and agriculture "by closing down or selling off various state enterprises and converting others into joint state/private concerns" (Killick, 1978, p. 313). Yet by the time it was handing over the reigns of government to the Progress Party in September 1969, only four small enterprises out of the twenty state manufacturing and services enterprises earmarked for privatization were successfully divestitured. The only exceptions were the additional four that converted to joint state/private ventures (Killick, 1978, p. 313). It is essential to note here that the NLC government even created two more state enterprises--Cotton Development Board and Export Promotion Company (Annual Report of the Auditor-General, 1969).

The PP government did not fare any better in its attempt to divestiture state enterprises. By the time it was overthrown by the military in January 1972, it had added three more new state ventures--Task Force for Food Distribution, Grains Development Board, Bast Fibers Development Board--to the list of state-owned enterprises (Annual Report of the Auditor-General, 1971).

In effect, by the end of 1971, 43 out of the 53 state economic ventures created by the CPP socialist government of Nkrumah remained, and five new ones had been added (Killick, 1978, p. 313). It is therefore less surprising that the state's total share in manufacturing gross output had not experienced any significant reduction by 1970--19.5% in 1966 versus 15.6% in 1970. Even this reduction was offset by the rise in the share of joint state/private foreign enterprises (Killick, 1978, p. 313).

The situation has not changed very much since 1970. There was even more emphasis on state-owned enterprises from 1972 to 1978 under Acheampong's military junta--NRC/SMC I (Hutchful, 1979, p. 54; Price, 1984, p. 188). According to Price (1984, p. 188), "although the rapid expansion of the state into the economy was slowed during the 1966-1972 period, after the military coup of 1972 the Ghanaian state once again rapidly expanded into the sphere of the economy." Under the Rawlings' Armed Forces Revolutionary Council (AFRC) in 1979, the roster of Ghana's state-owned enterprises witnessed a further extension (Gyimah-Boadi, 1991, p. 195). The Provisional Defense Council (PNDC) government's attempt to divestiture state enterprises to reduce the state's direct involvement in economic activities as demanded by the IMF and the World Bank since 1983, has not achieved any appreciable success due to "strong forces of a political, institutional, and administrative nature prevalent in the environment" (Gyimah-Boadi, 1991, p. 206). In short, therefore, there has been very little reduction, if any, in the Ghanaian state's active participation in the economy. The greater majority of these nationalized/state enterprises failed to be viable but huge sums of public money continued to be poured into them.

2. For detailed discussion of the Human Factor and African entrepreneurship, see Adu-Febiri (1996).

REFERENCES

Adjibolosoo, S. 1994. "The Human Factor and the Failure of Economic Development Policies in Africa." In F. Ezeala-Harrison and S. Adjibolosoo, eds. *Perspectives on Economic Development in Africa.* Westport, CT: Praeger.

Adjibolosoo, S. ed. 1995a. *The Significance of the Human Factor in African Economic Development.* Westport, CT: Praeger.

Adjibolosoo, S. 1995b. *The Human Factor in Developing Africa.* Westport, CT: Praeger.

Adu-Febiri, F. 1996. "Entrepreneurship Development for Industrial Progress in Africa." In S. Adjibolosoo, ed. *Human Factor Engineering and the Political Economy of African Development.* Westport, CT: Praeger.

Adu-Febiri, F. 1995. "Culture as the Epitome of Human Factor in Development: The Case of Ghana's Collectivistic Ethic," In S. Adjibolosoo, ed. *The Significance of the Human Factor in African Economic Development.* Westport, CT.: Praeger.

Ahiakpor, J. C.W. 1987. "The Role of Statist Ideology in African Development Crisis: The case of Ghana", A Paper Presented at the Canadian Association of African Studies Conference, University of Alberta, Edmonton: May 7-9, 1987.

Babu, M. A. 1981. *African Socialism or Socialist Africa*? London: Zed Press.

Dia, Mamadou. 1961. "African Socialism." *Socialist International Information,* XI (18): 276-277.

Fitch, B. and Oppenheimer, M. 1966. *Ghana: End of an Illusion.* New York: Monthly Review Press.

Friedland, W.H. and Rosberg, C. G. eds. 1964. *African Socialism.* Stanford: Stanford University Press.

Government of Ghana. 1962. *First Seven Year Development Plan.* Accra: Office of the Planning Commission (pp. 1-4).

Gyimah-Boadi, E. 1991: "State Enterprise Divestiture: Recent Ghanaian Experiences." In D. Rothchild, ed. *Ghana: Political Economy of Recovery.* Boulder: Lynne Rienner Publishers.

Hutchful, E. 1979. "A Tale of Two Regimes: Imperialism, the Military and Class in Ghana." *Review of African Political Economy,* 14: 50-63.

Killick, T. 1978. *Development Economics in Action: A Study of Economic Policies in Ghana.* New York: St. Martin's Press.

Kitching, G. 1982. *Development and Underdevelopment in Historical Perspective.* Milton Keynes: Open University Press.

Mboya, Tom. 1963. "African Socialism", *Transition,* Vol. VIII, March 1963. Reprinted in W. H. Friedland and C. G. Rosberg, eds. *African Socialism.* Stanford: Stanford University Press (pp. 250-258).

Nkrumah, K. 1963. "Some Aspects of Socialism in Africa." *Pan Africa:* Nairobi, April 19, 1963 (pp. 1-14).

Ninsin, K. A. 1991. *The Informal Sector in Ghana's Political Economy.* Accra: Freedom Publication.

Nyerere, J. K. 1962. "Ujamaa: The Basis of African Socialism." An address by The President of Tanganyika to a conference on African Socialism held at Kivokoni College in Dar es Salaam (Reprinted in W. H. Friedland and C. G. Rosberg, eds.1964. *African Socialism.* Stanford: Stanford University Press (pp. 238-247).

Onimode, B.1988. *A Political Economy of the African Crisis.* London: Zed Books Ltd. (pp. 244-277).

Ottaway, M. D. 1986. *Afrocommunism.* New York: Africana Publishing Company.

Price, R. M. 1984. "Neo-colonialism and Ghana's Economic Decline: Critical Assessment." *Canadian Journal of African Studies*, 8 (1): 163-193.

Senghor, L. 1961. "African-Style Socialism." *West Africa*, November 11: 1235-1237.

Sklar, R. 1975. *Corporate Power in an African State.* Berkeley: University of California Press.

PART III

GENDER, ENVIRONMENT AND RURAL DEVELOPMENT

5

ENVIRONMENT AND GENDER-BASED DEVELOPMENT STRATEGIES: NEW DEVELOPMENT DIRECTIONS FOR AFRICA OR ANOTHER SET OF FALSE STARTS?

Benjamin Ofori-Amoah
Department of Geography & Geology
University of Wisconsin-Stevens Point

INTRODUCTION

Over the past decade or so, environment and gender issues have produced a band-wagon effect among those involved in development thinking and research. Not only has the number of governmental and non-governmental agencies and research funds for these issues increased but also, as a result, the number of researchers and "experts" on these two issues has gone up considerably (World Bank, 1989; Miller, 1995). Among the several outcomes of this surge in interest has been the reinterpretation of long-standing economic development problems in environment and gender terms. Thus, in Africa problems of declining agricultural production, the food crisis, stagnant industrial production, problems of the structural adjustment programs, rural-urban differences, AIDS, and general economic, social, and political decline have all been somehow linked directly or indirectly to gender relations and environmental issues (Kamarck, 1976; Lofchie and Commins, 1984; Timberlake, 1986; McPherson, 1984; Henn 1983; O'Barr, 1975; Guyer, 1981; World Bank, 1989).

Scholars in these areas and their supporting agencies seem to agree about the need to address these issues in Third World development, and the tendency for dissenters to be ridiculed and labeled as sexist, anti-environment, or ignorant has overshadowed questions of validity regarding these two strategies. However, as I have argued, new development concepts, theories, or strategies can become counterproductive when used indiscriminately (Ofori-Amoah, 1995a, pp. 15-24). In particular, they can lure nations to sidestep development problems that really need to be accorded topmost priority and instead focus on ones that are of less priority, a situation Rene Dumont (1969) has referred to as a false start. Given Africa's historical record, with new development directions, it is important to examine these two development strategies to see whether they hold the future to Africa's economic development.

This chapter, therefore, is written neither from a sexist nor an anti-environment perspective. Rather it is written from a deep concern I have about a malady that has pervasively plagued economic development practice in Africa, namely the indiscriminate adoptions of new pathways to development, which in turn have produced a series of false starts in economic development on the continent (Rene Dumont, 1969; Ofori-Amoah, 1995a, pp. 15-24). In particular, the chapter questions the portrayal of environment and gender-based development strategies as new development directions for Africa. It argues that both environment and gender-based development strategies rest on false premises and have doubtful applicability to African countries. This, in turn, stems from the way the two strategies evolved and how they are being applied to Africa. As a result, the two strategies have a higher potential for constituting another set of false starts instead of being new development directions.

The chapter is divided into four sections. In the first section, I outline a conceptual framework that shows how new development directions can become economic development false start. In the next two sections, I present in detail the main features of the environment and gender-based development strategies and examine how these two strategies constitute the commencement of another set of false starts in Africa. Finally, I give some concluding thoughts about what really needs to be addressed.

NEW DEVELOPMENT DIRECTIONS AND THE PROBLEM OF FALSE START

Economic development implies positive changes in the living conditions of people, and oftentimes positive changes cannot occur without new development directions. By new development directions, I mean new ideas, concepts, prescriptions, and strategies for achieving economic development. Throughout the history of development, new directions have provided significant breakthroughs for general economic and social advancement. New development directions become necessary when existing pathways to development have reached their ends and have nothing more to offer. They also become necessary when existing directions are just not working. The tendency to seek for new avenues of development is thus part of human nature.

However, not all new development directions will lead to the "promised land" of economic development. In particular, new development directions can become economic development false starts because of their failure to articulate, for the recipient society, the real problems that need to be dealt with at a given point in time. Such a situation can arise for three reasons. First, new development directions can become false starts if they are based on false premises. Second, new development directions can become false starts if they have doubtful feasibility or applicability. Third, new development directions can become false starts if they result from the saturation hypothesis syndrome (Ofori-Amoah, 1995a).

To be successful, new development directions must be based on a true and/or real life premise or rationale. This premise provides the hope, motivation, and the conviction that the direction will achieve something better than the previous one. It also makes the new direction a venture worth following. However, if this premise itself is in error, then all the hopes and expectations will not only enslave a people, but will also destabilize the very foundation of the existing development program. In the end, the new development direction will become a false start, leading to perpetual underdevelopment.

Equally relevant is the question of feasibility or applicability. In order for new development directions to work, they must be amenable to practical translation and implementation in terms of the locale's economic, social, political, and technological contexts at both national and global levels. Although many new ideas sound theoretically appealing, they may not be easily implemented. Sometimes, society would be fortunate to sense this right from the beginning of the implementation. In other cases, however, society can only know after the implementation is well underway. In either case, a great deal of effort, time, and scarce financial resources will have to be spent only to learn later that all those resources have been misapplied.

In the final analysis, the problems of false premise and doubtful applicability that may characterize new development directions derive from the saturation hypothesis syndrome. The saturation hypothesis syndrome is the tendency for development practitioners to conceive of development problems and solutions in developing regions in terms of what is currently considered to be the most important and pressing needs or issues in developed countries (Ofori-Amoah, 1995a, pp. 15-24; 1995b). This syndrome has its roots in the mechanism by which development theories evolve, a mechanism I term the saturation hypothesis (Ofori-Amoah, 1995a, pp. 15-24). This hypothesis conceives of economic development as a problem-solving process that moves society from one stage to another. Each stage defines its own problems, which are in turn prioritized in order of importance by society. As solutions to highest priority problems are found and perfected in terms of methods, technologies, and institutional support systems, society reaches a stage of saturated development. Problems, which were formerly less important, come to the fore, while established solutions may themselves expose new problems. In the process, society is pushed to reprioritize these new problems. Solutions to these new prioritized problems raise society to a new and a higher stage of development, and the process repeats itself. The way development problems are conceived, defined, and proposed to be solved then constitutes the core of development concepts, principles, theories, and strategies (Ofori-Amoah, 1995a).

As a result, all new development ideas are primarily meant for solving the problems within the society from which the theory, concept, or principle originates. The apparent projection of such new ideas as something beneficial to other societies is necessitated by the originators' desire to gain access to the uneven geography of all the resources, both human and natural, required to fulfill their own public and hidden agenda. Thus, the full benefit of such new ideas to other societies can be achieved only (1) If the recipient societies are at the same stage of the evolutionary process as the originating society. (2) If the recipient societies have the same definitions and conceptions of problems that need to be solved; and (3) If the recipient societies are pursuing these from the same perspectives and with the same order of priorities as the originators (Ofori-Amoah, 1995a, pp. 15-24). However, if recipient societies are at different development stages and differ in their perceptions of what constitute the most important problems and how those problems could be solved, then the indiscriminate adoption of the new ideas and concepts embedded in the new directions will eventually produce dismal results. At that point, it would be clear that the new development direction was nothing more than a false start.

These then are the three main features of new development ideas that can become false starts. New development directions can become false starts if (1) they are based on false premises, (2) they have doubtful applicability or (3) they result from the saturation hypothesis syndrome. In the remaining sections of the chapter, I will show that, as far as Africa's development program is concerned, both environment and gender-based development strategies are false starts because both of them are characterized by all three features. To do this, I will first outline the main features of environment and gender-based development strategies.

ENVIRONMENT AND GENDER-BASED DEVELOPMENT STRATEGIES

The most distinguishing features of both environment and gender-based development strategies lie in the factors they seek to emphasize. Thus, environment-based development strategies advocate a form of development, which is environmentally friendly in its impact. The rationale for these strategies is rooted in the conviction that the world's physical environmental system is under serious threat. This threat manifests itself in widespread deforestation, desertification, soil erosion, depletion of renewable and nonrenewable resources, production of toxic waste, high levels of concentration of pollutants in the earth's atmosphere, climatic change and drought. In the belief that this threat has resulted from two main sources, (increased economic development and rapid population growth) those advocating environment-based development strategies offer solutions, which range between two extremes (see Miller, 1995).

The conservative environment-based development strategies lean toward the preservationist view that economic development is totally incompatible with environmental health and safety (Lorraine, 1972; Carson, 1965; Goldsmith et al., 1972; Curry-Lindahl, 1972; Caldwell, 1972; Brown, 1993; Goodland, 1991). They not only advocate for an end to rapid population growth, but they also strongly urge or seek to prevent developing regions, and for that matter Africa, from following the development experience of the developed countries. They romanticize a modest form of development and lifestyle, typical of tribal living within the Amazon, because of its compatibility with the so-called environmental constraint. In the same spirit, they oppose any project with "development" connotations, from the construction of hydroelectric power projects and highways to the use of modern production technologies, on the grounds that they cause environmental destruction.

In their most liberal form, environment-based development strategies assume the conservationist view that economic development must be compatible with environmental quality and safety, a view which has been best expressed by the buzz word of current development literature--"sustainable development" (UN, 1973; World Commission on Environment and Development, 1987). Defined by the World Commission on Environment and Development (1987) as "the development that meets the needs of the present without compromising the ability of future generations to meet their own needs," sustainable development identifies four critical but integrating areas of action: economic, human, ecological, and technological. Economically, sustainable development implies committing resources toward the improvement of living standard. In human terms, it entails making full use of humans but at the same time curbing rapid population growth, which underlies environmental degradation. Ecologically, it involves protection of natural resources, avoiding overuse of modern agricultural and industrial technologies, as well as avoiding practices that increase the incidence of resource depletion, global warming and pollution of all forms (World Commission on Environment, 1987; World Resources Institute, 1992). In order to implement all these, environment-based development strategies emphasize the need to build and strengthen appropriate institutions (World Bank, 1992; The Stanley Foundation, 1992).

In general, environment-based development strategies prescribe solutions, which range from extreme preservation of existing resources and complete avoidance of certain established development practices to a combination of use-with-restraint and use-with-preservation practices. In addition, they prescribe subjection, approval and implementation of all major development projects to environmental impact assessment; and the building of an institutional framework capable of supporting these. The assumption is that these solutions will lead to a better development.

In contrast, gender-based development strategies focus on the role of women in the economic development process and advocate a form of development that is achievable by concentrating on women and their problems. These strategies rest on the premise that, in spite of the important role played by women in Africa, women have become marginalized in the development of the continent (Boserup, 1970; Hutson, 1985). Thus, these strategies seek to redress the plight of African women by identifying these problems and providing solutions to them. Five main areas requiring action are identified: agriculture, technology transfer, structural adjustment programs, cities, and AIDS (Schoepf, 1992, pp. 203-241).

In agriculture, it is claimed that women produce an estimated 60-80% of all the food produced in Africa. In addition, women constitute the primary processors and distributors of the food supplies consumed in Africa. Yet, they lack the land, the most basic resource needed to produce food. It is therefore argued that the devotion of the best lands and infrastructure to export crops marginalizes small food crop farmers, especially women. This hinders expanded cultivation of food crops for the growing urban population and causes environmental effects (Siedman and Ohiorhenuan, 1992, pp. 23-67). Besides, women spend so much time doing other chores such as fetching firewood and cooking that they do not have enough time to raise their food production capabilities.

In the case of transfer of technological innovation, the claim is that this has not been gender neutral. Instead, transfer of technology has avoided the peasant women and sought to help "lazy" peasant men. As a result, women become doubly disadvantaged by losing their control not only over land but also over their labor.

Poor women and children have also been singled out as the group most negatively affected by such programs as structural adjustment that have been implemented in Africa (Bujra, 1990; Pittin, 1989; Dennis, 1988). The implementation of these programs has resulted in increasing the cost of certain services such as health and education, which in turn makes them inaccessible to poor women.

Within the cities of Africa, women are also claimed to be the most disadvantaged group. Most women here are traders who eke out a meager living. Economic crisis severely limits the opportunities for women, while the double-load of generating income and providing domestic labor is taxing. Many middle class women are overtaxed by the responsibilities of large extended families. In addition, women have become targets of revolutionary governments as they are accused of high food prices, profiteering and illegal currency smuggling (Dennis, 1988; Clark, 1990; Schoepf, 1988).

African women are also claimed to be at greater risk of AIDS in part because poverty forces many women to use sex with multiple partners as a means to ensure their own and family survival. Even faithful wives are at risk if their husbands have sex with multiple partners.

In general, therefore, gender-based development strategies rest on the premise that women's contributions to Africa's economic development are neglected. Development projects have bypassed women and concentrated on men. The result is that gender-based development strategies seek to alleviate the plight of the African woman through a series of projects, which can be collectively called "women-only" projects. These include putting gender issues at the center of Africa's development process by providing rural women opportunities to increase their incomes; improving women's access to land; training women field workers and women rural development workers; forming women co-operatives; and increasing the representation of women in government.

The attention that both environment- and gender-based strategies have drawn among development researchers and policy makers in Africa cannot be overemphasized. However, are these two strategies really new development directions for Africa to follow or nothing more than another set of false starts? I try to answer this question in the next section.

NEW DIRECTIONS OR FALSE STARTS?

It is my contention that environment- and gender-based development strategies are false starts to economic development in Africa for three main reasons. First, both environment and gender-based strategies are based on false premises. Second, they both have doubtful applicability. Finally, they both exhibit strong symptoms of the saturation hypothesis syndrome.

False Premises

Both, environment-based and gender-based development strategies rest on false premises. They both assume that by focusing on the environment and gender issues respectively, Africa's development problems will be alleviated. As a result, the diagnoses and prescriptions of the two strategies are couched in a language that trivializes Africa's development problems. Let us look at some examples.

Environment-based development strategies rest on the premise that too much economic development and rapid population growth cause environmental breakdown. Yet, in Africa the real cause of environmental problems is lack of economic development and especially the existence of a weak technological base. Thus, lack of adequate electricity for fuel leads to the use of wood and subsequently the disappearance of the forest. Lack of better farming techniques leads to frequent clearing of forests and grasslands as well as overgrazing, both of which lead to soil erosion. Lack of good waste and sewer disposal technologies and use of outmoded industrial technology lead to the accumulation of toxic waste and ecological breakdown in both rural and urban Africa. Finally, lack of economic development has left intact some of the cultural beliefs that tie people down to the need for large families. Thus, contrary to popular perception that a greater part of Africa's development crisis can be attributed to environmental decay, lack of economic development has created the environmental decay.

In the same vein, the diagnoses and prescriptions of gender-based development strategies give the impression that African men and women are two homogenous groups that have benefited in completely different ways from the development process in Africa, a point which Mohanty (1988) has eloquently argued. Thus, economic development has benefited and empowered all African men while it has both suppressed and subjugated African women. All African men are said to be powerful. They control the means of production. They benefit from government development projects. They are better off than women. They do not suffer any discrimination, and do not take care of their wives and children. In contrast, all African women are described as being poor and powerless, and as having no control over any means of production. They do all the farm work and the household chores as well as take care of the children without reaping any benefit at all.

These descriptions do not only grossly overgeneralize the issues at stake, but also reveal the ignorance of such scholars regarding the problems of underdevelopment in Africa. Thus, if all entitlements and privileges claimed to be enjoyed exclusively by African men were true, then one has to find an explanation for Africa's "brain drain" problem that is very high among educated African men. Specifically, why would educated African men want to emigrate from the continent or choose to stay abroad after studying there? Why would they choose to live in places where they can at best end up only as second class citizens, losing all the power, respect, dignity, and privileges they would enjoy by living in their respective African countries?

The fact is, under conditions of continuing economic underdevelopment, it is not surprising to see that most of benefits are concentrated in the hands of the few who constitute the dominant political, economic, and social faction. In many African countries, this faction is not defined so much on the basis of gender, knowledge, and qualifications, but on the basis of one's personal and social relations with those in responsible positions in government, and business and on whether one is living in the urban or rural area. Most of the arguments that have been used to bolster the need for gender-based development strategies also hold true for African men who are outside the dominant social, economic, and political faction.

Apart from the weaknesses of the general premises of both environment and gender-based development strategies, there are also problems with the data and information base of the two strategies and how these data are processed and interpreted. In particular, most of these databases are mere estimates (see, for example, FAO, 1993; The World Resources Institute, 1994). We know little about who does the estimation, for what purpose, and by what methods. None of the expert individuals and organizations has definitive information as to what the real picture is. Thus, no one knows whether these trends are being overestimated or even underestimated. Ironically, these estimates have become the bases of unsupported overgeneralized statements and forecasts, which constitute part of the premises of the two strategies.

Similar observations can be made about gender-based development strategies. Consider the claim that technological development and transfer in agriculture in sub-Saharan Africa has bypassed women and concentrated on men alone. If this were the case, it would be expected that these developments would have erased the burden of farming for men while women farmers would still be stuck in the same old tedious nature of farming. Yet, the cutlass, the machete, the manual sharpening stone, the axe, and the hoe continue to be the main tools for farmers in the forested regions of sub-Saharan Africa. Thus, male cocoa farmers in Ghana, Cote d' Ivoire, Nigeria, and Cameroon, for example, still use the cutlass or the machete just as their female counterparts in the food sector. They endure the same ordeals of blistered palm, sore back, and stiff waist that result from the use of the cutlass, or machete, as do their female counterparts in the food sector. They still have to endure the stiff neck and sore eyes that result from trying to pluck that one elusive cocoa pod hidden somewhere up in the heavy canopy of cocoa trees with the primitive *cocoa coba,* during the harvesting season. As one of the leading commercial agricultural activities in West Africa, cocoa growing has not seen any major technological development since the seedlings were planted on small holdings during the late 19th century, except the introduction of the insecticide which serves as an antidote to the capsid insect. So, where is the technological development that has so much relieved men from the tedious nature of the African farming?

The whole premise that economic development in Africa has bypassed women is also a red herring. Gender-based development strategies belittle the importance of the export sector in the economies of African countries. Thus, while acknowledging that men largely dominate this sector, some advocates of gender-based development strategies have referred to these same men as "lazy." Yet, this export sector has to date provided all the necessary foreign exchange that has gone into the importation of most of the manufactured products found in African countries, as well as the providing transportation, education, health care facilities, and power supplies. Even though these infrastructures are inadequate, in every African country, there are definitely more schools, more hospitals, more roads, better drinking water quality and more goods and services than there were during the colonial era. These have not benefited men alone. Indeed, given that most of these developments have concentrated in the few large urban areas, if there is any group of people who have been bypassed by the economic development process in Africa, it is the rural dwellers, and it cannot be said that it is only women who live in rural Africa.

Besides, while it is essential for a nation to be able to feed itself, every nation need not grow all its food. In fact, few nations are able to grow all the food they need. Instead, by having a strong export sector, most nations are able to feed themselves through food imports. Thus, had the export sector been efficient, and the proper use and management of foreign exchange as well as shrewd economic development planning prevailed, the food sector could have been made efficient. In that case, the double-day shift of Africa's women farmers would have been reduced considerably since not much time would be required by food crop farmers to produce food. Unfortunately, a hostile global economic and political system that depresses the prices of the so-called primary products and jacks up the so-called manufactured value-added products, coupled with internal mismanagement of scarce foreign exchange, have stifled the development that needs to occur in both the export and food crop sector. As Dolphyne (1991) has pointed out, it is this same hostile international context that has reduced the ability of the African man to care for his family, thereby passing the burden onto the African woman.

The fact is environmental and gender issues in Africa do not derive simply from neglect by the economic development process. Rather, they derive from a perpetual process of economic underdevelopment that draws its support from both external and internal forces. Externally, these forces include an oppressive global political and economic system that has directly or indirectly created an unfavorable system of checks and balances to maintain the status quo between developed and developing regions of the world. Internally, these forces include a weak mix of the appropriate human factor characteristics required to envision, initiate, design, implement, manage, and manouver the economic development process (Adjibolosoo,1994, pp. 25-37). Among these characteristics are dedication, accountability, responsibility, and sense of duty. In the absence of these, corruption, mismanagement, incompetence, and selfish motives have become a feature of the entire political, economic, and social leadership of African societies, creating a major hindrance to the economic development process. They lie at the root of the apparent neglect of the environment and women by the development process so it is these issues that we really need to address.

Doubtful Applicability

Environment- and gender-based development strategies also raise questions of feasibility or applicability. Environment-based development strategies involve conflicts between preservationists and conservationists. The former upholds the view that economic development ought to stop in order to save the environment, while the latter believe that the two are compatible. In reality however, neither view is accurate, at least not within the context of Africa's present economic condition. This is because economic development, as we know today, involves interaction of both human and natural resources. Never, in the history of modern economic development has the process of development occurred in peaceful co-existence with the biophysical environment. In particular, at the initial stages of development, there is bound to be some disequilibrium between the need to develop and the need to care for the environment. Only after the ability to provide certain basic needs has been attained and become sustained may such disequilibrium be corrected.

It could be argued that precedence is not a necessary condition for implementing the environment-based development strategies being proposed. However, we are dealing with more complex issues than mere implementation of ideas. Here we are dealing with the global political and economic system. At the core of all these is the problem of technology. Most of the technologies that are required to deal with the problems of balance between development and the environment are not even in existence. Most of them are being researched at the moment.

However, as a result of the increasing bond between technology and national sovereignty, the chances that these new technologies will become available to Africa are quite slim (Juma and Ojwang, 1989; Ofori-Amoah, 1994, pp. 85-102). Efforts on the part of developed countries to avoid any discussion about making environmentally friendly technologies available to developing countries at the UN Conference on the Environment in Rio de Janeiro in 1992, are a further testimony to this. Even if we assume that such technologies will become available, what sort of economic development will emerge from those technologies? The experience from the appropriate technology movement shows that Africa cannot rely on another nebulous concept as environmentally friendly technology to achieve economic development. The implication is that the future of Africa's economic development from both the preservationists' and conservationists' standpoint does not hold any good news. On the one hand, Africa stands condemned to perpetual poverty. On the other hand, everything is uncertain.

Similar observations can be made about gender-based development strategies. African women do not exist in isolation. As members of the African society, they exist within cultural, economic, political and spatial systems, all of which are intertwined and cannot be isolated from one another. Focusing on women's problems alone as a means of economic development will not work unless the systems within which African women live are all included. Thus, development projects that have addressed the needs of married women without involving their husbands have failed not only in Africa but in other parts of the Third World (see Lewis, 1988 pp. 177-200; Hale, 1985).

In the same way, providing credit access to women farmers living in remote countryside will not enable them gain control over their labor and resources when there is no adequate transportation systems that will bring easy access to such supporting services as market outlets and other service centers. Talk of empowering women without easy access to improved food production, storage and processing technologies as well as easy access to good drinking water and medical facilities will not achieve anything. Thus, legislating women's representation in government and positions of responsibility will not necessarily improve the status of women unless it is accompanied by adequate educational facilities and resources within reasonable reach of not only women but men as well. Above all, focusing on women without doing anything about the ills of exploitative domestic and global political and economic systems within which African women live will provide only a false sense of hope. It will not lead to women's liberation. This same sense of false hope has resulted in the brain drain among educated Africans.

The point is the context of the "plight of the African woman" is intertwined with the economic underdevelopment of the continent. The use of women's issues as the integrating core of the development agenda for the continent, as being advocated by experts, is not only mythical but also a false start. Thus, as Dolphyne (1991, p. xiv) writes:

> for most African women living in the rural areas with no good drinking water, with no hospital or clinic within easy reach, no motorable roads to centers where certain essential services can be obtained, living in a drought-stricken area where there is a constant threat of famine and so on, the issue of women's rights is inextricably linked with that of survival. Their concerns relate to the provision of basic necessities of life that will relieve them from the anxieties inherent in their existence, so that they can direct their energies towards making a worthwhile contribution to the achievement of a sustainable improvement in the conditions in which they live, and to the development of their society.

Finally, both environment- and gender-based development strategies are top-heavy with institution building (see World Bank, 1989, 1992; The Stanley Foundation, 1992; Shoepf, 1992, pp. 203 - 241). The problem is institutions do not run themselves. To be effective, they need the appropriate human factor, "a spectrum of personality characteristics and other dimensions of human performance that enable social, economic, and political institutions to function and remain functional over time" (Adjibolosoo 1994 p. 26). Africa's record with institution building shows that without addressing these elements, the creation of additional new institutions will not solve the pertinent problems of underdevelopment.

All these clearly show that both environment and gender issues in Africa have their roots in the fundamental problem of Africa's economic underdevelopment. As a result, any effort at dealing with environmental and women's issues without addressing the problem of underdevelopment itself leaves much to be desired. This cast doubt on the applicability of environment- and gender-based strategies as they are being advocated in Africa.

The Saturation Hypothesis Syndrome: The Real Roots of the Problems of Environment- and Gender-Based Development

The final reason why both environment and gender-based development strategies are potential development false starts for Africa is that they both exhibit symptoms of the saturation hypothesis syndrome. The saturation hypothesis syndrome is the tendency of development practitioners to conceive of development problems and solutions in developing regions, in terms of what is currently considered to be the most important and pressing needs or issues in developed countries (Ofori-Amoah, 1995a pp. 15 - 24, 1995b). The implication of this is that both environment- and gender-based development strategies as applied in Africa grew out of economic and social development problems of developed societies and not those of Africa. They therefore have some features that make them incompatible with the African condition. To see this, we have to examine the historical evolution of the two development strategies.

Historically, concerns about the environment and women's role in economic development are not new. In the United States, for example, concerns about the environment date back to the late 19th century. In 1864, Marsh's book on Man and Nature was published. In 1872, the conservation movement culminated in the creation of the Yellowstone National Park. In 1891, the Yosemite National Park was established, and a year later, the Sierra Club, a private conservation organization was established. Concerns about the role of women goes back even further to the 18th century, as evidenced in the "feminist" writings of Mary Wollstonecraft, John Stuart Mill, Karl Marx, and Frederich Engles (see Tong, 1989)

However, it was not until the latter part of this century, indeed in the 1970s, that both the environment and gender became paramount issues. Thus, in the United States, for example, it was not until January 1, 1970, when President Nixon declared the 1970s to be the years that America paid back its debt to the environment. In April that year, the first Earth Day was held. The following months and years saw a proliferation of Acts of Congress on the environment. Among these were the National Environmental Policy Act, 1970; the Clean Air Act, 1972; the Clean Water Act, 1972; the Pesticide Control Act, 1972; the Endangered Species Act, 1973; Resource Conservation and Recovery Act, 1976; and the Surface Mining Control and Reclamation Act, 1977. At the international level, the UN Environmental Program (UNEP) was not put in place until after the First UN Conference on the Environment in 1972.

Women's role in economic development followed a similar pattern. It was not until 1973, when the US Congress enacted the Percy Amendment to the Foreign Assistance Act, requiring bilateral programs to give particular attention to those projects that focused on women. Two years later, in 1975, the UN General Assembly endorsed the recommendation of the International Women's Year Conference in Mexico and declared the period from 1975 to 1985 as the International Decade for Women and Development. In 1979, the UN General

Assembly adopted the Convention on the Elimination of All Forms of Discrimination against Women and established the United Nations Fund for Women and the International Research and Training Institute for the Advancement of Women (The World Resource Institute, 1994).

The question is, "Why did it take so long for these two issues to gain the recognition they have now?" The answer is simply that these issues were not thought to be important then. This is not to discredit the role played by Carson's (1962) and Friedan's (1963) works as well as the role played by the 1969 California oil spills in creating an awareness of the environment and the status of women in society. However, if these were the main reasons, the concern about the environment and women should have been more prominent in economic development issues at a much earlier date. Yet, even the conservation movement saw the environment as a necessary input for economic development.

The fact is that developed countries had more pressing problems to grapple with than with the issues of environment and gender. As Smith (1992) has argued, the dominant social paradigm (the cluster of beliefs, values, and ideals that influence the thinking about society, government, and individual responsibility) at that time accepted laissez-faire capitalism, economic growth, progress, and a faith in science and technology. In order to conquer material poverty, developed countries focused on mass production of basic necessities of life. In the process, large scale mechanized agriculture with its associated irrigation schemes and heavy use of organic and inorganic manure became the order of the day. Massive manufacturing plants led to incredible consumption of natural resources while producing massive industrial effluents into rivers, the ocean and the atmosphere. Immense network of highways, railroads, airports, and seaports and sprawling megalopoli all took thousands of hectares of both forest and grassland and destabilized the natural environment. At that time, the environment and gender issues were not thought to be important.

However, after resolving the most important problems of the time, developed societies reached a saturated stage. Some of the solutions which had made developed societies so efficient and so competent, such as advanced technological systems and mass production technologies as well as social systems that required women to be homebound and men outside workplace-bound, began to have positive feedback on the system. Environmental degradation and the frustration of educated middle class white women began to explode right in the face of the established order of things, forcing the social system to reorder its priorities (see, for example, the World Commission on Environment and Development, 1987; Hooks, 1984). Environment acquired a new priority status, and so did gender. Thus, the serious concern with the environment did not happen until most of the nations and peoples who now show the most concern had solved the basic problem of survival and achieved sustained development, namely provision of food, shelter, and clothing.

However, these domestic movements needed the support of global resources, human and natural, in order to succeed, partly due to the nature of resources and the environment and partly due to the politics of the whole business. While environmentalists invoked the idea of the "global village," feminists invoked the concept of "sisterhood" (World Commission on Environment and Development, 1987; Hooks, 1984). The rain forest became a global resource overnight, while all women became victims of the male-dominated economic development process. With these two concepts as bridges, advocates of these two strategies and their supporters in the developed world began to launch a global crusade to save the environment and free all women from bondage. With respect to activities at the United States Agency for International Development (USAID) Lewis (1988, pp. 177-200;) shows that women did not get on the agenda of the USAID until the Percy Amendment to the Foreign Aid Bill in 1973 and the subsequent establishment of the Women In Development (WID) office at the agency. She writes:

> The USAID launched its New Directions Policy, which mandated equitable development. WID became a base from which feminist activists could seek to educate, persuade, and pressure decision makers responsible for designing and authorizing projects initiated by country teams. By making women's interests a criterion of project acceptability, the WID advocates sought to move planners toward their position. Finding the USAID bureaucracy recalcitrant, the WID office reached out to feminist scholars working on development to build their case. This literature not only documented the extent to which women had been overlooked in past policies and projects but also sought to build the positive case: that inclusion of women in development projects furthered, or was even imperative for, the achievement of USAID's development goals (Lewis, 1988 p. 182-183).

What these advocates, knowingly or unknowingly, failed to realize was that the contexts of environmental and gender problems in both the developed and developing worlds, and especially in Africa, were different. Thus, rather than too much economic development causing environmental degradation in the developing world, and in Africa in particular, it was lack of economic development that was causing environmental degradation. Similarly, gender-based development strategists, deriving their strengths from feminists, were faced with a different African woman, who rather than being a housewife who needed to be liberated and accepted into a formal workforce, was already integrated into the productive workforce.

Clearly these two different contexts demand different questions and tactics. With respect to developed countries, the question for environment-based development strategies is, "How do we maintain the current standard of living within present environmental constraints?" In the case of Africa, the question is, "How do we advance the current level of development for the better within the current environmental constraints?" In the case of gender-based development, the question in the developed countries is about the distribution of the benefits of economic development through active participation in the labor force by women. In Africa, it is a different issue. African women are already part of a workforce of an economic system, which cannot even adequately feed itself, let alone generate surpluses of wealth. In this context the question is what can be done to make such a system more efficient and effective so it will not only provide for its people's basic necessities but also generate surpluses to make the system self-sustained. Thus, as Johnson-Odim (1989, pp. 314-327) has pointed out, in undeveloped societies, and for that matter Africa, it is not just a question of internal redistribution of resources but of generation and control. It is not just equal opportunity between women and men, but creation of opportunity itself. It is not only the position of women in society, but also the position of the societies in which, Third World women find themselves.

Instead of modifying their central questions to fit the African context, environment and gender-based development strategies went on to ask the same questions and follow the same approaches they had followed in the developed countries. Not only has this failure led to problems with the premise and applicability of the two strategies, but it has also led to sharp divergences between the views of leaders and delegates from Africa, and the views of their counterparts from the developed world. Thus, it did not take long for the international environmental efforts to come up against strong opposition. Developed countries saw population growth as the prime cause of environmental degradation, while developing countries saw the uncontrolled consumption of developed countries as the real cause of environmental degradation. Similarly, the differences between African delegates and their western counterparts regarding issues and methods to be addressed at the UN Mid-Decade Conference on Women and Development held at Copenhagen in 1980, was followed by other delegates giving a hostile reception to the lesbian group attending the Nairobi End-of-Decade Conference. (Dolphyne, 1991). Since these early warning shots were fired, it has been claimed that some progress has been made on both grounds, but the roots of these differences still remain.

CONCLUSION

Economic development is a problem-solving and learning process. As a result, new directions, pathways, or trajectories from both within and without a given society are both indispensable and inevitable, especially when existing pathways have reached a dead end. However, because of the nature of the evolution and application of such new ideas, there is also the danger they will become economic development false starts, especially when they are indiscriminately adopted.

In this chapter I have argued that, as a result of how they evolved and how they have come to be applied to Africa, both environment and gender-based development strategies have false premises and doubtful applicability which make them strong candidates for economic development false starts. At issue here is neither an anti-environmentalist nor anti-feminist sentiment. I recognize the need to control deforestation and soil erosion. In fact the need for forestation and forestation programs and methods of preventing soil erosion have long been part of the African schools' curricula. As a victim of the abuses and injustices of the matrilineal inheritance system of the Akans of Ghana, I am also aware of the treatment African women are subjected to in various traditional settings. However, most of this treatment is culturally determined and continues to persist not because women have been bypassed by economic development but because economic development has not gone deep enough to cause transformations in such cultural practices.

At issue here is whether environment and gender-based strategies can deal with what Ezeala-Harrison (1994, pp. 1-24) has referred to as an over-stretched underdevelopment of Africa, a situation where economic underdevelopment has become a quasi-permanent feature. From my perspective, this feature of over-stretched underdevelopment derives from a complex set of both internal and external forces, which are much more fundamental than environmental degradation and neglect of women. Externally, these fundamental forces include an oppressive global political and economic system that has directly or indirectly created a system of unfavorable checks and balances to maintain the status quo between developed and developing regions of the world. Internally, these include a weak mix of appropriate human factor characteristics required to envision, initiate, design, implement, and manage the economic development process (Adjibolosoo, 1994, pp. 25-37). In the absence of such characteristics as dedication, accountability, responsibility, integrity, and sense of duty, corruption, mismanagement, incompetence, and selfish motives have become lasting features of the entire political, economic, and social leadership of African societies, creating major hindrances to the economic development process.

Economic development, as presently conceived, is "western," even though some academics and Third World nationalists would not agree. This implies that developing regions, such as Africa, cannot completely escape from having to follow in some of the footsteps of the West. However, economic development is also an evolutionary and cumulative process, with each stage deriving its support from the one before it. Thus, if developed countries want African countries to follow them, or if African countries want to follow developed countries, it is absolutely necessary for African countries to ensure that whatever is to be followed has an appropriate foundation to build on. To date, we do not know the full effects of environment- and gender-based development strategies on developed countries. We cannot know their effects on Africa's economic development process. In the final analysis, we cannot take care of the environment and bring women issues into the economic development process until the empty stomachs of the African people are filled. It takes more than environmental degradation and women's issues to do this.

The fundamental cause of Africa's overstretched underdevelopment lies first and foremost in the decay of its human factor. This has created a situation in which scarce economic development resources are misapplied. It has also led to a situation where the fruits of the little economic development that takes place is appropriated by the few in positions of power and responsibility at the expense of the rest of the people. These exploiters are able to get away with what they do because they are not accountable to the rest of the people. In turn, the people let them off the hook because they are ignorant of their rights and responsibilities or do not know how to assert them or even do not care. Africa needs first and foremost a development education that will instill such human factor characteristics as accountability, responsibility, sense of duty, dedication, and integrity into the people, both the rulers and the ruled, male and female, and old and young. When this is done, leaders will be accountable and responsible because the people will hold them to it. Resources will go where they are supposed to go. In the absence of this, all new development strategies will be hijacked by people who look after themselves at the expense of those they are supposed to help.

REFERENCES

Adjibolosoo, S. 1994. "The Human Factor and the Failure of Economic Development Policies in Africa." In F. Ezeala-Harrison and S. Adjibolosoo, eds. *Perspectives on Economic Development in Africa.* Westport, CT: Praeger.

Boserup, E. 1970. *Women's Role in Economic Development.* New York: St. Martin's Press.

Brown, L. R. 1993. "A New Era Unfolds." In L. R. Brown et al. eds. *State of the World 1993-A World Watch Institute Report on Progress Toward a Sustainable Society.* New York: Norton.

Bujra, J. M. 1990. "Taxing Development: Why Must Women Pay? Gender and Development Debate in Tanzania." *Review of African Political Economy,* 47: 44-63.

Caldwell, L. K. 1972. *In Defense of Earth: International Protection for the Biosphere.* London: Bloomington.

Carson, R. 1965. *Silent Spring.* London: Penguin.

Clark, G. 1990. "Class alliance and Class Fractions in Ghanaian Trading and State Formation." *Review of African Political Economy,* 49: 73-81.

Curry-Lindahl, K. 1972. *Conservation For Survival: An Ecological Strategy.* New York: Morrow.

Dennis, C. 1988. "Women in African Labor History." *Journal of Asian and African Studies,* 23 (1-2):125-140.

Dolphyne, F. A. 1991. *The Emancipation of Women: An African Perspective.* Accra: Ghana Universities Press.

Dumont, R. 1969. *False Start In Africa*. New York: Frederick A. Praeger, Inc., Publishers (Translated by P. N. Ott.).

Ezeala-Harrison, F. 1994. "What Ails African Economies: Lessons From Over-Stretched Underdevelopment." In F. Ezeala-Harrison and S. Adjibolosoo, eds. *Perspectives on Economic Development in Africa.* Wesport, CT: Praeger.

FAO. 1993. *Forest Resources Assessment, 1990: Tropical Countries*. Rome: FAO.

Friedan, B. 1963. *The Feminist Mystique.* New York: W. W. Norton.

Goldsmith, E; Allen; A Allaby, M; Davoll, J and Lawrence, S.. 1972. *Blueprint for Survival*. Boston: Houghton Mifflin.

Goodland, R. 1991 "The Case that the World has Reached Limits: More Precisely that Current Throughput Growth in the Global Economy Cannot be Sustained." In R. Goodland, H. Daly, S. El Serafy and B. von Droste, eds. *Environmentally Sustainable Economic Development: Building on Brundtland.* Paris: UNESCO.

Guyer, J. 1981. "Household and Community in African Studies." *African Studies Review*, 24 (2-3): 87- 137.

Hale, S. M. 1985. "Integrating Women in Development Models and Theories." *Atlantis,* 11 (1): 46-63.

Henn, J. K. 1983. "Feeding the Cities and Feeding the Peasants: What Role for Africa's Women Farmers?" *World Development,* 11 (12): 1043-1055.

Hooks, B. 1984. *Feminist Theory: From Margin to Center*. Boston: South End Press.

Hutson, P. 1985. *Third World Women Speaks Out*. Davao City, Philippines: Asian Women's Research and Action.

Johnson-Odim, C. 1989. "Common Themes, Different Contexts: Third World Women and the Politics of Feminism." In C. T. Mohanty, A. Russo and L. Torres, eds. *Third World Women and the Politics of Feminism.* Bloomington, IN: Indiana University Press.

Kamarck, A. 1976. *The Tropics and Economic Development*. Baltimore: Johns Hopkins Press.

Juma, C. and Ojwang, J. B. 1989. *Innovation and Sovereignty*. Nairobi: African Center for Technology Studies.

Lewis, B. 1988. "Getting Women on the African Agricultural Development Agenda." In H. Glickman, ed. *The Crisis And Challenge of African Development*. Westport, CT: Greenwood Press.

Lofchie, M and Commins, S. 1984. "Food Deficits and Agricultural Policies in Sub-Saharan Africa." *The Hunger Project Papers,* No. 2, San Francisco.

Lorraine, J. A. C 1972. *The Death of Tomorrow*. London: Heinemann.

McPherson, M. 1984. "Checking Land Destruction: Immediate Gains and Future Benefits." *Journal*. Washington: World Resources Institute.

Miller, Jr. G. T. 1995. *Environmental Science: Working With the Earth.* Belmont, CA: Wadsworth Publishing Company.

Mohanty, C. 1988. "Under Western Eyes: Feminist Scholarship and Colonial

Discourses." *Feminist Review,* 30 (Autumn): 62-88.
O'Barr, J. 1975. "Making the Invisible Visible: African Women in Politics and Policy." *African Studies Review,* 18: 19-28.
Ofori-Amoah, B. 1995a. "The Saturation Hypothesis and Africa's Development Crisis." In S. Adjibolosoo, ed. *The Significance of the Human factor in African Economic Development.* Westport, CT: Praeger.
Ofori-Amoah, B. 1995b. "Development Research and Africa's Development Crisis." *Review of Human Factor Studies,* 1 (1): 26-44.
Ofori-Amoah, B. 1994. "Technological Change Strategy for Economic Development in Africa." In F. Ezeala-Harrison and S. Adjibolosoo, eds. *Perspectives on Economic Development in Africa.* Westport, CT: Praeger.
Pittin, R. 1989. "Women, Work and Ideology in a Context of Economic Crisis: A Case Study." In *Women, History and Development WP 11.* The Hague: Institute for Social Studies.
Schoepf, B. G. 1988. "Women, AIDS and Economic Crisis in Central Africa." *Canadian Journal of African Studies*, 22 (3): 625-644.
Schoepf, B. G. 1992. "Gender Relations and Development: Political Economy and Culture." In A. Seidman and F. Anang, eds. *Twenty-First-Century Africa: Towards a New Vision of Self-Sustainable Development.* Trenton, NJ.: Africa World Press and African Studies Association Press.
Seidman, A. and Ohiorhenuan, J. 1992. "Towards a New Economic Strategy for Sustainable African Development." In A. Seidman and F. Anang, eds. *Twenty-First Century Africa: Towards a New Vision of Self-Sustainable Development.* Trenton, NJ: Africa World Press and African Studies Association Press.
Smith, Z. A. 1992. *The Environmental Policy Paradox.* Englewood Cliffs, NJ. Prentice Hall Inc.
The Stanley Foundation 1992. *Environment and Development: Institutional Issues. 23rd United Nation's Issues Conference.* Muscatine, IA: The Stanley Foundation.
Timberlake, L. 1986. *Africa In Crisis: The Causes, The Cures of Environmental Bankruptcy.* London: Earthscan.
Tong, R. 1989. *Feminist Thought: A Comprehensive Introduction.* Boulder, Col. Westview Press.
United Nations. 1973. *Report of the United Nations Conference on the Human Environment.* Stockholm June 5-16, New York: United Nations.
The World Bank. 1981. *Accelerated Development in Sub-Saharan Africa: An Agenda for Action.* Washington, DC: The World Bank.
The World Bank. 1989. *Striking A Balance: The Environmental Challenge of Development.* Washington DC.: The World Bank.
The World Bank. 1992. *The World Bank and the Environment.* Washington, D.C.: The World Bank.
World Commission on Environment and Development. 1987. *Our Common Future.* New York: Oxford University Press.
The World Resources Institute, et al. 1992. *World Resources 1992-93: Toward*

Sustainable Development. New York: Oxford University Press.

The World Resources Institute, et al. 1994. *World Resources, 1994-95: People and the Environment.* New York: Oxford University Press.

6

THE GENDER FACTOR IN RURAL ENERGY SYSTEMS IN AFRICA: SOME EVIDENCE FROM GHANA

William Yaw Osei
Department of Geography
Algoma University College

BACKGROUND AND SETTING

The ability of woodfuel systems to sustain the rapidly growing energy needs of rural populations of Africa is a central concern for sustainable development initiatives. Within traditional or near self-sufficient agricultural societies, indigenous energy sources such as wood provided adequate fuel requirements for domestic and limited agricultural and industrial activities. However, in an expanding and modernising economy, as most African countries hoped to become after attaining nationhood, traditional fuels which are generally poor in quality could scarcely generate surpluses beyond the household level to meet new challenges of production and distribution. Growth in the conventional energy sector has particularly stagnated over the past decade, even as oil prices fell. With increased population needs and pressures on national economies in general, serious constraints have been placed on the financial capacity of most of the oil-importing sub-Saharan African countries. It is estimated that in 1992, energy imports took over 50% of total merchandise exports of Ghana (52%), Mali (57%), Burkina Faso (58%), and Guinea Bissau (87%) while actual quantities of imported energy stagnated or declined (World Bank, 1994).

Most sub-Saharan African countries are placed in a very tight situation because while most of them are poorly endowed with exploitable conventional energy resources, they also do not possess the financial capability to import adequate amounts of energy to satisfy home demands. The general results are that scarce conventional energy resources, either imported or internally generated, are directed into sectors considered strategic by policy makers, who are faced with a number of critical choices within a fuel-scarcity situation. Most rural areas for that matter, are scarcely served by modern conventional fuels. Pressures on wood resources for energy and for other life-sustaining demands, therefore, continue to mount.

While the effects of over-use of wood for fuel has been amply documented in such negative terms as deforestation and increased monetary costs of fuel, the nature of human impacts in fuel-scarcity situations are not given much attention. For most areas of rural sub-Saharan Africa, harvesting, processing, and transportation of wood are still manual undertakings. Women are generally considered to be the major organizers of the supply and final use of woodfuel. They are therefore likely to be most affected by any negative trends in the system. Nonetheless, most current data on woodfuel systems appear inadequate and too inconsistent, and for that matter, women's work in rural energy production systems tends to be particularly clouded with inconclusive reporting and controversy. Wood is, generally speaking, potentially the most reliable source of fuel for most energy-starved African countries both now and in the future. Therefore, to meet the needs of overall strategic rural planning and for women's development in particular, an adequate and reliable information base is required.

In this chapter, an attempt is made to analyze the role of women in the rural energy sector in sub-Saharan Africa using information based on a comprehensive woodfuel study undertaken by the author in Ghana. The objective of this chapter is, therefore, twofold. First is to provide appropriate information on the complexity and dynamics of socio-economic relationships of rural energy systems. Second is to provide information that will help energy and development planners to evolve efficient rural energy systems in Africa for sustainable development initiatives. Specific patterns, constraints, future trends, and the extent and conditions under which women's development potentials are affected are comprehensively analyzed.

THE GENDER FACTOR IN AGRARIAN AND RURAL ENERGY SYSTEMS

Globally, the nature of women's involvement in work, and the type and value of work for both sexes, are now used to assess the achievements of socio-political entities in terms of frameworks for improving the quality of individual life and sustenance of the environment. It is argued that a principal characteristic of the overwhelmingly male-dominated structures of global socio-economic realities, has been a tacit exclusion of women from material benefits in larger political structures and in existing economic arrangements (Oakley, 1974; Brydon and Chant, 1989;

Joekes, 1992; Nelson and Chowdhury, 1994). Invariably, the overall participation of women in the productive sectors of most socio-economic entities has not received the required attention. Women are perceived to dominate in work roles that appear to enjoy relatively lower economic and social profiles, conditions which ultimately affect their remuneration potential, recognition, and decision making participation.

Within most rural and agrarian systems of Africa where technological adaptations have been slow to augment human labor, and improve productivity in general, an apparent segregation of work roles is discernible. Women are routinely involved in tasks making for general household management. Food crop farming and harvests, food processing, food preparation, food marketing, and fuelwood supplies are common female tasks. In a general sense, because most women's activities are not directly market-oriented, their contributions tend to be invisible on the basis of short-term household cash inflows. However, as most male work domains are perceived to be directly market-targeted, it is held that female income opportunities are inherently constrained, especially where accounting of personal contributions and effective access to within-household wealth are taken into account.

The nature and patterns of women's work and household/community decision making in general tend to be complex. In rural Africa, because of differences in local traditions and cultures, living standards, work opportunities, incomes, and access to life enrichment resources such as nutrition, health care, and education, fixed and absolute global standards tend to be almost impractical to adopt. In simple terms, patterns and trends vary over both space and time. Okonjo (Nelson and Chowdhury, 1994) commented that among the Muslim Habe-Fulani of Northern Nigeria, women were not allowed to perform such simple tasks as buying and selling, which are necessary functions for running households. Yoruba women (also in Nigeria) are however described as often enjoying considerable (economic) power (Townsend, 1991). Joekes (1992) confirmed that women in sub-Saharan Africa maintained a level of economic autonomy in agriculture and much control over specified income generating activities. In Nelson and Chowdhury (1994), however, Nzomo and Staudt noted that women in Kenya continue to feed and support their families but without the structural advantages which men enjoy in agriculture. In a case study in rural Ghana, most women respondents confirmed the existence of a sexual division of labor at the household level but maintained that there were times when activity roles switched between the sexes (Ardayfio, 1986).

Over much of sub-Saharan Africa, changing rural conditions are helping to break down rigid role segregation. In agriculture in particular, total household labor is often organized in both vertical and horizontal role linkages to ensure successful farming whether for food or cash cropping. Male migration and increased number of female-headed households are all contributing to the undermining of strict gender work segregation.

Many reports on women's work in traditional energy production systems indicate characteristics of female exploitation and household work segregation.

Reports indicate severe and excessive labor and time demands on women for fuelwood collection in many parts of Africa. Such demands are especially acute in areas where forest loss and vegetation degradation in general are leading to serious shortages of wood. About 250-300 woman-days per family are reported to be required for fuelwood collection in certain parts of Tanzania (Arnold, 1979). Similar estimates have been made for the Sahelian region (Postel and Heise, 1988). In a related survey in Ghana, women in a village near Accra were estimated to travel more than 11 km to woodfuel production sites (Ardayfio, 1986). Since most wood collected is used for household purposes rather than for sale, it is assumed that women gain little or no direct monetary benefits. They also lose potential time-opportunities for alternative income yielding ventures. Furthermore, research findings in India found that women who are normally exposed to the burning of wood and other biomass fuels for long periods of time were exposed to about 700 micrograms of particulates per/m^3 compared to acceptable limits of 75 (UNEP, 1985). The potential impact of woodfuel on women is therefore found to span socio-economic variables to health issues.

Recently, however, some field researchers of woodfuel systems have cast doubts on the validity of many of the existing woodfuel reports as most studies overstate negative impacts (Desai, 1985; Cecelski, 1987; Osei, 1987 and 1989; Postel and Heisi, 1988; Cline-Cole et. al., 1990). The complex nature of woodfuel systems and methodological deficiencies in particular may possibly contribute to overstatements and misconceptions, especially where long-term, on-site, and appropriate studies which are related to local environments are not followed. Notwithstanding the doubtful quality and validity of many of such rural energy reports, they are routinely used by researchers, agencies, commentators, and policy advisors. In the long term, women's socio-economic development issues may not necessarily be isolated from wider human institutional and ecological challenges in broader contexts of sustainable development. Women's needs require critical attention, but equity, partnership, and gender cooperation should guide new, balanced, sustainable development initiatives in Africa.

Ultimately, African researchers and policy makers need to critically evaluate existing shortcomings in their rural energy systems since wood is still the dominant source of fuel in the rural food system. To improve the rural energy sector, an adequate and valid information base will be needed to meet planning and managerial requirements and also to help provide understanding in the workings of rural energy systems in Africa.

Among the most critical areas of consideration of women's role in the rural energy system are (1) the potential loss of opportunity for women's self improvement due to time loss for wood collection; (2) the potential domination of women in the rural wood energy sector due to the low-valued nature of wood as an energy resource and therefore corresponding with their traditionally low-valued tasks; (3) a virtual male exclusion in rural energy production systems which may reflect power and subordination of women at the household level; and (4) the potential hazards of the wood system to women's health. A case study from Ghana provides a discussion setting for evaluating the gender factor in rural energy systems.

A CASE STUDY FROM GHANA

The Basis of Information

The information on which this work is partly based was gathered as part of a general wood energy study conducted by the author in Ghana (for details, see Osei, 1989, 1993). The study was undertaken on the basis of a series of formal objectives which combined both methodological and empirical requirements. A total of 371 selected households in three sample villages in South-eastern Ghana (Figure 7.1) were subjected to detailed studies involving both quantitative and qualitative methods. The methods aimed to assess the amount of wood used as fuel at the household level, the dominant species, the source, the mode of acquisition, and the actual and possible socio-economic and ecological impacts.

The weighing method was adopted to determine the actual amount of wood used for fuel in aggregate and sectoral terms and by species for each household and village and for the three villages together. Each household was covered a minimum of 20 times in both the dry and wet seasons. A charcoal conversion experiment was also conducted for an idea of raw wood to charcoal ratio and a means to convert charcoal to wood equivalence (see Osei, 1989, 1993). Interviewing, direct observation and participation, and diary methods were used to collect information such as household characteristics (number, size, age, sex, ethnicity, religion, taboos, etc.), occupational structure, income levels, land ownership, major and minor fuels, woodfuel use type, commercial operations, wood acquisition forms, time expended on wood collection, collectors, distance to collection sites, sites and conditions at sites, economic costs of fuel, social opportunity costs, health constraints, and conditions of common property resources opportunities.

ANALYSIS OF GENERAL PATTERNS

The results of the study provide information on general patterns of the rural woodfuel system as a way of providing a basis for assessing reported constraints and controversies and also as a way of examining conservation and/or planning directions. Patterns are first established, followed by comprehensive discussions of implications and impacts.

Empirical evidence from the field study in Ghana confirmed a general dependence on woodfuel. Of a total of 371 households studied, 369 reported woodfuel (firewood and charcoal) as their major fuel (Table 6.1). This trend is consistent with the country as a whole, where dependence on wood for fuel is estimated at between 70 and 76 per cent of the total national energy budget (Osei, 1989). In many of the rural areas, wood completely fuels all energy needs for cooking, due to a virtual absence of conventional alternatives such as electricity. A high degree of dependency on woodfuel is also common in most of the countries of sub-Saharan Africa (Postel and Heise, 1988).

In the three villages combined, 268 surveyed households (74%) collected all their wood needs for domestic purposes, and only 3.8% wholly used the market place (Table 6.2). A mean of approximately 8.6 bundles of wood (28 kg/bundle base) per month was returned to the household (Osei, 1989). Also, wood was collected in about 8 days of each month, with each collecting day taking approximately 1.24 hours. The average distance to wood collection sites, which tended to be multiple, was 2.79 kilometres, and wood from owned or leased property accounted for 66.5% of all sources (Osei, 1989). In 45.5% of the households, women were the sole collectors of wood, and in another 41.3%, women and children constituted the main collectors (Table 6.3). Wood was harvested mainly by the cutlass and simple axe.

The patterns of wood collection as established suggest significant implications for impacts. In human terms, it is confirmed that since wood is mostly self-collected, labor-time commitment is high. Women dominate wood collection. There is a level of drudgery involved in woodfuel systems which has health implications. The low contribution of adult males smacks of male domination and relegation of unvalued tasks to women. However, drawing easy conclusions from statistical information without the benefit of detailed analysis of the realities behind hard figures tends to depreciate credibility. It also constitutes a basis for misconceptions. It is therefore necessary to critically examine the extent to which the woodfuel sector constrains women's socio-economic advancement. In particular, it is necessary/important to examine the following four questions: How does the rural energy system hurt the socio-economic opportunities of women? Are women mostly responsible for wood harvests because of the low-value nature of the activity? Is there male exclusion, and if so, is it a reflection of male power and influence in decision making? Is wood gathering the most serious source of health hazard in the rural food system?

Rural Energy and Women Socio-Economic Opportunities

It is apparent that since women are the main collectors of wood, any time spent on wood collection could amount to lost time for other beneficial economic and social activities. In the study villages, the period for wood collection was found also to coincide with prime time for economic activities such as paid work and trading. Where wood collection took precedence over income generating activities, time-revenue loss could be assumed. At Okrakwadjo for instance (Table 6.1), some commercial operators reported potential losses of as much as 60% because they left their line of business for fuel search and/or for farm work (Osei,

1989). Some women also reported fatigue which sometimes excluded them from social meetings.

Field realities made it difficult for a conclusive determination of direct adverse effects of the energy sector on women's socio-economic development. As Table 6.2 indicates, about 59.3% of all households with wood-based commercial operations also did collect their own wood, either wholly or in part. This implies that there were no real lost opportunities since fuel search was also connected with commercial and/or income generating opportunities. Field observation also confirmed that whenever a line of business was vacated, the bulk of sales were already completed or arrangements made for sales to continue. According to Table 6.2, fuel purchases mostly benefited commercial operations. The implications are that households with profitable ventures bought supplemental fuel, helping to cut the time and efforts for fuel search, and thereby, reducing potential adverse economic effects. Improved household incomes could achieve similar results.

TABLE 6. 1
MAJOR AND MINOR FUEL TYPES (BY NUMBER OF HOUSEHOLDS)

Village	**Major Fuel Types**				**Total ** (Major)**
	Fuelwood	**Charcoal**	**Kerosene**	**Gas**	
Teacher Mante	126	2	1	1	130
Tontro	80	1	0	0	81
Okrakwadjo	150	10	0	0	160
Total	**356**	**13**	**1**	**1**	**371**
Village	**Minor Fuel Types**				**Total ** (Minor)**
	Fuelwood	**Charcoal**	**Kerosene**	**Gas**	
Teacher Mante	2	20	0	0	22
Tontro	0	14	0	0	14
Okrakwadjo	3	37	0	0	40
Total	**5**	**71**	**0**	**0**	**76**

Source: Field Data. Sample size = 371 households.

Note: The Frequency of charcoal use in one household at Tontro is less than 3 times in a year. All calculations involving minor use of charcoal in that village, apply to 13 households.

Direct adverse effects on social opportunities were also not confirmed. Other demands, such as crop planting and tending and household duties, demanded more labor time than wood harvests. Also making it more difficult was the fact that wood harvest was usually integrated with farm-related activities. Some women reported that some of the real quality breaks they had from their otherwise repetitive and boring household chores were during group fuel search expeditions. In such instances, more time was expended on "catching up" on issues than on actual wood harvests. Social engagements are not significantly affected since alternative arrangements for fuelwood are easily made.

TABLE 6.2
WOODFUEL ACQUISITION PATTERNS:SOURCES OF WOODFUEL

Villages	1*	2*	3*	4*
	%	%	%	%
1. Domestic Use				
	77.7			
Self collection	3.8	84.0	61.9	74.0
Purchase	10.0	1.3	5.0	3.8
Part collection/part purchase	0.8	6.3	22.5	14.6
Gift	6.2	1.3	2.5	1.6
Part collection/part gift		5.0	3.8	14.9
2. Commercial Use				
Self collection	37.1	83.3	33.3	49.7
Purchase	38.7	1.9	39.7	27.9
Part collection/part purchase	12.9	11.1	14.3	6.2
Gift	1.6	0	0	0.6
Part collection/part gift	6.5	1.9	1.6	3.4

Source: Field Data. Sample size = 371 households.

* Villages: 1. Teacher-Mante 2. Tontro 3. Okrakwadjo 4. All Villages

TABLE 6.2
WOODFUEL ACQUISITION PATTERNS: SOURCES OF WOODFUEL (CONTINUED)

Villages	1*	2*	3*	4*
	%	%	%	%
3. Primary Source				
Own property	71.5	80.2	55.3	66.5
Friends	12.3	9.9	10.7	11.1
Property of extended family	3.8	4.9	6.3	5.1
Purchase	8.5	1.2	16.3	10.3
Gift only	2.3	1.2	0.6	1.4
Gift/part collection	0.0	1.2	5.0	2.4
Communal property	0.0	0.0	1.3	0.5
4. Secondary Source				
Own property	19.0	19.4	28.6	24.1
Friends	10.3	50.0	20.0	22.6
Property of extended family	3.4	5.6	7.6	6.0
Purchase	48.3	13.9	10.6	25.1
Gift only	12.1	8.7	0.0	5.0
Gift/part collection	1.7	0.0	3.8	2.5
Communal property	1.7	0.0	16.2	9.0

Source: Field Data . Sample size = 371 households.

* Villages: 1. Teacher-Mante 2. Tontro 3. Okrakwadjo 4. All Villages

Women, Woodfuel, and Low-Valued Tasks in the Food System

Societies rank and put value on activities and tasks with regard to antecedent historical traditions and practices, mode of production, societal needs, expectations, demand competition, labor input, and time expectations. In most traditional agrarian food systems, rankings and/or apparent "segregation" of certain tasks do not necessarily relate to monetary or specialized skills but to such locally relevant factors as effort required and a perception of hazard. In most of the forested areas of West Africa and in Ghana in particular, farm clearance, felling of trees and firing of cut brush, tend to be male domains because such tasks are traditionally considered physically demanding and potentially hazardous for women's health. Women tend to dominate planting and harvesting which are perceived to be less demanding and less hazardous.

No single household considered wood gathering as an inferior task (women were the main respondents). In a majority of households, woodfuel was considered "efficient" and very appropriate for village settings because such benefits as food storage and preservation is not possible with non-wood based energy sources. Women also dominated the market for woodfuel. Because income opportunities tended to be limited in the villages, the use of the market place was selective. Rather, complementary tasks by members of a household made it possible for most needs to be met, without resorting to the market. Such survival mechanisms tended to avoid any deliberate gender games or value assignment. Wood collection was not an exception.

Low Male Involvement in Wood Collection

A low adult male involvement is confirmed by Table 6.3. A critical scrutiny of the whole system, however, revealed a level of adult male participation which tended to be disguised, particularly in predominantly cash cropping areas, and areas with abundant sources of wood. Male contributions took place mostly on site, such as cutting and processing large stems or branches to be ready for transportation. In some cases, adult males carried loads of firewood and then deposited them at village perimeters for "children" to take them home.

Women routinely left farm work early to get firewood so that meals could be prepared while the men worked late on the farm. In all households where wood supply was acute, increased male involvement at all the stages of wood harvesting was found, possibly to avoid the potential burdens of fuel purchases. In the past, labor for fuel search was not an issue because of large households. Such conditions are changing as the youth migrate to urban settings for better opportunities. Male contributions will be more crucial as "free" household labor shrinks.

In the study villages, the low rate of male involvement was not seen as a reflection of a power imbalance. It was regarded as part of rural production relationships and convenience of household division of labor. As socio-economic dynamics change and the mode of production adapts, changes are expected to occur in such village production relationships.

TABLE 6.3
WOOD COLLECTION: DISTRIBUTION OF HOUSEHOLD LABOR

Collector	1*	2*	3*	4*
	%	%	%	%
Women	43.8	28.8	53.4	45.6
		61.3		
Women and Children	34.6	5.0	33.8	41.3
		2.5		
Women and Adult Males	6.6	1.3	2.7	4.6
Adult Males	6.6	1.3	2.0	3.0
Children and Adult Males	0.8		0.0	0.6
Children	3.3		7.4	4.6

Source: Field Data . Sample size = 371 households.

* Villages: 1. Teacher-Mante 2. Tontro 3. Okrakwadjo 4. All three

Percentages apply to number of households in each category against the total number of households within that category for a village or the three villages together as appropriate.

Woodfuel and Women's Health

The woodfuel system like many aspects of the rural food system is fraught with potential adverse health implications. Most tasks in the woodfuel system such as cutting, processing, and transportation are hardly mechanised. Almost all households reporting health effects mentioned general bodily pains, a result of the arduous task of collecting and carrying heavy loads of wood over distances. Accidents did occur, such as trips and falls, and cuts from misplaced cutlasses and axes. Increased frequency of trips to farms also generated fatigue.

Several reports of adverse health instances were received during the survey. In the strictest sense, however, health problems were generally inferred since they were related to other factors. As an example, a respondent was injured from a fall on the way home from farm work. The primary motive of the trip was crop tending, but foodstuffs and firewood were obtained for home use. Such situations and others similar, made it difficult to isolate actual woodfuel-related causes. The study also concluded that increased frequency of wood search was not necessarily scarcity-related neither did it directly increase fatigue levels. Households which recorded the highest frequency of returning fuelwood to the household were those with plentiful sources of supply. In effect, a limited amount was returned home each day after farm work. Distances to sources of wood also did not necessarily increase linearly with wood shortages because of constraints of property location and trespassing. Rather, collection sites grew multiple with increased scarcity.

CONCLUSION

The preceding discussion indicated strong potentials for adverse affects of woodfuel on people intensively involved in its use. The woodfuel system is generally non-mechanised with very low infrastructural support. The very set up of the woodfuel system is liable to speculation and controversy, especially, where detailed local site level studies are non-existent. Data from the study confirmed that women dominate the system and are therefore likely to be the most affected when any adverse effects occur. Women do not suffer any real significant socio-economic impacts from woodfuel at this stage but that possibility could exist, particularly as wood shortages grow acute, incomes and household labor drop dramatically, and managerial attention ignores the rural energy situation. Health implications are real but are not unique to the woodfuel system. Lack of basic infrastructural support in the rural food system maintains practices and processes that tend to intrigue foreign observers. Men do not escape the impacts of any adverse situation because when women become ill or incapacitated for any reason, male partners become saddled with added responsibilities and vice-versa. This implies inherent partnership and cooperation in rural food systems. Power and control rarely enter into fuel needs decision making at the rural level. Household survival and support mechanisms propel partnership and diversity of tasks.

Planning and policy interests are required for effective response to constraints in the rural energy system. Rural energy problems do affect human development needs as they do environmental sustenance. A timely and appropriate response will enhance rural quality of life and promote African development in general. The lack of an adequate information base in the woodfuel sector requires continued site-level research to provide support for decision making.

REFERENCES

Ardayfio, E. 1986. *The Rural Energy Crisis in Ghana: Its Implications for Women's Work and Household Survival*. Geneva, Switzerland: International Labor Organization.

Arnold, J. 1979. "Wood Energy and Rural Communities". *Natural Resources Forum*,3: 229-252.

Brydon, L. and Chant, S. 1989. *Women in the Third World: Gender Issues in Rural and Urban Areas*. New Brunswick, New Jersey: Rutgers University Press.

Cecelski, E. 1987. "Energy and Rural Women's Work: Crisis, Response and Policy Alternatives." *International Labour Review*, 126 (1): 41-63.

Cline-Cole, Main, H, and Nichol, J, 1990. "On Fuelwood Consumption, Population Dynamics and Deforestation in Africa". *World Development,* 18 (4): 513-527.

Desai, A. 1985. *Ends and Means in Rural Energy Surveys*. Ottawa: International Development Research Centre Report No. 112e.

Joekes, S. 1992. *Women in the World Economy.* New York: Oxford University Press.

Nelson, B. and Chowdhury, N. eds. 1994. *Women and Politics Worldwide.* New Haven & London: Yale University Press.

Oakley, A. 1974. *The Sociology of Housework.* New York: Pantheon Books.

Osei, W. 1993 " Woodfuel and Deforestation-Answers for a Sustainable Environment" *Journal of Environmental Management*, 37: 51-62.

Osei, W. 1989. *Woodfuel Use in Ghana: Its Nature and Impact at the Village Level* Unpublished Ph.D Thesis, University of Western Ontario, London, Ontario.

Osei, W. 1987. "Woodfuel Research in Developing Countries: The State of the Art." *Ohio Geographers*, 15: 3 43.

Postel, S and Heisi, L. 1988 *Reforesting the Earth*. Washington, D.C.: Worldwatch Institute.

Townsend, J. 1991. "Towards a Regional Geography of Gender." *The Geographical Journal,* 157 (1): 25-35.

UNEP 1985. *The Environment News*. Nairobi, Kenya:UNEP News.

World Bank 1994. *World Development Report 1994*. New York: Oxford University Press, Inc.

7

AFRICAN TRADITIONAL MEDICINE: DANGEROUS, ANACHRONISTIC OR PANACEA?

Joseph R Oppong
Department of Geography
University of North Texas

INTRODUCTION

For centuries African traditional medicine was the only source of health care for most Africans, but today it has an identity crisis. Currently, many people view African traditional medicine in one of three ways. First, African traditional medicine is regarded as anachronistic, a component of the shameful past before civilization and "scientific medicine" came. A second viewpoint lumps traditional herbal medicinal cures with criminal abuses of western pharmaceuticals, under the generic title of "dangerous drugs." Traditional medical practitioners (TMPs) are then seen as criminal charlatans whose activities must be stopped. A third viewpoint romanticizes traditional medicine nostalgically as a panacea to the health problems of Africa. This approach downplays the limitations and problems of traditional medicine. Clearly, none of these viewpoints characterizes African traditional medicine accurately. In fact, such misrepresentations confuse the issues and undermine serious efforts to develop and preserve indigenous African health technologies.

The central thesis of this chapter is that the tendency to regard African traditional medicine as inferior to western medicine is simply Eurocentric. This tendency that emerged during Africa's colonial past was entrenched by post independence health care policies, but it has no factual basis. This chapter argues that traditional medicine is a bonafide part of the African cultural heritage and has valuable medical properties that should be preserved. Preservation, research and development of traditional African medical knowledge, practices and pharmacopeia are critical in a world of newly emerging killer viruses such as ebola and HIV that biomedicine is currently unable to cure. In fact, scientific research has confirmed the efficacy of many herbal medicines (Stock, 1995). Moreover, the fact that previously unorthodox "alternative medicine" practices such as acupuncture and chiropractic are now widely accepted in North America to provide relief for conditions that western biomedicine cannot cure underscores the urgency of preservation. Finally, the World Health Organization (WHO) responding to the problem of shortages in the formal health care system and renewed interest in ethnomedicine, has encouraged programs that involve traditional healers in national health systems. Nevertheless, such formal programs are currently relatively rare.

Thus, while African traditional medicine may be inexplicable to the western mind and the practice shrouded in magic and ritual, it is culturally appropriate to the African (Anyinam, 1987). Besides, since western medicine is expensive, geographically limited, alien and culturally unacceptable to many African people, African national health programs ignore traditional medicine at their own peril.

In what follows, the chapter starts by describing the nature and characteristics of traditional medicine and healing systems, and then deals with the sources of distortions of traditional medicine: colonialism, post independence policies and fake drugs. It ends by examining the strengths and weaknesses of the African traditional medicine.

TRADITIONAL MEDICINE AND TRADITIONAL HEALERS

Koumare (1983) describes African traditional medicine as the total body of knowledge, techniques for the preparation and use of substances, measures and practices in use, whether explicable or not, that are based on the socio-cultural and religious bedrock of African communities. African traditional medicine is based on personal experience and observations handed down from generation to generation, either verbally or in writing, and this knowledge is used for the diagnosis, prevention or elimination of imbalances in physical, mental or social well being.

African traditional medicine focuses on an illness in its social, cultural and familial settings, and often seeks explanations and cures far beyond the immediate disease itself. Among the Akan people of Ghana, land is communally owned and may not be sold because it belongs to the living, the dead and those yet to be born. Violating the land by outright sale, for example, is expected to bring appropriate curses upon the culprit including sickness and even death. Thus, an immediate ailment such as simple diarrhea, may result from a curse began by an improper land transaction. Treating the diarrhea, without pacifying the offended spirits or making appropriate restitution is unlikely to be effective. Social harmony must be restored. Through counseling with the patient and related family members, treating the individual in the context of the community, the traditional healer provides the required psychological framework necessary for healing.

In contrast, western biomedicine is based on standardized dosage drugs, germ theory and a social system that is based on individualism (Good, 1987). Disease and illness are reduced to essentially mechanical or organismic states, as physical manifestations that can be successfully diagnosed and treated separately from a person's psychological condition and social context.

This sensitivity makes traditional medicine very attractive, not only to rural residents with limited access to urban-based modern health care, but to many urban residents as well (Good, 1987). It is particularly important to the urban poor, and the underclass of modern society. In a study based in the Ivory Coast, Lasker (1981) found that many socioeconomic groups, not only the poor, use traditional medical services. In essence, traditionally based therapies are thriving in towns and cities because they fill a void for services that are in demand, they are accessible, and they offer culturally recognized responses to illness.

CATEGORIES OF TRADITIONAL HEALERS

Twumasi (1987) groups African traditional healers into four main types of specialties as: (1) Traditional birth attendants; (2) Faith Healers; (3) Herbalists; and (4) Spiritualists. Traditional birth attendants are specialists in obstetrics and pregnancy-related problems. They are the midwives during childbirth, serve as godmothers to young children and play a special role at puberty ceremonies. Their activities include sex education and contraceptive counseling. Faith healers are representatives and leaders of religious movements, especially the Syncretic Churches. Common among faith healers are the leaders of sectarian-based religious movements, the millennial and thurmaturgical Churches. These Churches are becoming second hospitals. Herbalists are healers whose approach to healing is often related to the use and application of herbs. Their methods of treatment and operational procedures are often similar to modern medicine. Spiritualists include fetish priests and priestesses, ritual leaders and others who are specialists in divination. Possession is a common feature of spiritualists and is considered a therapeutic resource. At times making a clear-cut distinction between faith healers and spiritual healers is very difficult. For analytical purposes faith healers operate from a religious movement whereas spiritualists are intermediates between a particular deity or spirit and the public.

FALLACIES AND MISCONCEPTIONS ABOUT TRADITIONAL MEDICINE

Until quite recently, there has been a widespread tendency in western societies to subscribe to one of two fallacies about health beliefs and behavior of indigenous societies. Steven Polgar (1962) labeled them the "empty vessel fallacy" and the "fallacy of the separate capsule." In the former, a territory and people are assumed to lack systematic health beliefs and therapy systems until western biomedicine arrives on the scene to fill the void. The "fallacy of the separate capsule" recognizes the existence of indigenous medical resources and theories of diseases, but maintains that they are inferior and not a viable alternative to biomedicine. Obviously, neither of these positions has any basis in fact.

Every human community has responded to the challenge of restoration and maintenance of health by developing a 'medical system'—the pattern of social institutions and cultural traditions that evolves from deliberate behavior to enhance health (Dunn, 1976). Consequently, medical systems do not stand alone, but are embedded in historically derived contexts of cultural meaning and social norms. In effect, Western biomedicine and African traditional medicine are particular instances or expressions of the broader range of realities surrounding health and healing in society. Expectedly, indigenous African etiological theory of illness is profoundly rooted in socio-cultural and spiritual foundations. Wyllie (1983, P. 46) writing about Ghanaian spiritual and traditional healers stated that "their explanations of illness are hopelessly embedded in a magic-religious theory of causation that is not amenable to testing in a laboratory or clinic." Nevertheless, this medical system evolved from, and is an integral part of the history, culture, traditions, beliefs and social norms of indigenous African society. Consequently, characterizing the African medical system expression as inferior to western biomedicine is simply ethnocentric.

The World Health Organization (1978) defines traditional healers as a group of persons recognized by the community in which they live as competent to provide health by using vegetable, animal and mineral substances and other methods based on the social, cultural and religious backgrounds as well as on the knowledge, attitudes and beliefs that are prevalent in the community regarding physical, mental and social well being and the causation of disease and disability. Since providing healing using culturally acceptable methods and substances is the basic function that physicians perform in any society, any negative characterization or labeling of traditional healers, for example as witch doctors, probably stems from ethnocentrism.

Research on health practices and beliefs suggest that people who seek the prevention and cure of an illness do so in a variety of ways and use various sources determined primarily by their socio-cultural and religious background (Airhihenbuwa, 1987; Airhihenbuwa and Harrison, 1993). Health systems do not exist in and of themselves, they exist as part of larger socio-cultural wholes. When indigenous people cope with physical or emotional symptoms, they classify them within a traditional taxonomy and seek help in the traditional health system. Thus, simply dismissing non-Western values and beliefs about health and healing as primitive, savage, or barbarian, being based on magic, religion or witchcraft is simply ethnocentrism based on ignorance (Seijas, 1975). African healing modalities and practices have been misunderstood and misrepresented in the same way as African culture has been misunderstood.

COLONIALISM AND TRADITIONAL AFRICAN MEDICINE

Before colonial contact, traditional healers were the sole practitioners of medicine throughout the continent. They treated ills and gave protective charms to people who asked for their services — all legitimate activity. Experienced healers instituted training programs based on the informal apprentice model, had consultations, referred patients and developed a medical culture. Amazingly, these traditional healing methods were significantly advanced and paralleled Western medicine in many ways. In 1879, Robert Falchion, a British medical missionary traveling in Baganda (now Uganda), reported a highly sophisticated level of medical practice. He observed the successful performance of a cesarean section with antiseptic technique by a native surgical team. He also saw experiments devised to discover a cure for a local epidemic (Davis, 1959). Although Falchion observed this barely two years after the use of antisepsis in surgery was introduced and advocated in London, it was clear to him that the team, surgical technique and public health experiments were a part of the tradition of the Baganda (Airhihenbuwa and Harrison, 1993). One wonders where African medical technology would be today if such traditions had been allowed to continue and develop.

Colonial rule and the spread of Christian missions in Africa posed an unprecedented challenge to the integrity and character of indigenous religions and their associated systems of traditional healing. Aided by the missions, colonial authorities vigorously repressed and officially banned some organized religious therapy systems. Suddenly, culturally sound health beliefs and practices became "superstitious" and laws were promulgated to criminalize the practice of traditional medicine (Airhihenbuwa and Harrison, 1993). Where it was not criminalized, a policy of "benevolent neglect" toward African medicine and practitioners was adopted (Beck, 1981). Colonial officials did not fully comprehend traditional medicine; they could not reconcile the mixture of supernatural explanations with the rational outcomes from the healers' medicines (Forje, 1989).

The case of Ghana, formerly the Gold Coast, provides an illustrative example. The coming of colonial rule introduced a new medical system in the country to cure and treat the many illnesses. Practitioners of the western system of healing were trained in formal schools of medicine with a distinct professional culture and used highly sophisticated western technological appliances in delivering health care. In essence, the practitioners of the new system of healing were organized under a formidable umbrella system — the British medical profession.

Contact with traditional healing practices produced conflicts in operational style, theoretical orientation, and organizational methods. The colonial government encouraged the institutionalization of the new system, western medicine, by giving it a legislative instrument in 1878. A primary goal of the colonial government was to liquidate native practice of traditional medicine (Fabrega, 1977). Traditional healers were thought to be insincere quacks who lived on the neuroses of their illiterate folks (Fabrega 1977).

Christian missionaries contributed to the denigration of traditional medicine. Because they did not understand the ritual practices inherent in some traditional medical practices, they condemned traditional healers as devilish. They failed to distinguish between traditional herbal medicine practice from witchcraft and psychic-based medical practices. Several generations of Africans educated in colonial government and mission schools and colleges were taught that indigenous religions and traditional healers were savage and primitive (Ademuwagun, et al 1979). Consequently, traditional healing lost its prestige and was stigmatized; healers became *persona non grata*. Yet, because these efforts did not rid the continent of devastating epidemics (Janzen, 1978), traditional healers continued to practice "illegitimately," in secrecy and isolation. Such officially instituted prejudice against traditional medicine persisted for a long time throughout the continent.

In short, the denigration of traditional African medical practices is directly attributable to colonialism and Eurocentrism, primarily due to the misunderstanding of African culture and belief systems. Unfortunately, the result of this deliberate denigration of African healing methods is still with us. For many people today, the mention of the African medicine person still conjures up the fearsome image of the "witch-doctor," clad in fur and feathers, prancing around a fire to the inexorable rhythms of the tom-tom (Maclean, 1971). To such people, traditional medical practitioners thus project an image of the backward, primitive, and the heathen, whom the elites regard as a relic rather than a contemporary force to reckon with (Senah, 1995).

POST-INDEPENDENCE POLICIES

Post-independence policies have been as varied as countries are different. Pillsbury (1982) identifies seven policy options adopted toward traditional medical practitioners (TMPs):

1. Legal prohibition (although impossible to enforce comprehensively

2. Official disregard (assuming they have nothing to contribute).
3. Informal recognition of and occasional cooperation with TMPs.
4. Formal recognition of TMPs and associated institutions.
5. Recruiting and training of TMPs to participate in biomedical health care programs, either through "upgrading" traditional skills or by training and assigning them new tasks as community health workers.
6. Licensing or registration of TMPs (with 4 and 5 above).
7. Integration of TMPs and the biomedical sector, with mutual referrals and two-way co-operation.

Most countries instituted a mixture of these policies. For example, after independence in 1957, Ghana's president, Nkrumah, sought to revive African arts, culture and medicine. A renewed interest in an African way of doing things to distinguish the African from the European became the standard. Within this frame of reference, in 1963, Nkrumah's government appointed a Ghanaian biologist, Mensah Dapaah, "to study and organize traditional healers to form an Association for the advancement of their art and techniques in the delivery of health care" (Dapaah, 1968).

This led to the formation of the Ghana Psychic and Traditional Healing Association in 1963. Mensah Dapaah's work showed that to understand the practice of traditional healing, one must be prepared to understand the healers in their own ways. The herbs can be studied from the scientific point of view but the total therapeutic process was hard to understand in a normal scientific way (Dapaah, 1968). In other words, the scientific method was inappropriate for understanding the therapeutic methods and treatment practices of traditional healers. Dapaah also drew attention to the therapeutic skills of traditional healers in treating ills mainly in the field of psychosomatic diseases (Twumasi, 1987).

The favorable political climate created by the Nkrumah government improved the public image and buttressed the confidence of traditional healers. Because they were not given any official recognition, the legal position of the healers remained fairly ambiguous. Nevertheless, it was no longer an offense to practice traditional healing or for people to use the services of traditional healers. Healers were prosecuted in law courts only when they used their medicine to harm or kill. At this point in national development, a national charter was established to organize traditional healers in the country. The objectives of the national association of traditional healers were:

1. To uphold, protect and promote the best in psychic and traditional healing in Ghana.
2. To encourage the establishment of advanced training programs in traditional healing.
3. To help to introduce and train medical students to appreciate the work of traditional healing.
4. To encourage research work into traditional medicine.

5. To establish clinics in remote places and educate traditional healers in the districts in order to improve on their practices.

In short, before independence, no national association of traditional healers existed. Political independence brought a social and cultural reawakening that culminated in organizing traditional healers. For some time, the role of indigenous healers in the deployment of health services by the Ghana government was purposefully kept ambiguous (Warren et al. 1979). However, the Ministry of Health showed an increasing interest in cooperation with the healers, and made recognizable, if cautious, moves toward rehabilitating indigenous healing systems. Evidence of this shift is the use of traditional birth attendants (TBAs) in Ghana's primary health care system, government support of the construction and operation of the Center for Scientific Research into Plant Medicine, and the recognition of the nationwide Ghana Psychic and Traditional Healers Association (GPTHA).

Government policy has clearly proclaimed the importance of traditional medicine in primary health care, but little money has been invested to develop traditional medicine. Ghana's primary health care program includes plans for TBA training and participation in health care delivery, particularly in rural areas. Currently, Ghana's Ministry of Health has an office for a ministerial secretary charged with responsibility for coordinating traditional healing methods, but a minuscule budget prevents any effective contribution from that office.

At the other extreme is Malawi, which continues to ignore traditional healers. Kalipeni (1995) observes that in Malawi, beyond the modern health care sector, there also flourishes a very large, traditional health care sector including about 18,000 traditional healers and 1,000 traditional birth attendants. So far this group of health care providers has been entirely ignored by the modern health care system and government officials. However, as noted by many scholars, coopting this sector into the modern health care delivery system would yield great benefits toward provision of primary care to the rural communities. The training of traditional healers in the basics of modern medicine and of traditional birth attendants in maternal and child care would complement the overworked personnel in the Western style health care delivery system (Kalipeni, 1995 p. 162).

Most national policies range somewhere between the two extremes of Malawi and Ghana. For example, the fourth National Development Plan of Kenya (1979-83) outlined policy measures governing the extent to which indigenous practitioners could be encouraged to render services in government health institutions (Forje, 1989). Many other countries have moved closer to integrating traditional and western medicines, partly because of the recognition that traditional medicines persist even when the health consumer has access to western medicines deemed more scientific.

Mali and Tanzania exemplify some of the more positive policies toward traditional medical practice. The National Union of Traditional Healers in Mali has established a successful marriage between traditional and modern medicine. Scientific investigation of traditional medicine has reached the industrial stage in producing medicines from local plants. The Mali model blends art, traditional science and technology, myth and magic. According to Forje (1989), many financial organizations are extending assistance to support the Mali experience. In Tanzania, the Medical Research Unit has established experimental farms in different parts of the country where both local plants possessing medicinal and aromatic qualities and plants from other parts of the world are grown. These farms enhance Tanzania's ability to harness local resources in manufacturing plant-derived pharmaceutical and aromatics within the country. In addition, the Traditional Medicine Research Unit has interviewed more than 1,000 traditional healers and 2,683 plant specimens have been collected of which 2,300 have been identified botanically. These plant specimens are claimed to be able to cure more than 100 diseases (Forje, 1989).

Despite increased interest, the character of traditional medicine and the medico-religious functions of healers remain misunderstood. While giving them "credit" is fashionable, indigenous medical traditions are often cast in a negative light. They are still viewed by many westerners and educated Africans, at least publicly, as the incarnation of a shameful legacy of paganism, barbarism, and black magic. TMPs are called "witch doctors" (a misleading term implying that practitioners are witches and therefore, bad people), and their skill dubbed a fetish. Their activities are often held up as examples of irrationality and malpractice, a mixture of superstition, deliberate deception, and ignorance (Maclean, 1971).

Throughout the continent then, TMPs coexist with and complement biomedical facilities. It is expected that they will continue to exercise an increasingly important role in the future as African countries are forced by scarcity and national debt to rely increasingly on indigenous medical resources. Obviously, policies that recognize traditional medicine and act to correct the negative images and stereotypes can be a catalyst for effective and purposeful collaboration. Traditional medical cures are an important component of Africa's rich cultural heritage and should be preserved.

Moreover, because of the enormous burden of ill-health, and the continuing — even increasing — dependence of Africa's people on traditionally based therapies, it makes little sense for traditional medicine to remain discredited because the official health establishment denies its worth or scientific intelligibility. Furthermore, in contrast to the limited reach of biomedical facilities, the influence of traditional medical practitioners is extensive in virtually every African country. Most of the African population has always depended almost exclusively on traditional health services. Less than 50% are considered to have reasonable access to biomedical care. For the entire continent, there is one traditional healer for every 500 people compared with one doctor for every 40,000 (Forje, 1989). In Tanzania at least 75% of the rural population depended on traditional healers by 1989 (Forje, 1989). In Swaziland, for example, Green and Makhubu (1984) report that there are more than 5,000

TMPs and thus a TMP/population ratio of 1:120. At least 85% of the Swazi population is said to use their services. Tanzania has between 20,000 and 50,000 traditional healers compared to between 800 and 1000 western-trained doctors. Traditional midwives are very active and the only providers of obstetrical services in most African villages.

Thus, in contrast to the limited reach of biomedical facilities, the influence of traditional medical practitioners is extensive in virtually every African country. After self-treatment, they are the main providers of health care to the rural poor. In fact, in Africa people use TMPs because biomedicine is unavailable (in many rural areas) or is not a comprehensive, interchangeable or automatically acceptable substitute. Contrary to what critics would have us believe, traditional medicine is not anachronistic, but is the preferred, dependable, and frequently only choice of health care for many in Africa. A recent survey by the Institute of African Studies, University of Nairobi, Kenya, revealed that even those areas where modern health care is available, traditional medical care is still widely used (Nyamwaya, 1986).

It is worrisome that traditional medical knowledge could disappear or become distorted as herbalists grow old. Indoctrinated in modern medicine, today's younger generations discount traditional medicine and associate its practice with backwardness, quackery and charlatanism. Consequently, diffusion of traditional medical knowledge from generation to generation is becoming ineffective (Forje, 1989). Clearly, urgent measures are necessary to preserve what is left of traditional Africa's body of knowledge regarding disease, health and healing.

COUNTERFEIT DRUGS AND TRADITIONAL MEDICINE IN AFRICA

A particularly difficult problem affecting the image of traditional medicine in Africa is fake drugs. Trade in counterfeit drugs in which corn meal, face powder, chalk, and other non-medicinal substances are packaged and sold, mostly as antibiotics, is booming. Indeed, it is estimated that 60-70% of all drugs in Nigeria are either counterfeit or contain only a fraction of the declared strength (Alubo, 1994). Consequently, drugs manufactured in Nigeria are banned in several countries. In a 1990 incident, counterfeit paracetamol syrup resulted in the tragic deaths of 109 children! Similar examples, with less tragic results have been reported in Ghana and Sierra Leone.

Unfortunately, there is a tendency to lump *bona fide* traditional medical practitioners with the poorly informed and deadly practices of some itinerant drug vendors, back street doctors and other fringe practitioners (Good, 1987). Dealing with the fake drug problem is difficult. How does government encourage the development of the African pharmaceutical industry, especially that based on traditional herbal remedies, without endangering the health of millions of Africans through fake and usually dangerous drugs? The privatization of health services currently advocated by the World Bank and IMF is bound to escalate this problem. In Africa, free enterprise medicine with its inherent profit maximization translates into many itinerant drug vendors who administer injections for every ailment or no ailment at all, often with questionable substances. Multiple usage of one needle for different customers, with or without sterilization, is certainly an effective way to cut costs and maximize profits. Nevertheless, it provides an optimal environment for spreading such illnesses as hepatitis and HIV/AIDS (Gould, 1994). Sadly, TMPs get blamed for the misdeeds of fraudulent con-artists pursuing self-enrichment schemes. Such practices undermine African traditional medicine. Urgent measures to protect authentic African pharmaceutical developments must be instituted and criminal western pharmaceutical pushers must be dealt with.

STRENGTHS AND WEAKNESSES OF TRADITIONAL MEDICINE

What are the strengths and weaknesses of traditional medicine? Good (1987) outlines several of them. Some important strengths are highlighted below:

1. TMPs are culturally more acceptable. They understand the belief system, needs, and fears of their patients and the necessity of treating not only the symptoms but also the social and spiritual causes of the disease.
2. TMPs are generally quite adaptive. They seek out and adopt innovations in healing.
3. TMPs perform primarily several psychological and sociological functions. Some of these include anxiety and stress relief, deviance control and minimizing the shock of cultural change. These are accomplished effectively through reinforcement of the patient and involving the primary social group of the patient in diagnosis and therapy.
4. TMPs collectively possess a large body of indigenous technical knowledge, ranging from individual and group psychology and psychotherapy to the properties and actions of local pharmacopoeias.
5. TMPs treat a broad spectrum of disease, including conditions that are not diagnosed, misdiagnosed, and incompletely diagnosed, or are no longer manageable by biomedical practitioners according to biomedical standards. Two of the best-known examples include hypertension and diabetes (Forje, 1989; Harrison, 1974).

Major weaknesses of traditional medicine include:

1. Lack of standardized training for TMPs. Much variation in length and quality of training of traditional healers results in great variety in expertise

and quality of care.

2. Dosage imprecision is another problem. Traditional medicine itself is ritualized, the medicine has no measurement, or at best, measurement is imprecise.
3. TMPS often lack elementary understanding of the functions of hygiene and sanitation.

Thus, while it would be naive to suggest that traditional medicine is a panacea for Africa's health problems, it has selective potential that should be encouraged and exploited (Airhihenbuwa and Harrison, 1993).

In contrast with traditional medicine, biomedicine is inaccessible to many Africans, and has a pervading urban bias due to its technological dependence and cost. Biomedicine, at least in Africa, over-emphasizes curative services rendered in hospital settings, and is unavailable to a large section of the population. Also, biomedicine fails to cope with a broad spectrum of illnesses because they are not recognized (no diagnosis), misdiagnosed, or incompletely diagnosed. Unless diagnosis and therapy proceed from a practical knowledge of the local human ecology and culturally derived labels, expectations and meanings of illness, even a conscientious indigenous biomedicine practitioner will frequently fail to recognize, or will misinterpret, patients' symptoms.

Given these limitations of both biomedicine and traditional medicine, the way of the future lies in active cooperation and collaboration between African traditional and western biomedicine. An impressive example of the potential benefit of such cooperation is the Korup Forest Project in Cameroon which has revealed many forest plants containing valuable chemicals such as fungicides, dyes, and even natural contraceptive and aphrodisiac compounds (Forje, 1989). More than ninety substances have been isolated of which 38 are new to science with potential commercial use in industry or medicine. Certain treatments against Hodgkin's disease and some forms of pediatric leukemia have been developed from plants grown in Madagascar (Forje, 1989). In Ghana, the Center for Research into Plant Medicine in Mampong-Akwapim is conducting clinical trials of herbal cures for diabetes, hypertension, asthma and several major diseases.

CONCLUSION

Until the arrival of colonialists, Africa had a well-developed medical system. Colonialist introduction of biomedicine and opposition severely undermined, but could not eliminate, traditional medicine. Post-independence policies toward traditional medicine have been lackluster and frequently inconsistent. Preference is usually given to biomedicine although it is inaccessible to most rural residents, while traditional medicine is merely treated with lip service or benign neglect. Such policies not only undermine Africa's cultural heritage, but deprive rural residents of a viable alternative system of health care. Moreover, they are based on a myopic and ethnocentric viewpoint. Sadly, it is the rural poor — with no modern health facilities, low incomes and poor sanitation — who suffer most from such policies.

Contrary to the western viewpoint, traditional medicine is neither anachronistic nor necessarily dangerous. In any medical system, not just African traditional medicine, the potential for danger through malpractice and abuse of medications is present. Such limitations as dosage imprecision and lack of standardized training for healers make African traditional medicine clearly not a panacea for Africa's health problems. Yet, it is an important component of Africa's cultural heritage that should be preserved and developed further. The increasing interest in alternative healing methods in the west should signal to African policy makers the importance of preserving traditional cures and remedies. Indigenous medicine is the only form of medicine available and acceptable to many rural residents. This is sufficient reason to encourage its preservation and development. Truly indigenous privatization of health care may begin here. Investing in and encouraging traditional medicine will surely extend health care to many people who currently have no access to essential health services. Perhaps the tried and tested herbs and cures of Africa can be made available globally.

Finally, whether they operate in the western scientific tradition or in the ethnomedical tradition, the goal of all health practitioners is to achieve and maintain a satisfactory level of health for clients and communities. Despite this common goal, the predominant attitude between the two systems has been mutual disregard. Due to significant differences in principles and practice, merging the disparate systems may not be a realistic option. The challenge is to identify areas where the two systems can complement each other and establish working, dynamic contacts in these areas. Such cooperation promises the only hope for providing health services to the millions of rural residents who lack access to the expensive, highly sophisticated, urban-based biomedical facilities.

REFERENCES

Ademuwagun, Z. A. *et al. 1979. African Therapeutic Systems*. Waltham, MA: Crossroads Press.

Airhihenbuwa, C. O. 1987. "Nigerian Heads of Households' Attitude toward Modern and Traditional Medicines." *Journal of Rural Health,* 3 (11): 21-30.

Airhihenbuwa, C. O. and Harrison, I. E. 1993. Traditional Medicine in Africa: Past, Present, and Future. *Health and Health Care in Developing Countries*. Philadelphia: Temple University Press.

Alubo, S. O. 1994. "Death for Sale: A Study of Drug Poisoning and Deaths in Nigeria." *Social Science and Medicine,* 38 (1): 97-103.

Anyinam, C. 1987. "Availability, Accessibility, Acceptability and Adaptability: Four attributes of African Ethnomedicine." *Social Science and Medicine,* 25:803-12.

Beck, A. 1981. *Medicine, Tradition, and Development in Kenya and Tanzania.* Waltham, Mass.: Crossroads Press.

Davis, J. N. P. 1959. The Development of Scientific Medicine in the African Kingdom of Bungakitara.*Medical History,* 3 (49): 47.

Dapaah, M. 1968. "Traditional Healing." *Ghana Journal of Science*, 21:16-21.

Dunn, F. L. 1976. "Traditional Asian Medicine and Cosmopolitan Medicine as Adaptive Systems. In C. Leslie, ed. *Asian Medical Systems*. Berkeley: University of California Press.

Fabrega, H. 1977. The Scope of Ethnomedical Science. *Cult. Med. Psychiat. 1:* 201-225.

Forje, J. W. 1989. *Science and Technology in Africa.* Harlow, Essex: Longman.

Good, C. M. 1987a. *Ethnomedical Systems in Africa*. New York: Guilford Press.

Good, C. M. 1987b. "Community Health in Tropical Africa: Is Medical Pluralism a Hindrance or a Resource?" In R. Akhtar, ed. *Health and Disease in Tropical Africa.* New York: Harwood Academic Publishers (pp. 13-50).

Gould, P. *1994. The Slow Plague - A Geography of the AIDS Pandemic.* Cambridge: Blackwell.

Green, E. C. and Makhubu, L. 1984. "Traditional Healers in Swaziland: Toward Improved Cooperation between the Traditional and Modern Health Sectors." *Social Science and Medicine,* 18 (10): 71-79.

Harrison, I. E. 1974. "First International Symposium on Traditional Medical Therapy." *Medical Anthropology Newsletter,* 6 (1): 10-13.

Janzen, J. M. 1978. *The Quest for Therapy in Lower Zaire.* Berkeley: University of California Press.

Kalipeni, E. 1995. Demographic and Spatial Aspects of the Health Care Delivery System in Malawi. *Global Perspectives on Health Care*. New Jersey: Prentice Hall Inc.

Koumare, M. 1993. Traditional medicine and psychiatry in Africa. In R. H. Bennerman, J. Burton, & C. Wen-Chieh, eds. *Traditional Medicine and Health Care Coverage*. Geneva: World Health Organization.

Lasker, J. N. 1981. "Choosing Among Therapies: Illness Behavior in the Ivory Coast." *Social Science and Medicine,* 15 (A): 157-68.

Maclean, U. 1971. *Magical Medicine. A Nigerian Case Study.* Baltimore: Penguin Books.

Nyamwaya, D. 1986. "Traditional Health Care in Rural Kenya." *The Courier,* No. 99, September/October.

Pillsbury, B. L. K. 1982. "Policy and Evaluation Perspectives on Traditional Health Practitioners in National Health Care Systems." *Social Science and Medicine,* 16 (18): 25-34.

Polgar, S. 1962. "Health and Human Behavior: Areas of interest Common in the Medical and Social Sciences." *Current Anthropology,* 3: 159-205.

Prince, R. 1964. "Indigenous Aerobe Psychiatry." In A. Kiev, ed. *Magic Faith and Healing.* New York: The Free Press of Glencoe.

Seijas, H. 1975. "An Approach to the Study of Medical Aspects of Culture." *Current Anthropology,* 14 (5): 344-345.

Senah, K. A. 1995. Ethnomedicine in the Context of Health Care Delivery in Ghana. *Global Perspectives on Health Care.* New Jersey: Prentice-Hall Inc.

Stock, R. 1995. *Africa South of the Sahara: A Geographical Interpretation.* New York: Guilford.

Twumasi, P.A. 1987. "The Role of Traditional Medicine in a Primary Health Care System: The Ghanaian Experience." In R. Akhtar, ed. *Health and Disease in Tropical Africa.* New York: Harwood Academic Publishers (pp. 497-512).

Warren, D.M. 1979. "The role of EMI Analyses in Medical Anthropology: The Case of the Bonn of Ghana." In Z. Ademuwagun, et al. eds. *African Therapeutic Systems.* Waltham, MA: African Studies Association.

World Health Organization. 1978. *The Promotion and Development of Traditional Medicine.* WHO Technical Report Series, 622. Geneva.

Wyllie, R. W. 1983. "Ghanaian Spiritual and Traditional Healers' Explanation of Illness: a Preliminary Survey." *Journal of Religion In Africa,* 14: 46-51.

8

SOME MISCONCEPTIONS OF AGRICULTURAL PRODUCTION, POPULATION, AND LAND RESOURCES IN AFRICA

Godson C. Obia
Department of Geology & Geography
Eastern Illinois University

INTRODUCTION

Agriculture is the backbone of the economies of most countries in Africa (Gyimah-Brempong, 1992, p. 22). The Economic Commission for Africa (1983) and the World Bank (1984) see the role of agriculture as vital and important in the economic and social development of Africa. The contributions of agriculture, measured in terms of agricultural population as a percentage of total population, agricultural exports as a percentage of total exports, and the share of total imports financed by agricultural exports, are paramount in the development of most African nations. For many countries, therefore, "agriculture is still the most important sector of the economy in terms of the large number of people who earn a living from it and also because it is the main source of food and raw materials for manufacturing" (Udo, 1982, p. 106). Particularly in the rural areas, agriculture continues to be the dominant economic activity among the majority of rural residents. For such people the availability of land for agricultural production is essential for subsistence and the conduct of daily living.

In spite of these advantages, agriculture has lost the security it once held for rural producers, and its contributions to social and economic development have become marginalized. The agricultural sector in Africa, therefore, faces several tough challenges: to feed the growing population, to preserve the basic resources of soil, water, crop, and stock inventories and varieties, and to properly manage these resources (McMaster, 1992, p.194). While some 70 percent or more of the population of most African countries are engaged in farming, pastoralism, and fishing, the vast majority of these people are still found in the traditional sector (Binns, 1992). According to O'Connor, ". . . for the great majority the past twenty years have brought very little change in material well-being [and] most rural households are producing and consuming much the same today as they were in the late 1960s" (O'Connor, 1991, p.109).

Most traditional farmers still have low technical skills and employ low levels of technological inputs in their production. Farm tools remain simple in their design and use. In most tropical farming areas, hoes, machetes, axes, and several kinds of digging tools are used to clear the vegetation, prepare the land for cultivation, and plant the crops. The human effort is, therefore, quite substantial and paramount, yet the return on human efforts is steadily declining (as measured by per capita production), while the quality of the land resource base is deteriorating. At the same time, population is growing rapidly, and, given present conditions of production and land use, has the potential to further reduce food production.

On the eve of the twenty-first century, Africa faces the daunting challenge of providing sustenance to a rapidly growing population from a steadily declining land resource base. However, efforts to isolate crucial causative factors and seek mitigating measures have been fraught with debilitating misconceptions. In particular, for almost four decades, there has been a steady proliferation of studies on Africa, with one common thread: to paint a gloomy and alarming picture of how Africa's population growth rate is causing food deficits, and creating irreversible environmental damage. The result (unintended in some cases) has been to cast Africa in a Malthusian trap, whereby the solutions to agricultural production problems and environmental degradation are seen to rest on the ability to control population growth. This perspective has hindered adequate and holistic assessments of the problem, thus ignoring other relevant factors.

The primary objective of this Chapter is to evaluate the conditions of Africa's land resource base, population growth, and agricultural production, and challenge some misconceptions associated with these conditions. The chapter will also focus on the interplay of agricultural production, population pressure, and environmental degradation in order to elucidate new directions for future socioeconomic development. It challenges the conventional wisdom that population growth and the quality of the resource base per se are responsible for the decline in agricultural production, and argues that human factors are at the heart of the misnomer in agricultural production and land degradation. For instance, the channeling of investment into urban-industrial complexes has, by fault or design, directly affected agriculture through divestment, and indirectly through the non-maintenance and deterioration of rural circulatory infrastructures -- roads, railroads, rivers, and the transportation systems associated with them. Decades of neglect and malignant overcultivation of the land resource base have left more and more people depending on a dwindling resource base. These conditions have led to a steady decline in per capita agricultural production, the degeneration of agricultural infrastructure, and the existence of pervasive poverty in predominantly agricultural settings.

The challenge to revitalize agricultural production is daunting, but must begin by debunking some of the harmful misconceptions or myths about the conditions of population growth, agricultural production, and the land resource base. Some pertinent questions must be asked: First, what are the conditions of population growth and the physical resource base? Second, what misconceptions about agricultural production, population growth, and the physical resource base inhibit a holistic assessment of the problem, and a search for more comprehensive solutions? Third, how do we challenge these misconceptions in order to chart a realistic course for future development?

CONDITIONS OF THE LAND RESOURCE BASE

The combination of physical land limitations and human land use factors can produce a precarious tangle of land degradation, in which deforestation, desertification, marginalization of agricultural land, and overpopulation contribute to the decline of agricultural production and the exacerbation of poverty. The condition of Africa's land resources is still marginally explored and understood, thus hindering the development of adequate measures to palliate production problems. Even what is known is not easily discernible, partly because of persistent misconceptions about the quality, quantity, and impact of these resources on production. Some characteristics and misconceptions of the African land resource base are discussed below.

Poor tropical and erodible soils and the conditions of Africa's tropical climates have been blamed for the deficiencies in agricultural production. Although very few substantive, confirmatory scientific studies exist to show a causal link between tropical environments and agricultural production, the misconceptions continue to be perpetuated. Although much of Africa suffers from land capability deficiencies, these conditions are not peculiar to Africa. Asia is suffused with arid and rugged topographies in areas such as western China and southern India, and dense tropical forests and destructive flood regimes limit agricultural production in such countries as Bangladesh and Indonesia. Yet countries such as China and India, with approximately two-fifths of humanity, have managed to feed their people within their environmental constraints. Why, then, is there such a global alarm about the conditions of the African land resource base, and its impact on food production? Although a good land resource base is a necessary condition for viable agricultural production, limitations thereof should not be a sufficient justification for Africa's declining agricultural productivity and the associated conditions of famine, hunger, and poverty. As the example of developed countries has shown, technology, education, skills, and proper management techniques have combined to enhance the productivity of arid and semi-arid lands through irrigation and other dryland farming methods, swamps through drainage and reclamation, mountain slopes through terracing, and cold lands through greenhouse techniques. There is, therefore, more to Africa's declining productivity than the limitations of its physical environment. Let us explore some of these factors.

Even for soils classified as suitable for agriculture, mismanagement could trigger irreparable damage. Oram (1988, p. 10) has suggested several reasons for the fragility of tropical soils, which characterize the environment of production in most of the continent. He argues that tropical soils are vulnerable for agricultural production because of several inherent characteristics. These include the following:

1. Soils in tropical rain forests are often extremely acidic and subject to severe erosion and loss of organic matter once the tree cover is removed.
2. Light-textured soils in semiarid, marginal areas, when cultivated and overgrazed, are vulnerable to wind erosion and desertification.
3. Poorly drained irrigated soils in arid lands easily become waterlogged and saline, unfit for cropping. Since there is a preponderance of land in the arid and humid equatorial climates, it would then stand to reason that any type of agriculture practiced in the continent is limited by these physical conditions.

Furthermore, soils in these environments have been characterized as "extremely fragile under agricultural use, have various combinations of difficult soils, climates, and topographies compounded by mismanagement" (Oram, Peter A.; as quoted in Mellor, 1988, p. 10). According to the World Resources Institute "Farming activities are major contributors to soil erosion, salinization, and loss of nutrients" world wide, but "most of the land damaged by agriculture and overgrazing is in Asia and Africa" (World Resources Institute, 1992 p. 96 and 97). While the conditions of the physical resource base, as pictured in the above statements, are hardly controvertible, accepting them as direct correlates of poor yields and limited agricultural productivity would seem to ignore adept management practices that have been successful elsewhere in the world, especially in similar environments. Yet it hardly matters; most publications on Africa harp on the limiting physical conditions to the extent that they ignore important human-cultural practices that are necessary to enhance production and conserve resources.

In contrast, another disabling misconception about Africa's land resource base (one that appears benign on the surface) is that Africa possesses an abundant supply of land. This is true only to the extent that the majority of Africans depend on agriculture for their livelihood and Africa is the second largest continent. Fueled from colonial stereotypes of Africa as "the dark continent," the perpetuation of this myth has produced a land use ethic that has neglected proper stewardship of the land. Agricultural systems that developed under conditions of low population density--for example, shifting cultivation and pastoral nomadism--have seen little change even at a time of high population density.

Overall, natural environmental constraints must be seen only as partial contributors to the alarming decline in food production that is now rife in Africa. Arguably, anthropogenic factors-- caused, in part, by the rapid growth of human and animal populations--coupled with human mismanagement of environmental resources, have compounded the problem of environmental degradation, especially in fragile, marginal areas. Consequently, increases in agricultural production have lagged behind dramatic increases in population, thereby resulting in per capita production decline. The process of production decline can be reversed, if African nations will take solid steps to reduce the frontier mentality that is pervasive in the rural areas. It is reversible because the United States did it in the aftermath of the Dust Bowl, when the agricultural land base was badly degraded. Rather than lament the deplorable condition of their land after the wind storms of the 1930s, or blame it on the growing numbers of farmers at the time, the United States government adopted technological alternatives and sound land use practices to raise agricultural productivity while conserving the quality of the land resource base. The challenge to boost agricultural production while conserving the resources was instrumental in creating such stalwarts of present day agriculture as the Soil Conservation Service, the Agricultural Stabilization and Conservation Service, and other such agencies of the US Department of Agriculture. Africa is at a critical crossroads in its agricultural production, and must seek comprehensive options that enhance production and protect the land resource at the same time.

Unless immediate action is taken, future levels of aggregate and per capita agricultural production in Africa will be seriously constrained by the combination of physical land deterioration and human resource mismanagement factors. Population growth will have the effect of increasing the man-land ratio and exceeding the carrying capacity of the land resource. The problem of land deterioration will be further accentuated by acute environmental conditions such as drought, leaching, and soil erosion, which either directly reduce the stock of good agricultural land, or attenuate land fertility. Unless concerted efforts are made (and soon), the crisis will grow deeper and the cost of abatement procedures will escalate. The African resolve to improve agricultural production and provide more raw materials for industrial expansion, has been the cornerstone of national policies and development plans in the majority of independent countries. In the 1960s, the future of Africa seemed so clear: a continent endowed with innumerable natural and human raw materials, to be integrated into a prosperous network of urban-rural, agro-industrial development. Thirty years later, the future seems very gloomy and population growth has become a common culprit as experts try to understand what went wrong. What then are the implications of population growth on land resource degradation and agricultural production decline?

POPULATION AND AGRICULTURAL PRODUCTION

Africa is a continent with a tremendous human resource capacity. Pessimists see the burgeoning numbers of Africans as a veritable threat to the physical and economic resources of the continent. These "experts" characterize population growth as the inevitable time bomb that will destabilize the continent. They pitch their sophistry by citing population growth rates and predicting future increases. It is not difficult to sense the alarm in statements such as: "Among world regions, Africa is experiencing the greatest proportional increase in population, projected to increase from 642 million in 1990 to 1.6 billion in 2025" (World Resources Institute, 1992, p. 245). A heightened sense of urgency and concern is often generated by emphasizing the high growth rate of the population and linking it to food production deficits and gross national product per person. This begs the question of whether rates of population should be the primary focus for solving the food production dilemma.

Let us state the facts and assess the problems. Between 1965 and 1989, the African population grew at an average annual rate of 2.9 percent (higher than the rates for Latin America and Asia--the other high growth regions). At the same time, the gross national product and private consumption grew at an average annual rate of 0.0 percent and -1.0 per capita, respectively. In the same period, the share of agriculture in GDP saw a negative percentage change of -2.3, and the percentage change in calorie supply per capita remained unchanged. Taken at their face value, rates of growth serve as deterrents to increased production per person, by adding more people to a population when resources are declining. However, to adopt such a monolithic interpretation of growth rates is retrogressive because it ignores the importance of other salient factors in the agricultural production equation. The problem with rates of growth is that focusing on the "alarming" rates, especially the rate of population growth, shifts emphasis from holistic planning to mere population planning. This seems to be the direction that African nations are being pushed to take. Quite clearly, this approach smacks of a Malthusian trap. If Africa consumes itself with population solutions per se in order to improve the well-being of its people, it would be following a path to social and economic development that most industrialized countries abhorred and side-stepped to get to their present state. As is all too well known, Europe defied Malthus by boosting its agricultural production and improving the socio-economic well-being of its people. It is here that Africa's problem lies: the inability to enhance agricultural production, and the slow pace of socio-economic development.

Unfortunately for Africa, the indiscriminate use of growth rates has enshrouded the continent in a veil of negativism. Consequently, rapid population growth is vigorously peddled as a scapegoat for the ills facing Africa. It is perhaps no small wonder that efforts to control the African population have become pivotal in setting international policies for developmental assistance. IMF and World Bank loans or development assistance to some African countries are pegged to some conditionalities which require population control measures. In some instances, loans are given for directly establishing population control measures, or executing existing policies. The problem with this attitude toward population is that African nations in dire need of development funds may be coerced into development paths that yield less than optimum dividends.

Population conditions are nonetheless critical in the planning for agricultural production expansion, and must be clearly understood in charting a path for the future. The result of increased population is that land resources for agricultural production are overused. In rural environments, where well-being and survival are directly tied to land availability, land-hunger is causing dire environmental problems, and poverty is prevalent. Once deemed adequate, arable land has become scarce, marginal land of low capability classification for production is being brought into productive use, and per capita yields have plummeted. In periods of desperation, farmers have cut down once thriving forests in order to bring more land into cultivation. This is a futile attempt, since the fertility of such forest soils quickly declines under frequent use and poor management commonly associated with the expansion of agricultural production into marginal lands.

Another dimension of the population problem is that the rural areas of Africa have historically been branded agricultural areas, in which the majority of the people derive their incomes or earn their livelihood from agriculture. Consequently, government involvement in creating non-agricultural or tertiary occupations has been slow, at the least. Moreover, the support for agriculture has always lagged significantly behind the support for city-based industrial activities or services. Therefore, rural people who have no access to land, or who have overcultivated their available land, have limited access to other economic activities. When alternatives are available, they may be at cross-purposes with environmental protection, and may indeed accelerate the rate of environmental and land resource deterioration. A good example is what happens when able young men resort to trading in charcoal and logged wood instead of moving to the city. The consequent deforestation is damaging to the land, and may, in some circumstances, render the land unproductive through loss of nutrients from soil erosion and leaching.

This is particularly detrimental to the youth, among whom unemployment rate is quite high. Disillusioned by the cruel realities of rural life, these young men often drift to the cities in search of perceived opportunities. For many the reality is cruel, as there exists an unprecedented level of poverty and despair among the ranks of the rural poor who move to the city in search of opportunities. The city is equally experiencing the overuse of resources, and urban population trends indicate that this dilemma is not abating. In 1960, urban population was 18 percent of total population; by 1990 the proportion had increased to 34 percent. During this period, urban population changed by approximately 5 percent. A detrimental consequence of this trend of emigration from the rural areas is that food production for both rural and urban populations is relegated to women and older men. This phenomenon is created, as experts believe, by the fact that rural-urban migration is sex- and age-selective; that is, more young people are prone to leave in search of a better life in the cities. Rural farm labor thus becomes scarce and costly. Without alternatives, the farmers barely manage to subsist with their families.

EVALUATING THE INTERPLAY OF FACTORS

Developing countries of Africa face the challenge to increase agricultural production, to assess and remediate the impact of population growth on agricultural production and consumption, and to stem the irreversible loss of environmental resources. This challenge must involve a holistic problem-solving framework. So far, the development of such a framework is marred by the persistent proliferation of misconceptions about African agricultural development. What follows is an evaluation of some misconceptions about the interplay of population and agricultural production, and the corresponding critique of such misconceptions. According to John Mellor (1988, p. 10): "the most pervasive manifestation of environmentally destructive poverty in developing countries is the dangerous exploitation of fragile resources by burgeoning populations. Deforestation and cultivation of easily eroded land and overgrazing of natural pastures are the most obvious examples." The conventional interpretation for Africa is that as more people stake their claims to a dwindling resource base for mere subsistence, more forests and hillsides will be cleared. Erosion-induced soil loss will increase. More marginal drylands will be overgrazed and overcultivated, and more scarce water resources will be depleted by both humans and animals (Oram, 1988a). Thus, as is typical, population is seen as the *raison d'etre* for food production deficits and degradation of the environment. It would be remiss to not acknowledge population as a contributory factor in food production problems, or to ignore the acute food deficit condition in many African nations. In his construction of potential food deficits and surpluses in Sub-Saharan Africa in the year 2000, Oram (1988b, p. 34) shows the *"agroclimatic population density"* by ecological zones. His assessment, based on a study by the FAO (1982), indicates that less than thirty percent of the countries of Africa are potential food surplus producers, and a greater percentage are potential (or actual) critical food deficit countries.

However, is population the cause of food deficits or just one of the myriad factors that help to exacerbate food production problems? I contend that population pressure acts to reduce land productivity only if other critical factors are absent--factors such technology, skills, education, political instability, foreign exploitation of resources, and domestic and international market conditions.

The inevitable competition for scarce resources and the continuing use of traditional techniques and equipment result in declining yields and productivity, widespread poverty, and the marginalization of the environment. Elsewhere in the world, the conditions are not markedly better than the ones in Africa. What is different is the varying combinations of technical and cultural factors that are needed to sustain agricultural production without causing irreversible damage to the physical resource base. Unfortunately, Africa is being told that the methods that worked for Europe, North America, and some countries of Asia are not possible for Africa, either because of the condition of African land resources or the rapid growth of population. Yet, hardly did any of the countries of the developed world attain high standards of development merely by waiting until population growth was controlled, or the quality of the land resource was upgraded. Even more disturbing is the fact that African nations are buying into the pernicious misconceptions being diffused about Africa, and are systematically abandoning potentially productive methods after a short period of experimentation. Consequently, it becomes convenient to acquiesce to the viewpoint that population growth and poor land resources are the cardinal problems facing agricultural production. Africa continues to face objections to the use of proven methods of production, and examples abound.

One measure that has been suggested to provide more food is to intensify agricultural land use in productive areas, and to seek alternative, environmentally safe methods for more fragile lands. Mellor (1988, p.11) suggests that "to relieve population pressure on the environment in developing countries, population control must be combined with increased intensity of land use in high-potential agricultural areas," which will in turn "relieve population pressures on more fragile lands." This has been done successfully elsewhere in the world. But rather than promote these methods for Africa, with an accent on environmentally appropriate methods in high-density areas, objections resonate and negativism prevails. The World Resources Institute objects to intensification on this basis:

> permanent cropping and cattle grazing deplete soil fertility or cause soil erosion if they are too intensive. As soil fertility declines, crop yields fall and more forest must be cleared to maintain the level of food production. When yields drop too low the land is abandoned" (*World Resources Institute*, 1988, p. 71).

Let us, for the sake of argument, confine intensification to dry areas of Africa. Conventional wisdom would have us believe that in dry environments, the overcultivation and overgrazing of grasslands exposes the land to wind and water erosion, desertification, and the irreversible loss of land for crop cultivation and grazing of livestock. If the fear of these problems should limit Africa's intensification, why do the United States, Russia, Australia, Israel, and Saudi Arabia, to name a few countries, continue to practice viable, productive agriculture in similar environments? The problem lies in the use of appropriate technology--technology that is appropriate to the culture and to the environment.

Africa has not made the proper technological transition that is a vital force in increasing agricultural production. Therefore, even when good land is available for cultivation, intensification of cultivation will involve the use of new methods of production and improved technologies, an effort that has met with limited success in many African countries. As Peter Oram argues, the challenge in making the transition to a more productive, intensive agriculture can be daunting because:

> In African countries with abundant tropical forests that should have the capacity to feed their own populations as well as those of other nations, this technological transition is not proving easy, and self-sufficiency has been falling. Farmers still cling to their traditional shifting cultivation practices (even where rising population pressures dictate a change) because they lack resources and because, thus far, the new techniques cannot sustain continuous annual crops in the fragile soils of the forest zone (Oram, 1988b p. 34).

But daunting situations are not necessarily destined for failure. If proper steps are taken, the difficult road to technological transition can yield rewarding dividends in the form of improved agricultural production. However, African nations must work systematically to reduce serious handicaps that stand to imperil any efforts to increase agricultural production.

A major handicap in the use of new techniques to increase agricultural productivity is the lack of skilled and trained humanpower for agricultural improvements. In the tradition of colonial education, rural education has traditionally prepared school-leavers to seek better opportunities in the urban areas, thus leaving the uneducated with farming and rural production activities. This trend exposes an obvious bias in rural development: the "identification of agriculture with lack of education and the latter with non-agricultural employment" (Ega and Famoriyo, 1988, pp. 157-165). As a result, parents encourage their children to use education as a ticket out of rural poverty, and a chance (even if far-fetched) at helping their parents. It is, therefore, a terrible irony that while urban-based technological innovations are expected to diffuse to the rural areas for improved production and well-being, those who stand to benefit from the new changes are making a speedy and mass exodus from the rural areas. One cannot ignore the traditional nexus between poverty, fuelwood cutting, deforestation, and desertification, and the increasing deterioration of the land resources base in both wet and dry areas. Although forestation projects have become popular in Africa, especially in the sub-Saharan region, there is growing concern that poverty is helping to accelerate environmental destruction (Mellor, 1988, p. 8). Of great concern are the permanent or semi-permanent clearance of forest for agricultural production or other purposes (Grainger, 1986), especially to meet increasing fuelwood needs.

ALTERNATIVE CONSIDERATIONS FOR IMPROVEMENTS IN AGRICULTURAL PRODUCTION

After attaining independence, most African countries began a march toward increased prosperity, based on the euphoria of technological emancipation. Technical solutions to agricultural and industrial problems were projected to lead Africa to increased productivity and consumption. The design of economic development plans was, therefore, predicated upon the urgent need to achieve rapid industrialization and mechanization. In the tradition of center-periphery models, which were employed successfully by Europe and North America, the concentration of technology in the cities would be the mechanism to erode rural backwardness by infusing new techniques of production into rural agricultural production. In retrospect, some experts have argued that for technology to be employed in creating acceptable levels of rural development (Stamp, 1989, p. 1), it must be seen as "an attitude of mind, not an assemblage of artifacts" (Achebe, 1982, as quoted in Stamp, 1989, p. 1).

Several questions must be asked about the present and future of African development. First, if past attempts at development through the "assemblage of artifacts" have "brought very little change in material well-being," what "attitude of mind" is needed to reverse the process? Second, given the fact that there is nothing inherently sinister about the use of technology, what options exist to ensure that technology works for, and not against, African development? Finally, what operational steps are needed to refocus African development to improve the Physical Quality of Life Index (PQLI) (Morris, 1979 and Nijim, 1990) of Africans?

The realignment of global economic and political power, which followed on the heels of the fall of communism, has marginalized African interests. As the number of competitors for foreign aid has increased, the modest share once received by some African countries has shrunk. This is perhaps the best medicine for African development. In these tough times, African countries must reevaluate their development strategies and, in the area of agricultural development, must go back to the basics of rural development. What are these basic steps?

Reestablishing Agricultural Productivity Security

African nations should try to regain the security that agriculture once afforded them, rather than continue to pursue misguided and misconceived policies of economic development. The trend in food exports and imports mirrors the tragedy of agricultural production--decreasing export production and increasing food imports to supplement domestic production declines. In the early years of the 1960-1970 decade, when many African countries became independent, Africa was a net exporter of an average of 1.2 million tons of staple food (Eicher, 1992), with West Africa accounting for "all of Africa's net exports of staple foods (mainly non-cereals such as groundnuts and palm oil) at independence in 1960" (Paulino, 1987). The 1970s saw a disappearance of this net export trend in staples. Eicher (1992) summarizes the trend in this way:

1. In the mid-1970s Africa was importing 2.5 million tons of staple food a year, with West Africa contributing half of total imports;
2. The negative trends from 1960 to the mid 1970s reflected West Africa's change from exporter to net food importer; and
3. West Africa's decline in food exports resulted from the low growth rate of millet and sorghum production and the decline of groundnut production -- the three dominant crops in the region.

The decline in food exports would not be so critical, if agricultural production met domestic demands for food. Accelerated levels of food imports, especially in crops in which Africa enjoyed a comparative advantage in the past, underscore the failure of the economic development policies in some African countries to see domestic production as the benchmark of industrialization. Caught in a web of competing demands for scarce resources, decision-makers seem to have taken the road of rapid, large-scale industrialization, at the expense of agricultural production. Nigeria is an archetype of countries in this category. Nigeria, among other countries in Africa, imports large amounts of palm oil from Malaysia. While domestic demand for palm oil has increased for cooking, Nigeria cannot produce adequate amounts to meet the demand. According to Eicher, the experience is "humbling to Nigeria because at independence in 1960, it was the world's leading producer and exporter of palm oil" (Eicher, 1992, p. 80). Faced with food shortages, many African countries experience serious problems of rising food imports, rising prices, and decreased productivity (Binns, 1992). For countries such as Nigeria, it was neither the poor quality of the land resource base nor the growth in population that created this condition; it was the misguided policies of rapid industrialization, which neglected agriculture and rural development as the lasting foundations of economic development

Population Management

The management of a country's population is important to ensure improvements in resource productivity and reduction in environmental degradation. Such management should recognize the cultural, social, economic, and political realities of each country. The focus has been on controlling the growth of population per se, rather than on the integration of population issues within a broad framework of social and economic development. When family planning measures are available, cultural and economic factors continue to prevent widespread adoption. Especially among the urban and rural poor, limited household incomes preclude expenditures on family planning measures. In many cases, the humanpower needed to disseminate family planning methods and instruments is skeletal and experimental. Even where the resources are made available--sometimes this is done through the cooperation of foreign and domestic agencies--socio-cultural conditions may make widespread adoption difficult. For example, making birth control pills available to women does not guarantee effective use. Many African cultures still accept large families, and the decision to have yet another child is bestowed upon the man. Therefore, the western idea that accessibility to family planning measures will solve Africa's population problems is yet another pernicious misconception.

Africa should extricate itself from the tangle of population misconceptions. The population issue in Africa exposes some troubling paradoxes. For example, the United States, with about 5 percent of the world's population, consumes 25 percent of the world's energy resources. Moreover, 21 percent of the world's population (mainly in the developed world) consumes about 85 percent of the world's energy resources. For many decades, African raw materials have been the galvanizing force behind industrial development in the west. Now, what Africa needs (perhaps desperately) is a revitalization and an expansion of instruments of production in order to generate increased levels of social and economic well-being. These instruments will help reduce the dependence on human labor and subsistence agricultural production. This will in turn limit the demand for large families, thus limiting population growth. It will also reduce the impact on natural and environmental resource degradation, through proper conservation measures and other proven technological alternatives.

Affordable Low-Input Technology and Capital

Barbier (1989, p.14) sees the lack of affordable, low-input technology as "a major constraint on the ability of marginal-land farmers to improve yields and the sustainability of their agricultural systems under resource-poor conditions." Land-hunger is a primary cause of poverty in the rural areas of Africa. As population pressure increases, cultivable land per person declines, resulting in increased frequency of cultivation, expansion into marginal lands, and a reduction in yields. Extensive farming methods, such as shifting cultivation, which depend on long fallow periods for their effectiveness, are no longer viable. The focus should be on farming methods that do not emphasize extensive land use, and emphasize intensive production, but this would require more technological inputs, which are affordable and appropriate.

The diffusion of agricultural technology to rural areas must, however, recognize the role of women in production and consumption, and any constraints to full-scale participation should be corrected. The adoption of agricultural technology in rural areas is susceptible to the powerlessness of women. Although women constitute a large proportion of the rural labor force (whether it is in agriculture, trading occupations, or simply taking care of domestic duties), "rural women usually have no direct access to institutional credit or to independently disposable cash income to purchase new innovations/technologies; and they seldom have access to information on new innovations" (Agarwal, 1986, p. 370). Perhaps a more critical factor is the fact that, in many African countries, women do not own land; men do. Consequently, any new techniques or improvements to the land involving permanent (or even semi-permanent) land use changes are usually rejected by the men.

Low-input technologies can also effectively combat the chronic overgrazing and overcultivation of arid and semi-arid areas. For example, lack of appropriate land use and irrigation technologies and water conservation techniques in the semi-arid environment have increased the desertification process, especially in the Sahelian zone. These technologies, if well managed, will reduce the cultivation or grazing of marginal lands, thereby allowing such land more time to regenerate.

Alternative Energy to Save the Land and Decrease Poverty

Most rural people in Africa depend on fuelwood for their domestic energy needs. It was once common for the farmland near settlements to provide more than adequate supply of fuelwood for a family; only in rare occasions did fuelwood gathering extend into unfarmed wooded areas. Today, women and children could travel many miles in search of wood--an exhaustive and frustrating effort that is not always rewarded. Without choice, desperate rural women gather material that should be left to cover or fertilize the soil, thus exacerbating the problems of soil erosion, leaching, loss of soil nutrient, and serious decline in fertility and productivity. This condition creates a vicious cycle in which poverty begets land degradation and low productivity, which, in turn, create an environment for poverty to fester.

Although rural development efforts are extending electricity and water to rural areas, sometimes with community participation, the heart of the problem remains unresolved. Poor rural people can least afford the expense of conventional energy, leaving them hard-pressed to continue with the usual practices, which exacerbate environmental degradation and poverty. Future development must identify clear alternatives to wood fuel in order to curb the impact of wood gathering on productivity and the environment. Such development should be targeted to the women who constitute the primary workforce in rural areas. This is particularly important for the fact that a primary reason often cited for the ineffective application of technology to rural production and consumption is the lack of support for women. As Agarwal (1986, p. 370) argues in the case of wood-stove adoption in India:

> The status of women within the household could be a significant factor in wood-stove adoption, especially where adoption requires cash

> expenditure, by virtue of the fact that although women are the potential users of the innovation, and therefore in the best position to assess its advantages and disadvantages, it is men who usually handle the household cash and make decisions on how it is spent . . .

Education for Rural Agricultural Development

Despite proclamations to the contrary, educational systems are still elitist, technocratic, and urban-biased. Whether it is by fault or design, the attainment of educational qualifications is perceived as a preparation to escape the tedium of rural life. The irony is that "while urban-based technological innovations are expected to diffuse to the rural area for improved production and well-being, those who stand to benefit from the new changes are making a speedy and mass exodus from the rural areas" (Obia, 1994, p.8). African nations should educate rural people on the techniques of sustainable agriculture. Because old methods of production are firmly ingrained in the rural culture, governments must provide incentive programs to help with the experimentation of new productive systems. Past experience indicates that regimented, return-to-land policies are not the answer, as is supported by the failure of the Farm Settlements in Nigeria and the Ujaama program in Tanzania. Incentives should include providing adequate infrastructure in the rural areas, rewarding the initiative to experiment with new techniques by giving farmers access to special funds and capital, using agricultural extension programs to teach combined methods of yield improvement and land conservation, and helping farmers find new markets for experimental crops which may not be part of the domestic staple.

CONCLUSION

Africa possesses the human and natural resource capacity to help it attain high levels of social and economic development. The development of agriculture is critical to providing food and agricultural raw materials for industrialization. The road taken has been one of "muddling through" without a clear focus on priorities. This chapter has highlighted some serious misconceptions that have forestalled efforts to put agricultural production, population, and environmental problems in their proper context. Many of these misconceptions have been propagated within Africa and externally. Africans have put themselves at risk by believing these misconceptions for too long, to the extent that some countries have lost the will to approach the future with any sense of decided optimism.

Focus of development needs to change from an emphasis on population control, to a restructuring of agricultural production and resource conservation. Alternative production technologies and methods of improving well-being should be explored. Africa must seek to expand levels of social and economic development through appropriate technological alternatives. This will ensure increased levels of agricultural production per unit area of land, reductions in the demand for human labor for agricultural production, and reductions in the amount of land needed for production. In turn, environmental damage will be abated as more marginal lands are left undisturbed.

On the issue of technological alternatives, the main cause of failure in the use of technology to spur desired levels of development centers on the inappropriate applications and adoptions of technology. While there is nothing inherently wrong with the use of technology, expected benefits must be weighed against social, cultural, economic, political, and environmental realities of adopting countries. As the experience of the developed countries has shown, production techniques and methods need time to work. Africa is replete with case after case of projects--farm settlements, resettlement schemes, experiment projects, irrigation projects, iron and steel complexes, and myriad agricultural projects--abandoned only after a short period of experimentation and trial. Any realistic plans for future development must trade ad hoc strategies for long-term planning. Such long-term, realistic planning has the promise of increasing agricultural production while controlling population and reducing environmental degradation.

REFERENCES

Achebe, C. 1989. (As quoted in Stamp, Patricia). *Technology, Gender, and Power in Africa*. Ottawa, Ontario: IDRC.

Agarwal, B. 1986. Cold Hearths and Barren Slopes: *The Woodfuel Crisis in the Third World.* Riverdale, Maryland: The Riverdale Co., Inc.

Barbier, E. B. 1989. "Sustaining Agriculture on Marginal Land: A Policy Framework." *Environment,* 31 (9): 12-17/36-40.

Binns, J. A. 1992. "Traditional Agriculture, Pastoralism and Fishing." In: Gleave, M. B. (ed.). *Tropical African Development*. Essex, England: Longman Scientific and Technical.

Economic Community for Africa 1983. *Situation of food and Agriculture in Africa, 1982: A Synopsis*. Addis Ababa, Ethiopia: E.C.A.

Ega, L. A. and Famoriyo, S. 1988. "Basic Contradiction Between Rural Development Strategies and Rural Welfare in Nigeria." *International Journal of Environmental Studies*, 31: 157-165.

Eicher, C. K. 1992. "African Agricultural Development Strategies." In: F. Stewart, S. Lall, and S. Wangwe, eds. *Alternative Development Strategies in SubSaharan Africa*. New York: St. Martins's Press (pp. 79-102).

FAO, United Nations Fund for Population Activities and International Institute For Applied Systems 1982. *Potential Population Supporting Capacities of Lands in the Developing World*. Rome: FAO.

Grainger, A. 1986. *The Future Role of the Tropical Rain Forests in the World Forest Economy. Ph.D. Dissertation.* Oxford: Department of Plant Sciences, University of Oxford.

Gyimah-Bempong, K. 1992. "Agriculture and Industrialization in Sub-Saharan Africa. "*Journal of Third World Studies*, IX (1): 22-39.

McMaster, D. N. 1992. "Agricultural Development." In Gleave, M. B. ed. *Tropical African Development* Essex, England: Longman Scientific and Technical.

Mellor, J. W. 1988. "The Intertwining of Environmental Problems and Poverty." *Environment*, 30 (9): 8-13/28-30.

Morris, D. 1977. *Measuring the Condition of the World's Poor*. New York: Pergamon Press.

Nijim, B. K. 1990. "The Physical Quality of Life Index in Arab Countries." *Journal of Third World Studies*, VII (2): 204-215.

Obia, G. C. 1994. "Technological Change and Rural Development in Africa: Constraints and Prospects." Unpublished paper presented at the annual AAG Meeting, San Francisco, California.

O'Connor, A. 1991. *Poverty in Africa: A Geographical Approach*. London: Belhaven Press (A Division of Pinter Publishers).

Oram, P. A. 1988a. "Land Capacity and Environmental Fragility." *Environment*, 30 (9): 10.

Oram, P. A. 1988.b "Building the Agroecological Framework." Environment, 30 (9): 14-17/30-36.

Paulino. 1987. As used in: Eicher, Carl K. 1992. "Africa In Agricultural Development Strategies," page 81. In: Stewart, Frances, Lall, Sanjaya, and Wangwe, Samuel (eds.). 1992. *Alternative Development Strategies in SubSaharan Africa* New York: St. Martins's Press (pp. 79-102).

Stamp, P. 1989. *Technology, Gender, and Power in Africa*. Ottawa, Ontario: IDRC.

Udo, R. K. 1982. *The Human Geography of Tropical Africa*. Ibadan, Nigeria: Heinemann Educational Books (Nigeria) Ltd.

World Bank. 1984. *Towards a Sustained Development in Sub-Saharan Africa* Washington, D.C.: World Bank.

World Resources Institute. 1988. *World Resources 1988-89: A Report by The World Resources Institute, in Collaboration with The United Nations Environment Programme and The United Nations Development Programme*. New York: Oxford University Press.

World Resources Institute. 1992. World Resources 1992-93: A Report by The World Resources Institute, in Collaboration with The United Nations Environment Programme and The United Nations Development Programme. New York: Oxford University Press.

PART IV

REGIONAL ECONOMIC DEVELOPMENT ISSUES

9

ACHIEVING A COOPERATIVE INTEGRATION IN SUB-SAHARAN AFRICA: A VOLUNTARY PIECEMEAL HARMONIZATION PROCESS

Senyo B-S. K. Adjibolosoo
Faculty of Business & Economics
Trinity Western University

INTRODUCTION

In the later 1950s and the early 1960s, winds of political independence began to engulf many African countries (ACs). As such, those countries that gained political independence from the colonial administration began to group together to pursue economic integration. Yet almost every attempt made to date seems to have failed in establishing a meaningful economic integration in Africa. The continuing failure being experienced by African countries to achieve economic integration has led many academicians to conclude naively that African countries cannot pursue economic integration successfully.

In view of these conclusions, the primary objective of this chapter is to argue that these conclusions are based on incomplete examination of historical stylized facts and perfunctory philosophical theorizing and/or reasoning regarding past attempts at integration and/or cooperation in Africa in the last several decades. Drawing on the unique experiences of the United States of America, Canada and the European Economic Community, it is argued that past efforts regarding economic integration in Africa have been pursued too ambitiously (and too hastily?) and in unproductive directions, always putting forward the weaker foot. The chapter suggests that true integration and/or cooperation can be achieved, when it is pursued on a piecemeal basis with individual country commitment rather than as it was done in the past.

The chapter is organized into four sections. In the first section I define integration, its rationale and Africa's integration efforts. Next, I review the theoretical perspectives on why integration fails and advance another view of why integrations fail, that is based on process rather than content or structure, a view I call a piecemeal harmonization approach. In the third section, I test the validity of the approach by examining the formation of the United States of America, Canada and the European Economic Community and comparing the processes of integration with Africa's case. In the final section, I suggest ways by which the piecemeal approach can be pursued by African countries.

ECONOMIC INTEGRATION EFFORTS IN AFRICA

In general, integration as a process is the coming together of countries to work together to achieve common political and/or economic purposes. These purposes may include the total elimination of existing discriminatory (tariff) barriers. By so doing, the countries involved work to create a viable environment for either economic development or industrial progress or political emancipation or all together.[1] In an evolutionary sense, nations involved in the establishment of this union start with a free trade area and then proceed through the rest of the stages including customs union (i.e., a common tariff barrier against outsiders), common market (i.e., allowing for the mobility of factors of production), and the economic union (i.e., complete synchronization and coordination of policies, programs and so on).[2] The achievement of continuing interdependence and mutual benefits are integral elements of viable integration programs among friendly countries. These are some of the major reasons, in addition to many others, why African countries made many efforts in the past to establish a workable integration among them.

As such, when ACs began to experience the winds of political independence, there were very strong desires among some of the first generation African leaders regarding regional integration/cooperation and later, a continental unity. Among these regional and/or country cooperation groups were the Casablanca and the Monrovia groups. Both groups were at variance with each other regarding their ideologies about cooperation and integration in Africa. The Casablanca group was led by Ghana and Guinea. Other members of the group included Mali, Egypt, Morocco, Libya and Algeria. This group believed in the political unification of all ACs (Cervenka, 1977). From this group, Ghana, Guinea and Mali formed a tripartite union in 1960. This union did not last for any extended period of time due to some pertinent problems. The Casablanca group maintained quite clearly that through policy activism and African initiatives, regional unions and continental unity could be attained in Africa.

The Monrovia group was forged by Ivory Coast, Liberia and Senegal. Other participating members included Nigeria, Egypt, Cameroon, Chad, Central African Republic, Congo Brazzaville, Benin, Gabon, Malagasy Republic, Sierra Leone, Mauritania, Niger, Somalia, Togo, Tunisia, and Burkina Faso (Wallerstein, 1967, p. 55). Although the Monrovia group believed in and encouraged economic cooperation among ACs, it strongly maintained that each independent African country must be allowed to maintain its sovereignty, that is, to maintain political boundaries inherited at independence. It also encouraged the relentless pursuit of evolutionary policies and development programs that possessed the potential to result in meaningful cooperation in such areas as education, economics, science and technology, and others.

On May 25, 1963, 32 African states met in Addis Ababa and embraced the Charter that birthed the Organization of African Unity (OAU). All member states agreed to "coordinate and intensify their cooperation and efforts to achieve a better life for the peoples of Africa." The purposes and principles of the Charter were carefully crafted to reflect a compromised vision of the views and desires of these two groups. Although these groupings did not see eye to eye with each other and viewed each other's ideologies and the corresponding policy suggestions with squint eyes, the tides turned slightly in favor of continental cooperation in the early 1960s.

Many more regional groupings mushroomed later. Notable ones among these include the formation of the Economic Community of West African States (ECOWAS) in 1975 (Asante, 1984 and 1986) and the creation of the Economic Community of the Great Lakes Countries-- Burundi, Rwanda and Zaire in 1976. The Southern African Development Coordination Conference (SADCC) came into existence in 1980. Its members include Angola, Botswana, Lesotho, Malawi, Mozambique, Swaziland, Tanzania, Zambia and Zimbabwe. In 1981, the Central African Customs and Economic Union was formed by Cameroon, Central African Republic [CAR], Congo and Gabon. Membership was extended to Angola and Democratic Republic of Congo (Zaire) in 1982 (Banks and Overstreet, 1983, pp. 635-640). Other regional groupings include the *Union Douaniere Economique de l'Afrique Centrale* (UDEAE). This group is made up of Cameroon, the Central African Empire, the Congo and Gabon. There exists also the West African Economic Community (WAEC). Its members include Ivory Coast, Mali, Mauritania, Niger, Senegal and Burkina Faso, all French-speaking countries.

Existing intergovernmental organizations (IGO's) are the Mano River Union made up of Guinea, Liberia and Sierra Leone. The union was inaugurated in 1973 (Clapmann, 1976; Commonwealth Secretariat, 1978 and 1979). Other notable agencies include the Niger Basin Authority; (revamped in 1980 and membership extended to embrace the 12 countries from Mali to Cameroon accessible through the Niger and its tributaries; the Gambia River (Gambia, Guinea, Senegal); the Senegal (Mali, Mauritania, Senegal); the Kagera (Burundi, Rwanda, Tanzania, Uganda); and the East African Development Bank. The creation and operation of these groupings at the grassroots level have revealed the benefits, costs and problems of integration in Africa. A listing of regional groupings and institutions in Africa can be found in Salvatore, 1989, pp. 257-260. This list is indicative of the fact that many different types of regional integrative types have been tried in Africa in the past. Yet few of these attempts have made any significant progress. Many scholars have explained this poor performance in many different ways. In what follows, a brief presentation is made regarding the views about why some groups succeeded while others failed.

PERSPECTIVES ON THE SUCCESSES/FAILURES OF INTEGRATION

The Conference of African Heads of State and Governments held in Addis Ababa in May 1963 was aimed at bridging the gap between the various groups that were proposing various paths to the political integration in Africa. At the conference, Emperor Haile Selassie noted that "through all that has been said and written and done in these years, there runs a common theme. Unity is the accepted goal. We argue about means; we discuss tactics. But while we agree that the ultimate destiny of this continent lies in political union, we must at the same time recognize that the obstacles to be overcome in its achievement are at once numerous and formidable." (see Thompson, 1969, p. 183; and Elaigwu, 1984, pp. 131-151).

As is clear from Haile Selassie's speech, it was obvious then that African leaders were aware that integration was not going to be easy to achieve, and rightly so. The many problems and difficulties they experienced made many scholars present their own perspectives on what makes it possible for one set of countries to achieve integration successfully while others fail. Axline (1984, p. 7-9) noted that the necessary requirements for successful integration include (1) a high degree of political cooperation; (2) the ability of all group members to negotiate and develop appropriate policies and programs; (3) the establishment of relevant policies and/or programs aimed at the equitable distribution of gains (see also Elkan, 1965, p. 74); (4) a greater unified bargaining power against the rest of the world; (5) the ability to create and utilize investment opportunities and also to attract foreign capital; (6) a high degree of independence which minimizes the excessive dependence of member countries on the rest of the world (see Kitamura, 1966, pp. 50-51; Demas, 1965, p. 32 & 36); (7) continuing growth in domestic income and savings (Mikesell, 1963, pp. 205-229; Kitamura, 1966, p. 54; and Demas, 1965, p. 89); and (8) the ability to create a great volume of trade among member countries (see Kitamura, 1966, pp. 42-63). These conditions must exist for integration to be successful.

As such, the thrust of the theoretical argument is that groups of countries that possess these abilities and/or conditions or both will be able to pull together successful integration programs. In the event these are non-existent, no group of countries can be successful in terms of creating viable integration. Africa's failure at its past attempts at integration is usually blamed on the absence of these abilities and/or conditions. In addition, it is usually argued that the sordid African experience regarding integration is also due to other drawbacks such as the fear of some African countries that they would be swallowed by others. There is also the fear of losing individual country sovereignty and bargaining power. For example, the break-up of the East African Common Market was due partly to the belief that while Kenya was experiencing industrial growth, both Tanzania and Uganda were experiencing severe balance of payments problems (Langhammer, 1984, pp. 203-215). The basic conclusion arrived at by many scholars, therefore, is that conditions existing in African countries have been very unfavorable to the attainment of successful integration. Some argue that subcontinental nationalism killed African nationalism (Elaigwu, 1984, p. 138). In some cases, it has been pointed out that many African states were unwilling to delegate any authorities to the Organization of African Unity. These countries were not willing to relinquish power to a supranational organization. For example, in the case of Nigeria, Balewa once said "Nigeria has not the slightest intention of surrendering her sovereignty, no sooner had she gained independence, to anyone else" (Elaigwu, 1984, p. 137-138). Other reasons given for the failure of integrative efforts in Africa include ethnic strife, ideological (i.e., capitalism and socialism) struggles, the production of similar crops by many African countries, racial intolerance, allegiance to colonizers, self-aggrandizement, misunderstanding, linguistic barriers, *ideological flirting and diplomatic roller-coasting,* and many others. Membership contributions quickly fell into arrears. This, I believe, can be adequately explained as being the result of member states who were neither committed to the goals and principles of the OAU nor clearly perceived the depth of the long-term net benefits to be derived. There are many more problems of integration in Africa.

Yet, all these arguments regarding the failure of integrative efforts in Africa are misplaced because scholars who maintain that African countries cannot achieve successful integration have failed to realize that past efforts have been made on false starts. Truly, African countries can attain integration successfully through the model I refer to as the *piecemeal harmonization process*.

In the next section of the chapter, I present three relevant case studies from which Africans can draw principles for inspiration. Drawing conclusions from the empirical cases presented and the observations made, *the piecemeal harmonization model of integration* is then presented. It is then argued that with a fully developed human factor (HF)[3] in African countries, the persistent and continuing pursuit of cooperation as suggested by this model holds the key to successful integration in Africa. The three cases are the USA, Canada and the European Community.

EXAMPLES OF SUCCESSFUL ECONOMIC INTEGRATION

Vivid illustrative examples can be found in historical records from all over the world to support the principle that whether one talks about economic regional integration or political unification, it is necessary and sufficient to pursue the process with evangelical commitment and determination on a piecemeal basis. In what follows, I present a detailed discussion of some of these examples to support the principal argument in this chapter.

Canada

Canada, a nation made up of ten provinces is still in the making, having begun some two hundred years ago. Yet regardless of these many years, what has been achieved to date did not happen overnight. Since the idea of bringing all the provinces together, each of these provinces had its own pertinent and nagging problems/concerns. These problems of concern were, at the beginning, a formidable threat to the successful creation of what is presently called Canada. Yet the founding fathers of the nation were aware of the various hindrances and were ready and willing to do their best to make sure that their intended goals of an all-inclusive economic and/or political integration were achieved. As such, they were fully prepared to tackle the daunting task of nation building through both economic and political integration.

The situation of British Columbia is quite intriguing because the people had three appealing possibilities. First, it was the most emotionally favored province to be used as a nucleus for the continuation of the British colony. Second, those who wanted to increase British Columbia's trade with its American partners were in strong favor of the province's annexation to the USA Third, most people born in the Maritimes and Canada, and those who "saw Confederation as the best means of protecting British institutions on the North Pacific and of developing British Columbia's resources" wanted union with Canada (Francis, Jones and Smith, 1992, p. 401). As such, the dilemma in which British Columbians found themselves was extremely great.

In the case of Nova Scotia, the British Crown replaced Nova Scotia's Governor with someone else who was very sympathetic to Confederation. New Brunswick's Governor was ordered to step into the politics of his province to ensure the success of Confederation. The Crown also guaranteed loan interest for the Intercolonial Railway. This was aimed at providing additional incentives to the Maritime Provinces to unite with the rest of Canada. Soon after the end of the American Civil War in 1865, there were very strong fears that the Northern army might be employed to incorporate other provinces into the United States of America. As it turned out, this fear of many facilitated the process of the Canadian Confederation (See details in Francis, Jones, Smith, 1992, pp. 416-417).

In Canada West (Ontario), many were of the opinion that "if federation were necessary to achieve *representation by population*, that was perfectly satisfactory." In the views of Canada West, since Confederation was of practical utility, a local government system was to be added in order to minimize "the heavy load of sectional differences they had hitherto been obliged to carry." (Waite, 1962, pp. 132-133).

In Canada East (Quebec), Waite (1962, pp. 158-160) noted that the choice was for Confederation rather than annexation after the battle was fought and won. Prince Edward Island joined Confederation when it was in deep financial stress and also was experiencing severe land controversies, religious difficulties, educational setbacks, and the splitting of the Island's political parties into very fickle factions. (Waite, 1962, p. 192). Recall that most of the provinces joined the Confederation at different points in time[4] and had different problems that needed to be addressed. A basic principle pursued was that most of these problems were either dealt with immediately or structures were put in place to help address them effectively at subsequent dates.

Some Nagging Setbacks

As noted above, each province began with its own concerns. Although these seemed to be insurmountable to the formation of the Confederation in the initial stages, they were overcome in due course. For example, New Brunswick also had many problems with the Confederation. (1) There was a strong fear that an intercolonial railway could not be guaranteed. (2). The existing pattern and direction of trade of the province were north-south rather than east-west. (3). There was also the fear that the province would be forced to accept the Canadian debt incurred from canal and railway building. (4) The province had only 15 members of parliament in a house of 194 seats; and (5) There were strong feelings that Protestant Canada could attack New Brunswick's Roman Catholic Church and Schools.

Many other provinces also had their own pertinent problems. Nova Scotian opposition to Confederation was not only due to the fear of identity loss and the possible cessation of being an important colony in a great empire. It was also the belief of Joseph Howe, a great political figure, that Nova Scotia looked to the Atlantic region and Britain rather than the western part of the North American continent. The leaders of Nova Scotia registered their objections to the Confederation because they felt that it was being imposed without proper consultation with the electorate. In the case of Prince Edward Island (PEI), the sentiments to reject the Confederation were based on the view that it (i.e., the Confederation) was another procedure aimed at replacing distant landlords in Britain with another one in Ottawa. (ibid., p. 415). Similarly, there were tremendous fears regarding the imposition of high taxes to support the railway and also the expectations of higher tariffs to be imposed on non-members to create interprovincial trade. In addition to all these, PEI wanted better terms of representation in the Senate and House of Commons, and better economic terms. Otherwise, the people wanted nothing of Confederation. Through debates regarding the Confederation, Newfoundland lost faith in the Confederation and did not believe that it would solve their economic ills. To them, Canada seemed to be so far away. In addition to these, they, like the other Maritime colonies, looked eastward not westward.

Canada East struggled for identity in Confederation. The fear of the French speaking people regarding loss of their identity and/or culture was real, scary and always threatened the successful achievement of the Confederation. However, in order to bring Quebec into the Confederation, French was to be made the official language of the province as well as one of the two main languages of the federal administration. The rights of religious minorities in relation to schooling (i.e., education) were also to be acknowledged in every province. In order to prevent the dominance of English Canada from happening, the newly created nationality was to be a political rather than cultural nationality (ibid., p. 412).

In an attempt to bring British Columbia into the Canadian federation, Ottawa agreed to assume the province's accumulated debt, and also gave full promises regarding the building of a railway from the east coast to the Pacific coast to guarantee that British Columbia did not decide to join the United States of America.

United States of America

The American experience of integration was similar to that of Canada because it was pursued on piecemeal basis and was not accomplished instantaneously. The American process was a very long one and took over two centuries to accomplish. The process was set in motion on January 7, 1789. This was the birthing day of the American Republic. At this point in time, only 11 states ratified the American Constitution. These states were South Carolina, Maryland, Pennsylvania, Virginia, Georgia, New York, Connecticut, Massachusetts, Delaware, New Hampshire and New Jersey. The rest of the other states joined the republic at different dates as presented in Table 9.1 below.

The whole process was not achieved without the writing and signing of specific treaties. For example, a treaty was signed in Washington that allowed the USA to buy Alaska from Russia for $7.2 million. On July 7, 1898, William McKinley, the US president, signed a bill that allowed for the annexation of Hawaii. In the case of Nevada, the Treaty of Guadalupe Hidalgo was signed in 1848 between the USA and Mexico. As such, Nevada was quickly rushed to statehood (Encyclopedia Americana, 20, 1985, p. 148). When the Mexican War broke out, New Mexico was proclaimed by General Stephan Kearny as belonging to America. During the Civil War, therefore, the Confederate Army quickly took possession of New Mexico. The building of the first railroad in 1879 led to the beginning of a long struggle for statehood (Encyclopedia Americana, 20, 1985, p. 214). In the case of Ohio, the fast and continuing growth of the territory led to the agitation for and a movement toward statehood (Encyclopedia Americana, 20, 1985, p. 669).

TABLE 9.1
DATES ON WHICH EACH STATE JOINED THE UNITED STATES OF AMERICA

Nov 21, 1789 North Carolina 12th May 29, 1790 Rhode Island 13th Jan 10, 1791 Vermont 14th Jun 1, 1792 Kentucky 15th (a slave state) Jun 1, 1796 Tennessee 16th (a slave state) Mar 1, 1803 Ohio 17th (a free state) Apr 30, 1812 Louisiana 18th Dec 11, 1816 Indiana 19th (a free state) Dec 10, 1817 Mississippi 20th (a slave state) Dec 3, 1818 Illinois 21st (a free state) Dec 14, 1819 Alabama 22nd (a slave state) Jan 3, 1820 Maine 23rd (a free state) Aug 10, 1821 Missouri 24th (a slave state) Jun 15, 1836 Arkansas 25th (a slave state) Jan 26, 1837 Michigan 26th (a free state) Mar 3, 1845 Florida 27th (a slave state) Dec 29, 1845 Texas 28th Dec 28, 1846 Iowa 29th (a free state) May 29, 1848 Wisconsin 30th (a free state) Sept 7, 1850 California 31st (a free state)	May 11, 1858 Minnesota 32nd (a free state) Feb 14, 1859 Oregon 33rd (a free state) Jan 29, 1861 Kansas 34th (a free state) Jun 20, 1863 West Virginia 35th Oct 31, 1864 Nevada 36th Mar 1, 1867 Nebraska 37th Aug 1, 1876 Colorado 38th Nov 2, 1889 North Dakota 39th Nov 2, 1889 South Dakota 40th Nov 8, 1889 Montana 41st Nov 8, 1889 Washington 42nd Jul 3, 1890 Idaho 43rd Jul 10, 1890 Wyoming 44th Jan 4, 1896 Utah 45th. Its constitution includes woman suffrage and prohibits polygamy. Nov 16, 1907 Oklahoma 46th Jan 6, 1912 New Mexico 47th Feb 14, 1912 Arizona 48th Jan 3, 1959 Alaska 49th Aug 21, 1959 Hawaii 50th

The European Community

Many years ago, Europe was filled with ethnic, religious and linguistic problems. On several occasions, the competing interests of these European nations led them to go to war against each other. It was Jean Monney of France who once suggested that European nations would benefit more if they all moved towards unity on an economic basis rather than through wars or military incursions. In 1951 the Suchman Declaration relating to coal production came into effect. In the same year, the European Coal and Steel Community (ECSC) was formed. The success of the coal and steel unions paved the way for the creation of the European Economic Community (EEC) in 1957.

The evolutionary process of the EEC began with France, Belgium, Luxembourg, The Netherlands, Italy and West Germany. In 1964, Turkey became an associate member. The United Kingdom, Denmark and Ireland became part in 1973. While Greece joined in 1981, Portugal and Spain entered in 1986. In 1987, the Single European Act, was ratified to complete the phasing out of all nontariff barriers among all member states so as to achieve economic union in 1992. In 1991, both the Economic Union Area and the Maastricht Currency Accords were signed. Although the European Monetary System (EMS) was created to link the currencies of all EEC members, England and Greece opted out from its use to avoid the experiences of large day-to-day fluctuations in currency rates. Although capital markets integration was slow due to many existing institutional restrictions, restraints on free labor mobility were dismantled (Encyclopedia Americana, 1985, pp. 600-610).

Efforts to integrate Eastern Europe into the European Community began soon after the former's revolutionary experiences of 1989-1990. In December 1991, Poland, Hungary and the former Czechoslovakia signed agreements to become associate members of the European Community. In 1993, Romania and Bulgaria joined. There exists an agreement between Community and the Eastern European countries to trade freely in industrial goods. The Eastern Europeans are, however, allowed to maintain tariffs for ten years. The basic goal is to encourage and draw the Eastern European nations closer to the European Community. They will be consulted when areas of common interest arise on foreign policy. The Poles, Hungarians, and Czechs are very anxious to become full members of the EC.[5]

Denmark signed the Maastricht Treaty on May 18, 1993. *Business Week* of May 31, 1991 reported that "a unified monetary system, planned for the end of the decade, was to help transform Europe into an economic superpower to rival Japan and North America." Note, however, that Denmark, England and France all experienced oppositions to the Maastricht Treaty due to their respective fears regarding how immigration could create a great deal of social unrest and crime.

The Economist of May 22, 1993 observed that since the Danes were afraid of losing national prosperity, they voted *YES* to the Maastricht Treaty. They also did not want to leave the EC. In 1996, as stipulated in the Maastricht Treaty, all members are expected to meet at a conference to revise the treaty. Relevant institutions will be reformed and updated in order to equip them to be more capable in addressing the needs of existing and newly admitted members. Above all, the treaty provides *opt-outs* for countries that find immediate adherence to certain stipulations of the treaty, especially on monetary union and social policy issues too problematic in their earlier years as members. The bigger this organization grows in numerical strength, the stronger it is becoming. It is creating massive advantages for its members.

OBSERVATIONS

As is obvious, the historical records seem to suggest that nations that went through the processes of political unification and economic integration had to do it on a piecemeal basis. No single one of the cases reviewed suggests a once and for all achievement of unification and/or integration. In addition, the leaders were dedicated and committed to their original ideals and visions.

Most treaties of integration and/or co-operation in Africa have been mere carbon copies of those existing in the developed regions of the world. Africans have been unable to create and develop their own unique and workable parallels that will fit their specific needs. Scholars and African leaders who advocated for strong efforts toward African co-operation and/or unity in the past seemed to have been oblivious to existing historical records regarding patterns of integration among other peoples of the world. The Canadian, American, and the EEC experiences presented are indicative of how to pursue piecemeal integration. A few states or provinces will begin the program for co-operation, and others will join at different points in time by their own choice. The gradual piecemeal integration process will admit new members into the group, deal with their pertinent problems, and then work together with them to solve problems of general interest. The growing and continuing strength of the co-operating countries will lead to the discovery of opportunities that must be jointly exploited for mutual gain, and new procedures for dealing with sub-Saharan African problems. The resulting net gains will then serve as sources of continuing bonding together among current members, and also as incentives to attract other countries to apply for membership. If pursued in this gradual and non-coercive manner, a strong core of countries would evolve, which will lead the way for successful total integration in future. With group dedication and commitment to seeing this process through, the most difficult problems will be solved. Other peripheral ones will fade away.

With the exception of the now defunct Union of Soviet Socialist Republics (USSR)--whose unification program was forged through coercion, wars of intimidation and force--others were more peaceful, although not without some fighting. Renninger (1982, p. 161) observed that "because of the heavy reliance on foreign models, the goals of economic cooperation in Africa have never been sufficiently clarified. Too often the primary goals have been trade creation or import substitution. The primary goal should, of course, be the transformation of the structure of production, but few economic cooperation schemes have set out with that goal specifically in mind." For example, Article 2 of the 1975 ECOWAS treaty says that:

> It shall be the aim of the community to promote co-operation and development in all fields of economic activity particularly in all fields of industry, transport, telecommunications, energy, agriculture, natural sciences, commerce, monetary and financial questions and in social and cultural matters for the purposes of raising the standard of living of its peoples, of increasing and maintaining economic stability, of fostering closer relations among its members and of contributing to the progress and development of the African continent.

To achieve these objectives, the treaty stipulated that all member states must work towards the elimination of all forms of duties and taxes, the establishment of a common market, free movement of people and resources, the harmonization of all policies regarding human activities and all facets of human life, and schemes that can help facilitate the joint undertaking of programs as prescribed in Article 2 of the ECOWAS agreement.

In my view, however, signing any kinds of agreements, ratifying treaties, putting in place the necessary protocols, organizing and attending of summits and/or conferences, adopting multilateral agreements, and so on will not in themselves help Africans to attain effective integration. It is one thing writing up excellent articles on co-operation, it is quite another ball game trying to put into practice what is stipulated in such agreements.

The problems are usually compounded because such integration schemes in Africa are too grandiose and, therefore, do not only complicate the difficulties of the group under formation, but also pressurize and highlight the problems of individual nation states. What this does is to magnify individual country setbacks and cloud prospective long-term goals. In reality, it hinders the abilities of national leaders to perceive the long term advantages of the co-operative efforts. Robson (1983, p. 170) argued that regional groupings that lack the required institutions and the ability to identify and jointly undertake meaningful projects and their corresponding net benefits will fail to create the necessary incentives required for effective co-operation. In many African cases, instead of focusing on HF development, effective grassroots programs and institutional structures that can help create relevant solutions to the pertinent problems, the focus is rather placed on forcing out and signing mere agreements among a large number of nations, usually followed with emotionally charged speeches that usually contain little substance, relevance or realism.

If Africans are going to achieve any successes in their programs of co-operation, they have to pursue first a thorough study and critical evaluation of how other nations pursued similar or comparable objectives in the past. The goal of this exercise, however, must not be geared to simply copying verbatim what others did in the past, but to draw meaningful and relevant principles that can be used for guidance as ACs search for better ways to achieve successful co-operation and/or integration. The HF is again the relevant feature in this case. In view of these hindrances and perceived difficulties, to pursue continental integration as has been done in the past will, therefore, be a misdirected effort. That is, an all-inclusive, all-African political integration may not be the primary thing to seek after as Africans enter into the twenty-first century.

The historical data and/or evidence presented above strongly support the view that there is no way a group of states or regions can attain co-operation and/or political unification without experiencing many problems, most of which will be specific to prospective members that are sovereign states or provinces. Integration through piecemeal cooperative efforts and programs definitely has greater chances and brighter prospects of success in sub-Saharan Africa. This procedure will transcend all problems relating to ethnicity, allegiance to former colonial powers, linguistic barriers, mistrust, suspicion, and so on. It also has the potential to diffuse the influences and/or powers of extracontinental relationships that may vie to divide the commitment of sovereign member states to the integrated cooperative enterprise. Critical to the whole undertaking is the political will of each individual country to seek co-operatively for solutions to existing problems. In case this fails, merely signing extensive agreements on paper will not necessarily lead to any progress. At every stage in the process, those who agree to be part of the co-operative integration program must not only be in the frame of mind to commit to the program, but also must be strongly co-operative in putting their maximum effort into helping find solutions to their formidable problems.

This was how the founding pioneers of Canada, the United States of America and the European Community pursued their process of political unification and economic integration. They were not really discouraged by the problems presented by each individual state. Instead, much effort was expended in seeking solutions to visible drawbacks because they were convinced beyond all reasonable doubts that expected gains would more than outweigh existing pertinent problems presented by each province or state. Although the African situation is much different from those of Canada, the United States of America and the European Community, African leaders still have many lessons to learn from their experiences.

In the African case, any two or three countries that choose to work together voluntarily in cooperation must define clearly its vision, the relevant functional areas of co-operative effort and the activities they are determined to work at together to foster a viable integration. Countries that agree to enter into functional co-operation to form the initial *kernel of integration* must develop a sense of purpose based on sound and appealing principles regarding expected problems and gains. Knowledge of this will produce an unflinching commitment to objectives and corresponding programs. Fragmentation in Africa will not produce any welfare gains for Africans.

Where then does Africa go from here? What is a workable vision? How must it be pursued? In what follows, a vision is articulated for Africa. In addition, a series of specific suggestions are put forward regarding how to successfully attain co-operation in Africa.

ECONOMIC INTEGRATION: A PIECEMEAL HARMINIZATION MODEL

A detailed study and analysis of the cases of the USA, Canada, the United Kingdom, and many others reveal that Africans can achieve co-operative integration. What is necessary is for two or three countries to decide and determine to pursue the project regardless of the intensity of any initial problems. Once they can agree on the guiding principles, rules, and regulations, the stage would have been set for the development of further structures and relevant institutions necessary for the accomplishment of objectives.

To begin a nucleus, it is critical to take into account the existing patterns of nonofficial direction of flow of people and merchandise goods and services in Africa. The countries that begin the nucleus take these patterns into consideration. After having identified and documented the true patterns of movement of goods, services, and people, the two or three nations that have participated in this initial program may consult their citizens about the intended co-operative integrative program. In due course, the agreement should be signed to officially recognize the already existing unofficial patterns of flow of people and merchandise goods and services. The signing of this agreement will, therefore, establish the foundation for co-operative integration in Africa and also give credence and recognition to the flow. As continuing progress is made, the program can be extended to include the dances, art, crafts, and other cultural activities. The creation and establishment of an *All-African Countries' Center* may be exploited carefully. The center must be given the sole mandate to oversee the whole program.

In view of the piecemeal harmonization model of integration, Elaigwu's (1984, p. 146) view that "the future of continental unity lies in the priority given to several stages of integration" is severely flawed. This is so because functionalism, although, may lead to the development of viable joint ventures at the onset, does not have the power to sustain the continuing survival of and/or relationship between member countries. As such, the whole process will crumble sooner or later (i.e., the case of the East Africa Economic community). African countries should not begin the integrative process by using the functional patterns of cooperation. Those who believe that by merely developing intra-continental highways, railways, air routes, communications systems, etc. will lead to successful integration are mistaken. These infrastructural projects do not have what it will take to achieve successful integration (be it economic or political or both). African countries need to pursue this integration program by following closely the piecemeal harmonization model.

Relevant Action Programs

The principle described above must, however, be propped up by a series of other programs and activities. Relevant goals and principles may include the following:

1. Integrity and open-minded communication to facilitate activities that possess the potential to enhance the cooperation process and relevant programs.
2. There must exist efficient mechanisms and many opportunities for frequent dialoguing and round table conferences to iron out bottlenecks and disputes. Negotiations, mediation, arbitration, and many others must be used effectively and judiciously.
3. Each member must honor the goals and programs no matter what. Openness and willingness must exist to admit prospective members into the co-operative program. The long-term objective of the embryonic membership must be the total emancipation of Africa. This must neither be forced through coercion nor wars, but through the willingness of other sovereign ACs who have assessed the initial performance of the countries already involved and have perceived what their expected long term contributions to and gains from the venture would be when they join the co-operative program.
4. Member states must promote unity and solidarity among all countries involved in the program, and insist on the attainment of improved welfare for the citizens of every member country. Where a member country is under severe economic, political and social stress, the others must come together to help solve the problems. These imply that human rights regulations must be enacted and observed in all participating countries.
5. It will be productive to develop sporting and athletics programs between the nucleus countries. As is well known all over the world, the development of good relationships between countries can also be accomplished through well-crafted sporting and athletics programs. These programs must be aimed at bringing deeper levels of awareness regarding relationships between the citizens of countries forming the core of the co-operative union. Through annual athletic competition programs, citizens of both countries will learn not only to tolerate people from other ACs, but also to work in cooperation with them.
   An expected outcome of this co-operative program is to have Acs present only one contingent to such world events as the World Cup Soccer Tournaments, the Olympic Games, and so on. This will provide many opportunities for Africans to learn to work together with people from other ACs. It will also allow them to learn to deal with differences since they will have to learn to deal effectively with pertinent problems.
6. It is crucial to educate and train all citizens of the nucleus countries to know and understand the welfare implications of the integrative

cooperative process. As has been the case in the past, most Africans did not really know about the various measures of integration being pursued by their leaders. African governments and/or leaders are in the habit of signing protocols, bilateral, trilateral, multilateral, etc., agreements, without necessarily making their citizens aware of what is at stake and what the expected net gains/losses will be.

To avoid ignorance and foolish oppositions to such programs, national awareness education and training programs must be instituted and carried on in the nucleus countries. Citizens of these countries must be provided with the fora to discuss, debate and analyze both the general and specific implications for their own long-term welfare. Such programs will also help people to perceive the need for cooperative programs and policies.

7. Another useful program to have in place is a Private Citizens' Organization (PCO) that possesses the power and authority to serve as a vigilant *watchdog* regarding the institution and operation of programs and agreements signed. In developing the nucleus, it may be necessary to have an existing independent body of citizens from the kernel countries to follow events of cooperation as they enfold and present people with their assessments regarding what is being done and how. If there be any violations and/or mistreatment of citizens of one member country by those of other member nations, the PCO must be in position to receive such complaints and bring them into the limelight for effective redress.

   The basic goal of the PCO will be two-folds. First, to collect data on citizen moods, views, expectations, and so on; second, to present these to governments of every nucleus member and also insist that leaders of such nations put their best into the cooperative agreement. Their objectives must revolve around collecting and disseminating relevant information; and above all, exerting sufficient pressure on all national governments to do their best for the success of the cooperative program. This organization may also want to identify prospective leaders in the nucleus countries, raise financial resources; educate and train them; and encourage them to take up relevant positions in their individual countries and help to develop creative and effective procedures for dealing with problems and hindrances.

8. Programs, institutions, rules and regulations must be developed to help facilitate the cooperative process. In this case, the field of coverage must be wide and diverse. The guiding philosophy for achieving this goal must be based on problem solving. Available historical records of regional cooperation and political unification programs in Africa abound and must be effectively used to determine the more pressing problems and issues that must be addressed in succession in all nucleus countries.

Whatever program is pursued to attain the intended goals of the founding members, it must be borne in mind that without well-developed HF to help sub-

Saharan Africans to initiate and oversee every plan and project, the whole program may be doomed to failure. This is one reason why at the initial stages, it is essential for member states to develop efficient joint education and training programs to prepare the people to develop the necessary HF (Adjibolosoo, 1995a & b).

CONCLUSION

African countries have struggled for the last four decades to achieve development and welfare improvement for their citizens. To date, very little has been achieved. Past attempts at regional and/or continental integration seem to be failing. Many ACs seem to be losing hope in their ability to achieve viable co-operation. But there still exists another opportunity for Africa. As discussed in this chapter, co-operative integration can be achieved in Africa if and only if it is pursued with determination and commitment on a piecemeal basis. Adjibolosoo and de Wolf (1994, p. 176) noted that "in the development-transformational perspective, new arrangements for effective development are also required. The prescriptions of import-substitution industrialization and export expansion may not deal effectively with Africa's economic underdevelopment."

The success of the piecemeal program, however, will require a properly carved vision to which an unflinching commitment is necessary. Above all, every other vision, plan and program is bound to fail in the absence of people who possess the required human qualities and/or characteristics. It is, therefore, of primary importance for core members to establish institutional structures that have the capability to meet the challenges of preparing the African peoples to acquire the necessary HF that is crucial for the piecemeal integrative co-operative program (Adjibolosoo, 1995b).

NOTES

1. For a more extensive definition and detailed analysis, see Orantes (1984, pp. 51-66) and Machlup (1977, pp. 3-12).

2. See Orante's reference in note 1, p. 52.

3. The term, the HF implies:

the spectrum of personality characteristics and other dimensions of human performance that enable social, economic and political institutions to function and remain functional, over time. Such dimensions sustain the workings and application of the rule of law, political harmony, a disciplined labor force, just legal systems, respect for human dignity and the sanctity of life, social welfare, and so on. As is often the case, no social, economic or political institutions can function effectively without being upheld by a network of committed persons who stand firmly by them. Such persons must strongly believe in and continually affirm the ideals of society (Adjibolosoo, 1993, p. 142).

4. In sum the Canadian process happened as follows: July 1, 1867 (Nova Scotia, New Brunswick, Ontario and Quebec); July 15, 1870 (Manitoba: The Dominion purchases title to territories held by Hudson's Bay); July 20, 1871 (British Columbia: A condition of union was for the CPR to reach the Pacific. The CPR was completed in 1885): July 1, 1873 (Prince Edward Island); September 1, 1905 (Alberta and Saskatchewan).

5. See *The Economist* of May 1, 1993 for a more detailed analysis of this issue.

ACKNOWLEDGEMENT

I am very thankful to the contributions of the members of the International Institute for Human Factor Development (IIHFD) Discussion Group. All their contributions at the seminar held on October 9, 1993, where the first draft of this chapter was presented and discussed, have helped a lot in improving the content of this chapter.

REFERENCES

Adjibolosoo, S. 1993. “The Human Factor in Development.” T*he Scandinavian Journal of Development Alternatives*, XII (4): 139-149.

Adjibolosoo, S. and de Wolf, J. 1994. "Industrializing Sub-Saharan Africa A Cooperative Rather than a Competitive Effort." In F. Ezeala-Harrison and S. Adjibolosoo, eds. *Perspectives on Economic Development in Africa*. Westport, CT.: Praeger.

Adjibolosoo, S. 1995a. "The Significance of the Human Factor in Developing Africa." In S. Adjibolosoo, ed. *The Significance of the Human Factor in African Economic Development.* Westport, CT.: Praeger.

Adjibolosoo, S. 1995b. *The Human Factor in Developing Africa*. Westport, CT.: Praeger.

Asante, S. K. B. 1986. *The Political Economy of Regionalism in Africa: A Decade of the Economic Community of West African States*. New York: Praeger.

Asante, S. K. B. 1984. “ECOWAS, the EEC and the Lome Convention.” In D. Mazzeo ed. *African Regional Organizations*. New York: Cambridge University Press.

Axline, W. A. 1984. "Underdevelopment, Dependence, and Integration: The Politics of Regionalism in the Third World." In P. K. Ghosh, ed. *Economic*

Integration and Third World Development. Westport, CT.: Greenwood Press.

Banks, A. S. and Overstreet, W. 1983. Political Handbook of the World. New York: CSA Publications. Business Weekly: May 31, 1991.

Cervenica, Z. 1977. The Unfinished Quest for Unity: Africa and the OAU London: Friedman

Clapmann, C. 1976. *Liberia and Sierra Leone: An Essay in Comparative Politics*. Cambridge: Cambridge University Press.

Commonwealth Secretariat. 1978. *The Mano River Union: An Assessment of Past Performance and Some Guidelines for the Future*. London: Commonwealth Secretariat.

Commonwealth Secretariat. 1979. *Report on the Urbanization of Fiscal Incentives to Industry in the Mano River Union*. London: Commonwealth Secretariat.

Demas, W. G. 1965. *The Economics of development in Small Countries with Special Reference to the Caribbean*. Montreal: McGill University Press. Economist May 22, 1993.

Elaigwu, J. I. 1984. "Toward Continental Integration: Supranationalism and the Future of Africa." In T. M. Shaw, ed. *Alternative Futures for Africa*. Boulder, Colorado: Westview Press.

Elkan, P. G. 1965. "How to Beat Backwash: The Case for Customs-Drawback Unions." *Economic Journal*, 75: 47.

Francis, R. D. Jones, R. and Smith, D. B. 1992. *Origins*. Toronto: Holt, Rinehart and Winston of Canada Ltd.

Kitamura, 1966. "Economic Theory and the Economic Integration of Underdeveloped Regions." In M. S. Wionczek, ed. *Latin American Economic Integration: Experiences and Prospects* New York: Praeger.

Langhammer, R. J. 1984. "Regional Integration and Cooperation in Africa: A History of Disappointments?" In P. K. Ghosh, ed. *Economic Integration and Third World Development*. Westport, CT.: Greenwood Press.

Machlup, F. 1977. *A History of Thought on Economic Integration*. London: The Macmillan Press Ltd.

Mikesell, R. F. 1963. "The Theory of Common Markets as Applied to Regional Arrangements Among Developing Countries." In R. Harrod and D. Hague, eds. *International Trade Theory in a Developing World*. New York: St. Martin's Press.

Orantes, I. C. 1984. "The Concept of Integration." In P. K. Ghosh, ed. *Economic Integration and Third World Development*. Westport, CT:. Greenwood Press.

Renninger, J. P. 1982. "The Future of Economic Cooperation Schemes in Africa, with Special Reference to ECOWAS." In T. M. Shaw, ed. *Alternative Futures for Africa*. Boulder, Colorado: Westview Press.

Robson, P. 1983. *Integration, Development and Equity: Economic Integration in West Africa*. London: George Allen and Unwin.

Salvatore, D. ed. 1989. *African Development Prospects: A Policy Modeling*

Approach. New York: Taylor and Francis.
Thompson, V. B. 1969. Africa and African Unity. London: Longman.
Waite, P. B. 1962. *The Life and Times of Confederation, 1864-1867; Politics, Newspapers, and the Union of British North America*. Toronto: University of Toronto Press.
Wallerstein, I. 1967. Africa: The Politics of Unity. New York: Vintage Press.

10

GROWTH CENTER APPROACH AND REGIONAL ECONOMIC DEVELOPMENT IN AFRICA: FAILURE OR MISSED OPPORTUNITY?

Benjamin Ofori-Amoah
Department of Geography & Geology
University of Wisconsin-Stevens Point

INTRODUCTION

During the late 1960s and early 1970s, the growth center approach attracted a great deal of interest among regional development planners and governments the world over, as the approach that would resolve regional disparities in economic development within countries (UN, 1971; Darwent, 1969; Lasuen, 1969; Kuklinski, 1972; Hansen, 1972, Moseley, 1974; Lo and Salih, 1978; Glasson, 1978; Friedman and Weaver, 1979). On the premise that economic development cannot take place everywhere at the same time, the growth center approach specifically advocated concentrating development projects at certain locations from which economic development impact would diffuse to surrounding areas. In Africa, where acute rural-urban differences in economic development within individual countries were contributing to massive rural-urban migration, the growth center approach was also seen as a means of rural development and a solution to rural-urban migration.

However, by the end of the 1970s the growth center approach had passed into oblivion and was widely declared a failure. Several reasons were advanced as to why the approach failed (see, for example, Moseley, 1974; Stohr, 1981; Lo and Salih, 1978; Friedman and Weaver, 1979; Holland, 1976). Thus, the approach was criticized for being authoritarian and too much top-down in orientation. In addition, it was said to be more concerned with space than with people. It was also thought to be too ambiguous. It produced no method for selecting the centers. It had no way to ensure that growth impacts from the center would spread to other areas, and it had no method for measuring the growth impacts.

The debate over the growth center approach ceased long ago. However, against the backdrop of growing regional disparities in African countries, questions regarding where, when, and how the approach was implemented in Africa and the basis for considering it as a failure still remain without any satisfactory answers. As we look beyond the veil in this volume, it is therefore appropriate to revisit the issue to see whether or not the growth center approach really failed in Africa or whether it was another missed opportunity for regional economic development of the continent.

This chapter examines the rise and fall of the growth center approach in Africa. It argues that, with respect to Africa, the growth center approach was not so much a failure, as it was a missed opportunity for regional economic development. The rationale for this argument is fivefold. First, the growth center approach never got beyond verbal acceptance and written incorporation into economic development plans of African countries. Second, the rationale for the growth center approach was consistent with the nature of regional economic development problems that had to be resolved. Third, not only was the approach consistent but it was also the most feasible approach of all the existing ones at the time. Fourth, though criticized on several grounds, there was nothing in those criticisms that could not be redressed if in fact the approach had been implemented. Fifth, the problem of regional development disparity that was supposed to be resolved by the growth center approach still persists today, implying that no other suitable alternative has been found since the growth center approach was abandoned. The underlying thesis of the chapter is that while critical analysis of development approaches is an essential prerequisite of any successful development planning, it can also lead to missed opportunity.

The chapter is divided into four sections. In the first section I construct a theoretical framework to illustrate the problem of missed opportunity in the economic development process and set out criteria or tests for identifying it. In the second section I outline the evolution, development, and main features of the growth center idea and its rise and fall in Africa. In the third section I examine the question of whether the approach was a failure or a missed opportunity, using the criteria I identified in the earlier section. In the final section I draw from the experience of the demise of the growth center approach in Africa to provide some important lessons for the economic development process in Africa.

THE ECONOMIC DEVELOPMENT PROCESS AND THE PROBLEM OF MISSED OPPORTUNITY

The economic development process is full of risks and uncertainties. This is because the process involves a series of decisions, the full effect of which can only be seen in the future. If right decisions are made, society reaps the benefit in the future. If wrong decisions are made, society pays in the future. As a result, all parties involved in the economic development process, presumably, want to avoid making wrong decisions. In particular, they want to avoid failure, which is the situation whereby a development approach is unable to achieve its stated goals and objectives. To do this, development approaches, concepts, theories, and strategies are usually subjected to intense scrutiny and critical evaluation for any tendencies for potential failure, before they are implemented and also during the course of their implementation. However, this important check-and-balance mechanism in the process of development planning can also backfire creating a situation that can be as bad as failure, a situation I refer to here as missed opportunity for development. What then is missed opportunity for development?

By missed opportunity for development I mean the failure to implement or follow through a development approach that would have been successful, or the failure to abandon a development approach that was doomed to failure. The failure to implement or follow through with a development approach that would have been successful will be referred to as a Type One (Type I) missed opportunity. The failure to abandon a development approach that was doomed to failure will be referred to as Type Two (Type II) missed opportunity.

The effects of missed opportunities, whether Type I or Type II, on society are both similar and different from those of failed development. They are similar to failed development because both Type I and Type II missed opportunities also result in loss of improvement in living conditions of people. In the case of Type I, it is the improvement that would have occurred had the approach been implemented, while in the case of Type II, it is the improvement that would have occurred had resources not been wasted on implementing the approach. However, the effects of missed opportunity are different from those of failed development because they can be remedied or recovered with relatively less time, effort, and resources. This is particularly so in the case of Type I missed opportunity. The implication of this is that if we can identify missed opportunities in the development process, we will be able to help society get back on the right path toward development or guide it from making wrong turns in the development process. How then can missed opportunity be identified?

There are five main tests for identifying a missed opportunity in economic development. They are the implementation test, the rationale or premise test, the feasibility or practicability test, the critique, and the aftermath tests. Each of these tests is centered on a key question that can be asked with respect to the past, or the present, or the future. Thus, the implementation test asks the question as to whether the approach was implemented or not. The rationale test focuses on whether the rationale for the approach was logically and historically consistent with the nature of the problem to be solved. The feasibility or practicability test examines whether the approach could actually be implemented within the economic, political, and social resources of the place. The critique test raises the question as to whether all the criticisms that were advanced in favor of or against the approach were in themselves valid. Finally, the aftermath test examines the question as to whether the implementation or lack of it has resolved the problem that was originally meant to be solved.

While these tests and questions are the same for both Types I and II cases the answers do vary between the two as summarized in Table 10.1 below. Thus, in Type I missed opportunity, the approach was not implemented. However, it was not only logically consistent with the problems that needed to be solved, but also economically, socially and politically feasible. Besides, the criticisms that were leveled against it did not seem to be convincing after further scrutiny. In addition to all these, the aftermath has seen a further deterioration or worsening condition of the state of the original problem.

In a Type II missed opportunity, the approach was implemented. However, both the rationale and feasibility signs were all negative in relation to the needs of the region. In addition, the criticisms of the approach, when subjected to further scrutiny, proved sound. Finally, the original problem never was resolved and in fact grew worse after the approach had been implemented. In the rest of the chapter, I will show that the story of the growth center approach in Africa is a Type I missed opportunity. Before I do this, I will provide a theoretical overview of the growth center approach and its rise and fall in Africa.

TABLE 10.1
THE FIVE TESTS FOR MISSED OPPORTUNITY IN DEVELOPMENT

Test	**Questions**	**Test Results Missed Opportunity**	
		Type 1	**Type2**
Implementation	Was the approach implemented?	No	Yes
Rationale	Was the approach logically consistent?	Yes	No
Feasibility	Was the approach feasible?	Yes	No
Critique	Were the criticisms against the approach valid?	No	Yes
Aftermath	Was the problem solved?	No	No

THE GROWTH CENTER APPROACH

Origin of the Growth Center Approach

The growth center approach originated from Perroux's concept of growth pole, which in turn was born out of the debate over whether underdeveloped regions could be developed by "balanced" or "unbalanced" growth strategies (Gaile, 1976). Triggered by Cassel (1924) and extended later by Rosenstein-Rodan (1943), Nurkse (1953), Lewis (1955), and Nelson (1956), balanced growth strategy argued the need for a "big-push" or "frontal attack" on all sectors of an economy, which would result in proportional or simultaneous development of all the sectors in the economic development process.

In contrast, Perroux (1955) and other unbalanced growth advocates (Singer, 1949; Rostow, 1956, 1960; Hirschman, 1958; and Scitovsky, 1959), argued the need to concentrate investment in those sectors that had the highest potential for growth, with the conviction that growth that would be generated by those sectors would eventually spread through the rest of the economy. Perroux (1955, p. 94) wrote that "the bitter truth is this: growth does not appear everywhere at the same time; it becomes manifest at points or poles of growth, with variable intensity; it spreads through different channels, with various terminal effects on the whole of the economy." Perroux (1955) conceived a growth pole as a center in abstract field of forces, from which centrifugal forces emanate and to which centripetal forces are attracted. This propulsive nature of the center is made possible by four main conditions. First, it is large. Second, it has a high degree of dominance in the field. Third, it is highly innovative. Fourth, it has a high level of interaction within the field. Given these conditions, a growth pole can be regarded as a sector of certain large scale, innovative, and fast-growing industries from which economic growth and change are initiated (Darwent, 1969; Thomas, 1972).

According to Thomas (1972) the initiation of economic growth occurs when the large-scale, innovative, and fast-growing or propulsive industry decides to expand output. This induces growth in the industries that supply its necessary inputs. Under conditions of increasing scale economies, the propulsive industry is able to reduce its output price. Industries that depend on that output for their input thus increase their purchases, which is in turn accompanied by the purchases of other inputs, depending on the nature of their production functions. Thus, growth is stimulated in the industries that supply those inputs also (Thomas, 1972). The amount of growth that is generated therefore depends on the activity of the growth pole and interconnections between it and other industries within its dominance (Darwent, 1969). The key to economic growth, according to the growth pole idea, is not to spread scarce resources thinly, as advocated by the balanced growth strategy, but to put investment into high growth sectors or industries that serve as growth poles.

The Transition from Growth Poles to Growth Centers

The transition from the growth poles concept to that of growth centers was forged by increasing realization that economic growth takes place in geographic space, even though there is some controversy as to whether geographic space was completely ignored in the original growth pole formulation. Thus, while several commentators have referred to Perroux's growth pole as essentially sectoral, Gaile (1976) shows that Perroux indeed did not ignore the geographic implications of economic growth. This controversy aside, the most extensive and explicit transition from Perroux's abstract notion of growth poles to its geographical equivalent of growth center is due to the pioneering works of Hirschman (1958) and Boudeville (1961, 1966).

Hirschman (1958) argued that for an economy to lift itself to higher income levels, it must develop within itself one or several regional centers of growth. This need for "growing points" or "growth poles," according to Hirschman, is an inevitable concomitant of growth itself. Once growth becomes firmly established in one part of the national territory, it puts certain forces in motion that act on the remaining parts. For Hirschman, these forces are of two main types: trickling-down or favorable effects and polarization or unfavorable effects. The former includes the increase of the growing center's (the North) purchases and investments in the rest of the territory (the South) and the absorbing of some of the disguised unemployment of the South by the North, thereby increasing the marginal productivity of the South. In contrast, polarization effects include the stifling of economic activities in the South due to strong competition from the North, which eventually leads to labor and skill migration from the South to the North. Hirschman argued that at the initial stage, polarization effects hurt the South. Eventually, however, economic pressures from the deteriorating conditions of the South come into play and force the situation to be remedied.

In a similar fashion, Boudeville (1966, p. 103) argued that economic growth is not a spontaneous homogenous or harmonized phenomenon. It appears in dynamic regions through propulsive sectors and their spillover effects on other regions in a variety of different ways. This, Boudeville (1966, p. 107) noted, can be more realistically achieved not by a program of uniform growth but one of polarized growth models. These models take account of geographic poles and polarized regions as well as the concept of a propulsive industry and its associated sectors, and they estimate the basic investment requirements needed for their development. Boudeville (1966 p. 112; 11) wrote:

> Since we are examining the regional setting and not the national space, it would be preferable to describe poles as a geographic agglomeration of activities rather than as a complex system of sectors different from the national matrix. In short, growth poles will appear as towns possessing a complex of propulsive industries. [Thus] a regional growth pole is a set

of expanding industries located in urban area and inducing further development of economic activity throughout its zone of influence.

These industries are characterized by direct and indirect dominating influences over all other activities and an oligopolistic concentration of industry with price leadership. An increase in the output of the propulsive industries induces the creation of other activities not yet in the region through mechanisms similar to those described by Hirschman (1958).

Following Hirschman and Boudeville, a proliferation of research work on the growth pole concept occurred, in which the term growth center came to be used interchangeably with growth pole for both Perroux's original notion of growth poles and Boudeville's geographic translation. To avoid an emerging semantic confusion, Darwent (1969, p. 11) suggested that the term "growth pole" should refer to the aspatial set of industries and activities and "growth center" to the spatial location of this set of industries and activities and the study of effects of this set on the surrounding area.

Acceptance and Rejection

Regional planners, regional scientists, policy makers, and governments around the world rapidly accepted the growth center idea. According to Gaile (1976), about 26 countries around the world had either implemented, seriously discussed, or provided for the use of the concept by 1974. More countries were added to this list during the early 1970s. These included a number of African countries, such as Cote d'Ivoire, Ghana, Kenya, Liberia, Libya, Niger, Nigeria, and Tanzania. In these countries, as it was elsewhere in the developing world, the growth center had an intuitive appeal for solving the existing regional development problems. In particular, the rationale that it was not possible to spread development thinly across space, and that it is important to identify certain locations as centers of growth, was seen as a short-cut method for ending the spatial inequality that had come to exist (Gaile, 1979).

The issues of how to select centers, and what activities should be provided became the subject of conferences and symposia across the continent, as various African countries attempted to adopt the approach as their regional development strategy (see for example, Ghana, 1975; Pioro, 1972). A solution to these issues was sought through a combination of the growth center idea and the central place theory.[1] Thus, a hierarchy of growth centers, each associated with specific economic development facilities, social services, and other forms of incentives, emerged as the method of choice among African countries. At the national level were growth poles; at the regional level, were growth centers, and at the district level were growth points. The number of centers increased down the hierarchy, but the importance in terms of services and facilities decreased. Each of these centers had its own area of influence, which depended on the criteria used to define it.

However, most areas of influence were to be demarcated in such a way that it would be convenient for people to reach a center for services that were not found at their places of residence. A considerable number of proposals were offered on how to set up the criteria for selecting these centers, the most popular being the use of existing regional and district capitals and selecting new centers from the remaining towns, where appropriate.

However, just as African countries were gearing up for adoption and incorporation of the growth center idea into their regional development programs, the sun was already setting on the growth center idea among western academics and policy makers. The growing appeal of political economy theories of development began to undermine the practical utility of the approach, as the approach came under heavy but somewhat questionable criticism. By the end of the 1970s, the growth center approach had passed into oblivion, just like other development concepts and strategies before it, and the approach came to be widely considered a failure. The crucial question here is, "Did the growth center approach really fail in Africa, or was it a missed opportunity for regional economic development of African countries?" My submission is that the growth center approach did not so much fail, as it was a missed opportunity. In the next section, I will apply the five tests of missed opportunity to verify the validity of this assertion.

FAILURE OR MISSED OPPORTUNITY?

The five tests for missed opportunity are the implementation, the rationale, the feasibility, the critique, and the aftermath tests. I will apply each of these tests in turn.

The Implementation Test

The primary question here is whether the growth center approach was implemented at all. Of the five African countries identified by Gaile (1976), Kenya and Tanzania were listed as having implemented the approach, while the remaining three were listed as having discussed it. Thus, any verification of the implementation of the approach must start with Kenya and Tanzania.

The blueprint of the implementation of Kenya's growth center approach is found in the 1970-1974 plan (Gaile, 1979). The Kenyan government recognized the need to promote the growth of a number of towns to a size where they were large enough to provide the people of the surrounding districts with many facilities and amenities available in a modern city (Kenya, 1969). A selection and classification of 1,682 urban growth centers was proposed, of which 11 were to be principal towns, 86 urban centers, 150 rural centers, 420 market centers and 1,015 local centers. The overall objective was to locate these hierarchy of centers in such a way that there would be a local center for every 5,000 rural people, a market center for every 15,000, a rural center for every 40,000, and an urban center for every 120,000. In addition, each center was to be provided with a specific level of economic and social infrastructure (Kenya, 1969). The 1970-74 Plan identified seven intermediate and small centers. Two more were added in the 1974-78 Plan, while a further nine were added by the 1979-83 Plan, bringing the total number of centers to 18. Of these, Kisumu, Kenya's third largest city was to receive top priority, while the rest of the 18 centers were designated for specific investments in either agriculture or industry (Hardoy and Satterthwaite, 1986).

Examining the implementation of these plans, Gaile (1979) noted that the whole pattern of government expenditure was contradictory to the intent of the growth center strategy. Thus, Nairobi received 65.2% of the government housing expenditure in 1970, though it had only 4.4% of the population. Throughout the 1970s, almost all the public buildings went to Nairobi (Stren, 1984). The first two of the large industrial estates proposed to aid the development of the large growth centers were both built in Nairobi. Thus, between 1970 and 1976, five times more money was spent on electrical transmission between Nairobi and Mombasa than was spent on the entire rural electrification program. Similarly, Nairobi and Mombasa received twice as much money for water development as the entire allocation for rural water development (Gaile, 1979).

Stren (1984) also reports that the most significant exception to the dominance of Nairobi was in the field of tourism. He shows that, partly as a result of high tourist demand on the Kenyan coast and government promotion of coastal tourism, Mombasa has been able to move in on Nairobi. Thus, in 1970, Nairobi had 41.4% of the nation's hotel beds while Mombasa had 34.1%. By 1981, the share was 35.4% for Nairobi and 41.4% for Mombasa. Hardoy and Satterthwaite (1986) also report that a new Secondary Towns program, supported by the World Bank and the US Agency for International Development is seemingly replacing the concentration on the 18 growth centers. The focus of this program is on servicing urban land constructing residential and small enterprise development, and establishing other local authority revenue generating projects such as bus parks, markets, and workshops. In a metaphorical summary, Gaile (1979 p. 206) observes that "the government has constructed a spatial skeleton for national development, yet the bones remain bare. Only the heart of the nation thrives."

With respect to Tanzania, Pioro (1972) reports that the first attempts to make use of the growth center approach took place in the 1967-69 period, when three physical plans were established in the country, as part of the decentralization and self-reliant policy of the Arusha Declaration of 1967. The three were the Dar-es-Salaam Master Plan; the Dar-es-Salaam Sub-Regional Survey and Plan, and the Physical Development Plan of the Handeni District. Despite the Arusha Declaration, the Dar es-Salaam Master Plan was aimed at maintaining the dominant role of the city as the growth pole, the biggest center for education and scientific research, and the biggest attraction for industry. The Dar-es-Salaam Sub-Regional Plan envisaged the control of population increase in Dar-es-Salaam by the development of attractive centers, especially centers along the major modes of transportation and by providing water and electricity. The proposed network envisaged a three-step hierarchy of urban settlement oriented toward serving the rural areas. The hierarchy included 15 local service and industrial centers, five intermediate service and industrial centers, and one major sub-regional industrial and service center, Ruvu. In the Handeni district, planners proposed a five-tier hierarchy of centers: minor village, minor rural center, major rural center, minor district town, and major district town. All these centers, together with those identified for the Dar-es-Salaam, were to be provided with certain services.

The Dar-es-Salaam Master Plan was never implemented because it was too expensive. In addition, as the Ujamaa project got underway, the plans became distilled into the decentralization and self-reliant experiment. Thus, in the effort to decentralize certain government functions and to locate industries, where possible, away from Dar-es-Salaam, the Second Five Year Plan (1969-1974), selected eight towns throughout the country for concentrated urban development over the plan period (Stren, 1984). These towns were Tanga, Arusha/Moshi, Mwanza, Mtwara, Mbeya, Morogoro, Dodoma, and Tabora. The 1976-1981 Plan sought to support the development of basic consumer goods' industries and to promote small and medium industries at the centers Hardoy and Satterthwaite (1986).

Looking back at how these plans had performed, Stren (1984) reports that the decentralization of administrative functions had been far more successful, culminating in the 1973 decision to move the capital city from Dar-es-Salaam to Dodoma. In addition, Dar-es-Salaam's share of the country's urban population had fallen from 45.2% in 1967 to 34.8% by 1979, as smaller towns began to grow rapidly in population. However, in other areas the story was different. In terms of urban employment, for example, Dar-es-Salaam still dominated in the location of urban employment, accounting for 46% of the total in 1970, up from 44.2 % in the previous year (Stren, 1984).

However, to interpret this as a failed plan would be to assume that the plan was fully implemented and without any problems. The fact is some aspects of the plan never got off the ground. As Stren (1984) noted, no administrative machinery had been set up to influence the siting of new industries in the selected cities, at least not in the early years of the plan period. Besides, between 1973-1975, a series of crises hit the Tanzanian economy that made it difficult to embark on development projects. The severe drought due to shortfall of rain in 1973-74; the forcible movement of large numbers of peasants at the time; the oil crises which raised the cost of fuel, fertilizer and other industrial and commercial goods; the fallen price of sisal on the world market; the acceleration of armed conflict with Mozambique and Zimbabwe and later with Uganda; and the expectation of foreign aid that never materialized all combined to stifle the economic development efforts.

Some of the countries, which discussed the growth center idea also, incorporated it into their development plans, but the turbulent years of the 1970s did not allow implementation. A typical example of this is Ghana, which incorporated the growth center approach in its 1975-1980 development plan and yet never implemented it due to major internal problems. Thus, the plan was not launched until 1977, when it was already two years behind schedule. By the end of that year a "palace coup" within the Supreme Military Council, the then ruling body of the country, transferred power from General Acheampong to General Akuffo in order to stem the growing national unrest against Acheampong's government. With an increasing threat coming from within the military, the Akuffo regime had little time to follow through any economic development projects. Two years later, in June 1979, the entire regime disappeared with all its development programs when a group of young military officers, led by Flight-Lieutenant J. J. Rawlings, seized power and attempted to move the country toward socialism. In view of these, it can be argued that the growth center approach did not fail in Africa because it was never fully implemented.

The Rationale Test

If the growth center approach was not implemented, was it because it was rationally inconsistent with the problems it was supposed to solve within the African context? As already pointed out, the main rationale for the growth center approach was the recognition that, contrary to the balanced growth model, economic development cannot be spread evenly in space all at once within the constraint of limited resources. Instead, by encouraging the right kind of development or investment activities at a selected number of centers of growth, it is possible to reduce spatial inequities in development at less cost.

At the time the growth center approach emerged, this rationale was very much consistent with the solutions needed for the problem of regional disparities in economic development in Africa. The roots of this problem date back to precolonial times when, along with the establishment and rise of civilizations such as Egypt, Cush, Carthage, Ghana, Mali, Songhai, Oyo, Hausa, Asante, and Zimbabwe, certain cities emerged as political, economic and religious centers. Among these were Memphis, Thebes, Cairo, Karma, Carthage, Walata, Timbuktu, Gao, Ibadan, Kano, Katsina, Kumasi and Great Zimbabwe. (Chandler, 1994a and 1994b)

Colonial administration either sought to reinforce some of these existing centers by using them as seats of colonial administration or established new centers as deemed necessary. Whatever the case, the colonial administrative and commercial centers had to be developed to the level of comforts for colonial officials. These centers therefore got a boost in development as every colonial development project was placed there. Thus, they became the first sites for schools, hospitals, and other social amenities. Those cities, which were by the sea, also became the seaports (Christopher and Tarver, 1994; Obudho and Obudho, 1994).

In addition to these colonial capitals, important centers began to emerge in highly mineralized as well as rich agricultural and other industrial raw material regions, as they became the hubs for rail and road transportation, as well as sources of new jobs. Most of these were in the interior, even in coastal countries. As a result by the end of the colonial period a two-tier, non-integrated spatial system could clearly be identified: an urban system overwhelmingly dominated by a national capital with a distant following of regional administrative capitals, important mining centers, commercial or market centers, and a rural system of small towns and villages dominated by district capitals.

Postcolonial development accentuated the existing spatial system, with a greater share of the development projects going to the national capitals. Most of these capitals were modernized to the standards of European and North American cities. In addition, the import-substitution industrialization policy that was adopted by many African countries also helped to concentrate more projects and jobs in the cities. First, the cities already had most of the infrastructure needed and thus had an initial advantage. Second, the fact that most of the industries required imported raw materials made seaports the best locations for coastal countries. As new jobs were created in such cities, more people migrated into them, making it necessary to provide more social amenities. Thus, not only did the cities have the initial advantage, but they also had Myrdal's (1957) process of circular and cumulative causation working to their advantage.[2]

Admittedly, regional disparities are not peculiar to Africa. In every country there are some regions that, for a wide variety of reasons, are more developed than others. However, when such imbalances reach a point that they begin to hurt the regions which are lacking development and in fact become counterproductive, they can no longer be seen as normal. Thus, by the end of the 1960s, regional disparities in economic development in every country in the new Africa had reached such unjustifiable proportions that something had to be done about them (UN, 1971). Geographers, sociologists, and regional planners led the charge when they criticized economists, who had been the sole architects of Africa's economic development, for neglecting the spatial aspects of development. In searching for solutions to reduce this regional development imbalance, African governments found answers in a new development concept: *integrated rural development.* Integrated rural development was defined as "the outcome of a series of quantitative and qualitative changes occurring among a given rural population whose converging effects indicate in time, a rise in the standard of living and favorable changes in the life of the people concerned" (UN, 1971 p.1). Integrated rural development emphasized agricultural development, development of rural industries, and provision of social amenities, which in the end would transform the marked regional disparities between rural and urban areas into a rural-urban continuum (Rondinelli and Ruddel 1976). A key objective in implementing this strategy was access by rural dwellers to services and opportunities that would help raise the standard of living of the majority of the people that live in the rural areas. Among these services and opportunities were good drinking water, good education systems, good health care systems, good transportation systems, technical advice on the various economic activities, and alternative sources of employment in the rural areas.

With the limited development resources of African countries, it was realized that the most judicious way to achieve this objective was not to spread development evenly across space but to facilitate the provision of these services and opportunities in a selected number of centers that would be within reasonable reach of most of the rural dwellers. Thus, the growth center approach provided a good fit to the problem of regional development disparities in Africa.

The Feasibility Test

The argument that the growth center approach provided a good fit, however, is not sufficient to make its abandonment a missed opportunity. This is because an economic development approach can be very sound and convincing in theory and yet unfeasible. Such a situation may arise when an important condition that needs to be fulfilled is either nonexistent or could not be met. In most cases the condition is economical. In other cases it may be political, social, or physical. A good development theory, strategy, or approach is useless if it cannot be implemented for whatever reason. So, we can ask: "Was the growth center approach feasible?"

Economically, the growth center approach was more feasible than other economic development strategies that had been implemented before or were vying for attention at the time. As already pointed out, before the growth center approach the main stream prescription for economic development was the balanced growth model. This model advocated a frontal attack on all the sectors of the economy since the problems of poverty were multisectoral. Even though this was an appealing proposal, it was expensive and required large sums of capital that were relatively scarce in African countries. Besides, the model was too sectoral and paid little attention to the spatial or distribution aspects of development impacts. To use this alternative approach to solve a problem it had helped to create would be the most difficult task. In contrast, the growth center approach took into consideration the scarcity of financial resources. In addition, as Gruchman (1972) has pointed out, limited financial resource was not the only reason that the growth center approach was suitable to African countries. The other economic factor was limited trained workers. The growth center approach reduced the need to rely on large numbers of trained workers, characteristics of the balanced growth model.

In other areas there were no major political, social, and physical problems that made the growth center approach unfeasible. It could be argued that the approach required a decentralized form of government as well as a well-developed physical infrastructure. However, both requirements were part of the growth center package. Thus, the growth center approach was a facilitator in establishing a decentralized system of functions among centers. In addition, existence of local government personnel including chiefs and other community leaders, could serve as a source for mobilizing people to support projects that would benefit the people.

Socially, there was nothing inherent about the growth center approach that would have hindered its implementation. Rural dwellers in African countries are already used to market centers, places where needed goods could be purchased. Most of these places have no good roads and can only be reached by walking or by long waits for transport that cut into a good part of a working day. The growth center approach could have strengthened these centers and brought them within easy reach of the majority of the people. In addition, the spirit of self-help and communal labor is very much alive in Africa. Everywhere, people have risen to the occasion of self-help when given the right leadership and motivation. The growth center approach could have capitalized on this asset to a great advantage. It would also have been an opportunity for both the government and the people to come together. Rural dwellers in particular would have felt a sense of belonging to a nation, thereby ending some of the apathy and culture of silence that characterize many African countries.

The Critique Test

Critical analysis of proposed development strategies is necessary to ensure that appropriate strategies are implemented while inappropriate ones are avoided. An examination of whether or not the growth center approach was a missed opportunity will not be complete without reexamination of the criticisms that were leveled against it at the time. For purposes of discussion, I have summarized these criticisms that can be found in the works Moseley (1974); Holland (1976); Lo and Salih (1978); Friedman and Weaver (1979); Stohr and Taylor (1981); as well as several others, into four.

First, the growth center approach was criticized for being authoritarian, exploitative, and too much center-down in orientation. This means that it did not include the people at the grass roots. Second, the growth center approach was criticized for being too much concerned with space or place rather than people, thereby making a fetish out of space. Third, the growth center concept was criticized for being too ambiguous. It offered no guide for selecting the centers. It was not clear how it could be used for spatial allocation of investments. Government financial incentives offered to private enterprises to divert manufacturing activities from locating in "natural growth centers" were too weak to achieve a permanent restructuring and spatial reorganization. Even if this did not occur, it was also pointed out that as a result of the process of circular and cumulative causation, development would polarize at the center and would never trickle down. In addition, the approach had no way of measuring growth impacts from the centers, if any. Fourth, the growth center approach was criticized for its low labor absorption capacity and, with the large surplus of labor in Third World countries and for that matter Africa, the whole approach would be detrimental to the labor force. To what extent are these criticisms valid?

Critics who accused the growth center approach for being too much center-down proposed a bottom-up approach to development as a much better alternative. However, a careful analysis of the bottom-up approach shows that it is not radically different from the growth center approach. The single most important claim of the bottom-up development approach is that it includes the rural people right from the beginning of the development process. However, for purposes of national development and security, there is nowhere in the world that rural dwellers are left on their own to do whatever they want to do. Development always requires leaders who will bring up ideas or facilitate the development of new ideas, and motivate people to action. Even in the extreme cases of self-reliance and self-help development strategies, someone has to come up with the idea of self-reliance and self-help and motivate people to catch the same vision before its impact could be seen. This means that development from below may not be completely different from development from above. The difference may not lie so much in the origin of the ideas and activities as it does in how the idea is put into practice.

Besides, the idea of involving rural people right at the beginning of the planning process is the most practicable thing to do in development planning. However, it does not always lead to efficient use of scarce resources. For example, Oppong and Hodgson (1994) found that in spite of the "proliferation" of rural health centers in Ghana, rural dwellers in that country usually by-passed the health facilities nearest to them to go to more distant ones because the latter were better equipped. Yet, the proliferation of these health centers was largely due to the demand by every settlement for a health center. Even so, the growth center approach was less of a center-down approach and more of a bottom-up approach, since it at least sought to redistribute facilities and opportunities for social and economic advancement. In that case, it was no different from the development of the urban system that is so essential in bridging the gap between the city and the country. In addition, while critics advocate the bottom-up approach to replace the center-down approach of development at the regional level (Stohr, 1981), there is no indication of how "big ticket" projects which are essential to grass roots development will be distributed in the face of limited national resources.

The criticism that the growth center approach was concerned more with space or place than with people also needs to be countered. The original premise for embracing the growth center approach in Africa, as already indicated, was to help people who had been unjustifiably bypassed by the development process. These people were confined to specific places. The towns that would be selected to become growth centers were not uninhabited, isolated, and vacant lands. They were settlements, occupied by people that were in turn surrounded by other settlements also occupied by people, all of which were lacking in basic infrastructure and services. There was no prescription in the growth center approach to select an intermediate location in the middle of nowhere and devoid of people. Some of the facilities that were proposed for the centers, such as public bath houses, might have been out of place, but that did not make the growth center approach more concerned with space than with people. Moreover, as Johnson (1970) has forcefully argued, there is no living space that can be detached from the life of the people that live in it. Any effort that focuses on changing that living space, therefore, cannot be done outside the life of the people. In the same way, the effects of the so-called people-focused development must reflect the organization of their living space. To argue that the growth center approach was more concerned with space than with people is theoretically sound but practically untenable.

The criticism that the growth center approach was ambiguous seems to be rooted in the semantic confusion that developed with Perroux's original growth pole notion. Perroux's growth pole concept was abstract and had a number of key concepts (such as propulsive, key, and leading industries) that were not properly defined (Darwent, 1969; Lasuen, 1969). However, the idea of the growth center did not have that ambiguity, at least not in the minds of developing countries in Africa. As I have already pointed out, there was no ambiguity as to the selection of centers because of the existence of regional and district capitals. In fact, these came to be referred to as "natural growth centers." Where such natural centers were nonexistent, methods for selecting them were not going to be any different from those used for location of any major development project intended to influence its surroundings.

The trickling-down criticism also missed the point of the growth center approach and how economic development effects spread through a region. The whole criticism against the trickling-down approach assumes that the effects of the development process will trickle down by themselves. This assumption has also precipitated the belief that the trickling-down of development is a myth. Both views are inaccurate. If the trickling-down effects of development are mythical, how did the developed countries of today achieve the relatively better spatial equity in economic development than developing countries. Of course, the cities that dominate the centers of activity in the US, Canada, Western Europe, etc., did not all emerge at the same time. They emerged through a complex process of positive and negative trickling-down effects from the few that took the lead because of having some kind of initial advantages. Above all, they emerged as the result of some form of government intervention, as was the case with Britain's new towns or the many intervention programs in the US, after World War II, such as the location of defense and the aerospace industries

The fact is nowhere does economic development trickle down by itself. People make trickling-down happen. It occurs when people decide to locate businesses and residences in places outside the main centers of activities. In turn, such a trend can only occur when there are incentives and disincentives in other places and entrepreneurs to take advantage of them. The creation of such incentives and other motivating factors does not come from thin air. It comes from a government leadership that is committed to the ideal of improving the lot of the majority of its people instead of the members of its own institution. It comes from a government leadership made up of people with the appropriate human factor characteristics who will see to it that the scarce resources are used judiciously for the betterment of the people instead of themselves.[3] Thus, the solution to the problem does not lie in a development-from-below strategy per se, as the critics of the growth center-approach would like us to believe, but in the availability of incentives in other places through direct and indirect government policies that encourage local entrepreneurs to emerge or non-local entrepreneurs to go there. This is exactly what the growth center approach was supposed to do. The fact that the incentives being offered by governments were too weak to divert attention to other areas does not make the growth center approach useless. It means those incentives must be strengthened. Besides, as Hansen (1975) has argued, what might constitute trickling-down or spread effects depends on one's perspectives. Thus, migration of the unemployed from an area, for example, benefits the area of origin, while migration of the skilled and the employed hurts the area of origin. Above all, it is common sense that it will be a lot easier for development impact to spread from *Anycenter* to *Anytown* in the countryside than from *Anycapital* to *Anytown* in the countryside.

Finally, the criticism that the growth center approach had a low labor force absorption capacity and therefore would be detrimental to the labor force assumes that the approach had to be adopted wholesale without any adaptation. Thus, the only employment opportunity that the centers were going to create would be from the propulsive industry at the center. However, there is no reason why the so-called propulsive industry could not create opportunities that could enhance an important local activity or series of small-scale industrial activities. In the countryside of many African countries there are numerous crafts and small-scale industrial activities that have great potential for being viable economic activities. However, these activities are stifled because of lack of help in resource inputs, technological improvement, and marketing facilities (see for example Ofori-Amoah, 1988; Norcliffe, 1983; Freeman and Norcliffe, 1984). Beyond the provision of basic needs such as good drinking water, an equipped health care center, and the like, a growth center approach did not have to follow a one-size-fits-all strategy, especially in the area of economic opportunities. Where opportunities existed for establishing a modern industry, it would have been appropriate to do so. In the same way, where opportunities existed for mobilizing crafts or small-scale industries into an industrial complex, it would have been appropriate to do likewise. This criticism that the growth center approach was not appropriate because of its low job creating ability thus underscores both a "paternalistic" attitude and a lack of creative adaptability the inability often assumed by both local and foreign intervention leaders in Africa's development.

The Aftermath Test

The foregoing discussion so far seems to confirm that the growth center approach was an opportunity that African countries missed in achieving a better regional economic development. However, before we can arrive at this conclusion, we need to perform one more test, a postmortem one. Thus, we ask, "What has happened to the problem of regional disparities in economic development in African countries, that in the 1960s and early 1970s made the growth center approach so attractive? Has it changed for the better or for the worse?"

We have noted some answers to this question during our discussion of the experience of Kenya and Tanzania with the growth center approach. In Kenya, we saw that Nairobi and Mombasa still continue to dominate the distribution of development investments. In Tanzania, the decentralization aspect seemed to have taken root. However, progress in the development of Dodoma has been slow due to funding problems. In the remaining African countries the situation is not different. The capital cities continue to dominate in population concentration, the number of hospitals, hospital beds, and physicians. They dominate in the number of schools, other social amenities, as well as in job opportunities. This means that since the abandonment of the growth center approach, not much progress has been made in the effort to bridge the gap in economic development among regions. This also implies that no better alternative strategies seem to have been found to do the job that the growth center approach was supposed to do.

CONCLUSION

The demise of the growth center approach is another example of how international development thinking can influence, and in some cases dictate, what can practically work and not work in Africa. To a large extent, the growth center approach was a victim of the resurgence of interest among leading development academics in theories of political economy that characterized the 1970s. The irony of it all is that most of these critics were from developed countries, whose city systems exhibited the best examples of growth centers. In the US, such examples include New York, Chicago, Los Angeles, San Francisco, Seattle-Tacoma, Dallas-Fort Worth, Houston, Atlanta, Cincinnati, St. Louis, Denver, Phoenix, and Minneapolis-St. Paul. In Canada, they include Montreal, Toronto, Vancouver, Edmonton, Calgary, and Winnipeg. In France, they are Paris, Marseilles, Bordeaux, Lyons, Toulouse. In Germany, they include Essen, Berlin, Cologne, Frankfurt, Bonn, Dortmund, Munich, Hanover, and Hamburg. In the UK, they include London, Manchester, and Birmingham. It is true that the growth of these cities has been due to a complex set of factors, but there has been a strong direct and indirect central government role. In the US, for example, the interstate highway and urban freeway project, housing policies, and defense spending are classic examples of how direct government policy helped to shape the growth of these centers. Similarly, in the UK deliberate efforts have been made to curb the growth of London since the 1960s.

In this light, what the growth center approach was proposing for African countries was not unique. In every African country there are regional and district capitals of some sort that could serve as centers of growth. However, as Mabogunje (1994) has argued, these cities have been unable to serve as veritable engines of growth as compared to cities in other societies. Admittedly, the growth center approach did not have all the answers needed to make African cities move beyond this inertia. However, the need to boost infrastructures such as transportation and power supplies and other incentives at other centers that would encourage local and non-local entrepreneurial activities, could have been a step in the right direction.

I have argued elsewhere that the history of Africa's economic development process has been characterized by the tendency of African countries to jump on any new ideas, either without critically examining them or because of certain clauses of conditionality (Ofori-Amoah, 1994, 1995a and 1995b). The demise of the growth center approach in Africa is an example of this same trend that worked in the opposite direction. Instead of examining the validity of the critiques of the growth center approach, African countries easily gave in to the idea that the approach will not work and abandoned it. Today, the regional development disparities that generated the need to adopt the growth center approach has grown from bad to worse, as primate cities dominate one African country after another. The implication of all this is that for Africa to develop, not only is it important for it to identify the appropriate strategy to follow but it is also important to be able to stay on course, in the face of conflicting views and opinions. This requires an appropriate human factor (Adjibolosoo, 1994 and 1995) that can critically analyze, implement, and supervise development concepts, ideas, and trends within the context of Africa's development problems and priorities.

From my perspective, the growth center approach is still relevant to the regional economic development of Africa. Instead of pursuing policies that will continue to polarize development in Accra, Abidjan, Kinshasa, Khartoum, and other capital cities, Africa should attempt to promote other existing regional and district capitals as centers of economic development. This is a better strategy for regional economic development.

NOTES

1. The central place theory was formulated by the German geographer Walter Christaller in 1933. On the assumption that settlement existed solely on the basis of hinterland trade, the central place theory sought to answer the question as to the number, sizes and arrangements of settlements in an ideal geographic space. The theory shows that settlements can be arranged in a hierarchy on the basis of the goods and services they offer and their market areas. Settlements at the top of the hierarchy offer the widest range of goods and services, have the largest market areas, and are much fewer in numbers than settlements down the hierarchy. The theory goes on to indicate how settlements in the lower hierarchies could be located in relation to the settlement at the top of the hierarchy.

2. Cumulative causation is a process by which economic development tends to concentrate at a place that had an initial advantage. The Swedish economist Gunnar Myrdal (1957) argued that as a result of this process, economic

development's impact will backwash the prospects of surrounding areas rather than spread to them.

3. For detailed discussion of the human factor and its role in developing Africa, see Adjibolosoo 1994; 1995.

REFERENCES

Adjibolosoo, S. 1994. "The Human Factor and the Failure of Economic Development Policies in Africa." In F. Ezeala-Harrison and S. Adjibolosoo, eds. P*erspectives on Economic Development in Africa.* Westport: Praeger (pp. 25-37).

Adjibolosoo, S. 1995. *The Human Factor In Developing Africa*. Westport, CT: Praeger.

Boudeville, J. R. 1961. *Les Espaces Economiques*. Paris: Presses Universitaires de France.

Boudeville, J. R. 1966. *Problems of Regional Economic Planning*. Edinburgh: Edinburgh University Press.

Cassel, G. 1924. *The Theory of Social Economy*. Tr. by J. McCabe. New York: Hanout.

Chandler, T. 1994a. "Urbanization in Ancient Africa" In J. D. Tarver, ed. *Urbanization in Africa: A Handbook.* Westport, CT: Greenwood Press (pp. 3 -14).

Chandler, T. 1994b. "Urbanization in Medieval and Early Modern Africa." In J. D. Tarver, ed. *Urbanization in Africa: A Handbook.* Westport, CT: Greenwood Press (pp. 15-32).

Christopher, A. J. and Tarver, J. D. 1994. "Urbanization during Colonial Days in Sub-Saharan Africa." In J. D. Tarver, ed. *Urbanization in Africa: A Handbook.* Westport, CT.: Greenwood Press (pp. 33-48).

Darwent, F. 1969. "Growth Poles and Growth Centers in Regional Planning-A Review. *" Environment and Planning*, 1: 5-32.

Freeman, D. B. & Norcliffe, G. B. 1984 "National and Regional Patterns of Rural Nonfarm Employment in Kenya." *Geography,* 221-233.

Friedmann, J and Weaver, C. 1979. *Territory and Function: The Evolution of Regional Planning.* Berkeley: University of California Press.

Gaile, G. L. 1976. "Spatial Reorganization of Development." (A Ph.D. Dissertation). Los Angeles: Department of Geography, University of California.

Gaile, G. L. 1979. "Distance and Development in Kenya." In R. A. Obudho and D. R. F. Taylor, eds. *The Spatial Structure of Development*. Boulder, Co Westview Press (pp. 201-222).

Glasson, J. 1978. *Introduction to Regional Planning*. London: Hutchinson and Sons Co. (Publishers).

Ghana, Government of 1975. *The 5-Year Development Plan 1975-1980* Accra: Ghana.

Gruchman, B. 1972. "Growth Poles in the Spatial, Structure of the Libyan Economy." In A. Kuklinski, ed. *Growth Poles and Growth Centres in Regional Planning*. Paris: Mouton & Co. (pp. 195-206).

Hansen, N. M. ed. 1972. *Growth Centers in Regional Economic Development.* New York: The Free Press.

Hansen, N. M. 1975. "An Evaluation of Growth Center Theory and Practice." *Environment and Planning,* A (7): 821-832.

Hardoy, J. E and Satterthwaite, D. 1986. "A Survey of Empirical Material on the Factors Affecting the Development of Small and Intermediate Urban Centres." In J. E. Hardoy and D. Satterthwaite, eds. *Small and Intermediate Urban Centers: Their Role in Regional Development in the Third World.* Boulder, CO: Westview Press in association with the International Institute for Environment and Development.

Hirschman, A. O. 1958. *The Strategy of Economic Development.* New Haven: Yale University Press.

Holland, S. 1976. *Capital Versus Region*. London: Macmillan.

Johnson, E. A. J. 1970. *The Organization of Space In Developing Countries*. Cambridge, MA: Harvard University Press.

Kenya, Government of. 1969. *The 1970-1974* Plan. Nairobi: Government of Kenya.

Kuklinski, A. ed. 1972. *Growth Poles and Growth Centres in Regional Planning*. Paris: Mouton & Co.

Lasuen, J. R. 1969. "On Growth Poles." *Urban Studies,* 6 137-161.

Lewis, W. A. 1955. *The Theory of Economic Growth*. Homewood, IL: Richard D. Irwin.

Lo, F and Salih, K. (eds.) 1978. *Growth Pole Strategy and Regional Development Policy: Asian Experience and Alternative Approaches*. Oxford: Pergamon Press for the United Nations Centre For Regional Development

Mabogunje, A. L. 1994. "Cities and Africa's Economic Recovery." In J. D. Tarver (ed.) *Urbanization in Africa: A Handbook.* Westport, CT: Greenwood Press (pp. xxi).

Moseley, M. J. 1974. *Growth Centers in Spatial Planning*. Oxford: Pergamon Press.

Myrdal, G. 1957. *Economic Theory and Underdeveloped Regions.* London: Duckworth.

Nelson, R. R. 1956. "A Theory of Low Level Equilibrium Trap." *American Economic Review*, 46: 894 - 908.

Norcliffe, G. 1983. "Operating Characteristics of Rural Non-farm Enterprises in Central Province, Kenya *World Development,* 11 (11): 981-984.

Nurkse, R. 1953. *Problems of Capital Formation in Underdeveloped Countries*. Oxford: Oxford University Press.

Obudho, R.A and Obudho, R. A. 1994. "The Growth of Africa's Urban Population." In J. D. Tarver, ed. *Urbanization in Africa: A Handbook.* Westport, CT: Greenwood Press (pp. 49-64).

Ofori-Amoah, B. 1988. "Improving Existing Indigenous Technologies as a Strategy for the Appropriate Technology Concept in Ghana." *Industry and Development,* 23: 57-79.

Ofori-Amoah, B. 1994. "Technological Change Strategy for Economic Development in Africa." In F. Ezeala-Harrison and S. Adjibolosoo, eds. *Perspectives on Economic Development in Africa* (pp. 85-102).

Ofori-Amoah, B. 1995a. "The Saturation Hypothesis and Africa's Development Problems: .On the Nature of Development Theory and Its Implications for the Human Factor in Africa's Development" In S. Adjibolosoo, ed. *The Significance of the Human Factor in African Economic Development.* Westport, CT: Praeger.

Ofori-Amoah, B. 1995b. "Development Research and Africa's Development Problems." *Review of Human Factor Studies,* 1 (1): 26-44.

Oppong, J. R. and Hodgson, M. J. 1994. "Spatial Accessibility to Health Care Facilities in Suhum District, Ghana." *The Professional Geographer*, 46 (2): 199-209.

Pioro, Z. 1972. "Growth Poles and Growth Centers Theory as Applied to Settlement Development in Tanzania." In A. Kuklinski, ed. *Growth Poles and Growth Centres in Regional Planning*. Paris: Mouton & Co.

Perroux, F. 1955. "Note sur La Notion de Pole de Croissance." *Economiqe Appliquee,* 1 and 2, Paris: ISEA.

Rondinelli, D. A. and Ruddle. K. 1976. *Urban Functions in Rural Development: An Analysis of Integrated Spatial Development Policy*. Washington D.C: Office of Urban Development, Agency for International Development, US Department of State.

Rosenstein-Rodan, P. 1943. "Problems of Industrialization of Eastern and Southern Europe." *Economic Journal*, 53: 205-16

Rostow, W. W. 1956. "The Take-Off into Self-Sustained Growth." *Economic Journal,* 66: 25-48.

Rostow, W. W. 1960. *The Stages of Economic Growth: A Non-Communist Manifesto*. Cambridge, Eng.: University of Cambridge Press.

Scitovsky, T. 1959. "Growth: Balanced or Unbalanced." In M. Abramovitz, ed. *The Allocation of Economic Resources*. Stanford: Stanford University Press.

Singer, H. W. 1949 "Economic Progress in Underdeveloped Countries." *Social Research,* 16: 5-8.

Stohr, W. B. 1981. "Development from Below: The Bottom-Up and Periphery-Inward Development Paradigm." In W. B. Stohr and D .R. F. Taylor, eds. *Development From Above or Below?* New York: John Wiley & Sons Ltd. (pp. 39-72).

Stohr, W. B. and Taylor, D. R. F. eds. 1981. *Development From Above or Below?* New York: John Wiley & Sons Ltd.

Stren, R. E. 1984. "Urban Policy." In J. D. Barkan, ed. *Politics and Public Policy in Kenya and Tanzania.* Westport, CT: Praeger Publishers (pp. 233-264).

Thomas, M. D. 1972. "The Regional Problem, Structural Change and Growth Pole Theory." In A. Kuklinski, ed. *Growth Poles and Growth Centres in Regional Planning*. Paris: Mouton & Co. pp. 69-102).

United Nations. 1971. *Integrated Approach to Rural Development in Africa.* New York: United Nations

11

THE COLD WAR RECONSIDERED: THE POLITICS OF SURVIVAL IN AFRICA

Boniface Y. Gebe
Department of Political Science
Queens University

INTRODUCTION

Some comments and explanations, particularly by Western international relations practitioners and theorists, would seem to suggest that the cold war era was one conducive to systemic peace and stability. Conversely, the ending of the cold war has been depicted as one which tore apart the ideological bond that held fragile polities together and opened the floodgates to ancient antagonisms, and to nationalist and ethnic agitation.(Waltz, 1964; Mearsheimer, 1990 Gaddis, 1987, 1991). Thus, Waltz (1964) asserts that the bipolar global structure prevalent during the cold war provided the world with a stability seldom known. Similarly, Gaddis (1987) has referred to the absence of a major or global war between the superpowers or the great powers during the cold war as the 'long peace.' This was considered stability so far as there was no major threat to the leading or dominant powers in the system.

Without doubt, the superpowers and their respective allies faced tremendous challenges of a political, military and geo-strategic nature during the cold war. They frequently had to negotiate their differences through agreements such as Strategic Arms Limitations Talks (SALT), Strategic Arms Reduction Talks (START), and occasionally had to hypocritically bring the rest of the world on board for their own strategic calculations, characterized by the NPT--Non-Proliferation Treaty (Nye, 1985). Through such ploys, the potential for a nuclear catastrophe was reduced significantly. At the same time, these same powers were stockpiling the most deadly weapons known to humanity in both quantitative and qualitative terms while maintaining international outlets for the massive transfer of arms to the periphery. The reality of the cold war bipolar environment, amidst the ideological antagonism and geo-strategic maneuvers, was to push the entire world toward a precarious balance between thermonuclear catastrophe and survival. In Africa, for instance, the tilt toward a particular ideological persuasion meant the active hostility of the opposing ideological camp. The intensity of social strife, civil conflicts and ideological labeling had adverse consequences for national reconstruction, development and reconciliation. A clear manifestation of this was the high level of foreign intervention on the continent, unparalleled increase in arms sales and transfers, militarism, dictatorships, political corruption and institutional decay.

The central argument of this chapter is that the cold war never provided global systemic stability, nor was international politics peaceful. Instead, it was marked by turbulence, great power rivalry and catastrophic spill-over effects to the developing world and Africa in particular. If today the world is experiencing increased ethnic and civil conflicts, it is not, if one should face the facts, necessarily attributable to the end of the cold war but a reflection of the historical distortions, power inequities and structural imbalances that years of Western imperialism and colonialism have implanted globally. It is simply a continuity rather than change. Power relations have certainly changed among the former great powers but the global structure in place still limits independent action in the developing world. Ultimately, the significance of the collapse of communism and the demise of the cold war is not so much that a uni-polar power structure has emerged and the United States has won (Krauthammer, 1991) but that a new era should be welcomed as an opportunity for Africa in particular and the rest of the developing world to pursue self-reliant policies that obviate foreign entanglements.

A concise framework for this discussion would be to place the cold war in proper context, with a brief analysis of its dynamics, major participants and passive recipients of the fall-outs. Also within that setting, an assessment of the repercussions for Africa and the meaning and significance of the end of the cold war for the continent would be made.

THE COLD WAR AND BIPOLARITY

The aftermath of World War Two led to intense infighting, short of war, among the allies (the United States, Great Britain, France, the Soviet Union among others) which stood and fought together to contain the onslaught of the Central Axis (Germany, Japan and Italy). With Germany defeated and occupied by the allies, the stark realities of the ideological incongruity and the competing strategic calculations between the American-led Western liberal democratic posturing and the belligerent assertiveness of the Soviet Union became apparent. To begin with, they could not agree on how to share the spoils of war (the occupation of Germany and its subsequent division into East and West was critical to the unfolding of ensuing developments). When it became obvious that the Soviet Union was determined to use military occupation to hold on to those conquered territories in Central and Eastern Europe, overrun during the war (ironically intended as a gesture of national liberation from Nazi Germany), the process was irrevocable. Even before 1945, it was obvious that the Soviets and their Western allies were strange bedfellows. Ideologically, they were far apart. In terms of economic and social organization, free market and liberal democracy stood in sharp contradiction to a centrally planned economy and totalitarian rule, even if the latter was projected for public consumption as democratic centralism or international socialism.

The cold war should be understood in terms of a tension-laden international environment. The two leading and dominant actors--the United States and the Soviet Union--possessed enormous power--military, economic and technological. The conversion of these power resources (actual and potential) helped them to pursue and promote unlimited political objectives. Their vast nuclear arsenal, built progressively over the cold war years, transformed international relations from one of several great powers balancing each other on the international stage to one that revolved around two power centers. With this went policy coordination and planning by both poles to restrict an extension of each other's zone of influence or create a defense system capable of withholding any surreptitious military onslaught. While the American-led Western alliance was vigorously pursuing the policy of 'containment' of the 'red menace' or Soviet communism, it was soon realized that the principles of socialist planning and emancipation from the vestiges of capitalist exploitation equally had a large measure of appeal to intellectuals and governments in much of the Third World.

The issue of ideology became a serious obstacle to accurate perception, and foreign policy enactments were often skewed or handicapped in appreciating the values and vision represented by international organizations such as the United Nations. United Nations objectives and principles of peaceful co-existence, respect for territorial borders and the active promotion of international peace and security were often sacrificed on the altar of big power manipulation inside and outside the Security Council. Between 1945 and June 1990, 279 vetoes hindered the Security Council from reaching agreement on actions to promote common purposes.[1] One could appreciate the extent to which the cold war climate was virulently destructive in regard to international understanding and cooperation.

The combination of ideology and the arms race thus constituted veritable components of the cold war environment and the international system in general. Ali Mazrui made a relevant observation that the cold war was not simply "the product of confrontation between capitalism and communism but in reality an outcome of interaction between two important phenomena--ideology and nuclear power," in a period of history fraught with the danger of a nuclear holocaust (Mazrui, 1977). The push for military leadership and global hegemony soon transformed the competition into an arms race, and resources, which could have been profitably utilized in social transformation and economic development, were misused. The intensification of the arms race and nuclear military competition was accompanied by the fear of nuclear destruction. Deterrence became a catch word in military planning and strategic studies, and defense policy in both camps--the American-led North Atlantic Treat Organization (NATO) and the Warsaw Pact under the central command of the Soviet Union--assumed a framework of credible threat and pragmatic restraint.

Protection of alliance members within these camps against possible nuclear attack became a preoccupation and with it came the military praxis of 'extended deterrence' between North America and Western Europe. 'Non-use', flexible response', and 'tactical response' were often foreign policy pronouncements and assurances rather than any serious policy choice, for as any cautious observer would decipher, a nuclear confrontation or conflict is open to volatility, unpredictability and unimaginable escalation. Very soon, however, the entire international system was restructured. The pre-World War Two multi-polar power centers gave way to far-flung American and Soviet hegemonies. The bipolar underpinnings of the cold war were also evident by the fact that the two super-powers created unparalleled and often unchallenged political, military and economic magnetism that determined the policy choice of their respective allies and proxies. The few daring challenges or differences on both sides arose either out of disaffection with certain institutional arrangements and policy enactments (British and French decisions to build their own nuclear capabilities) or ideological differences that destroyed the fundamental basis of cooperation (China and Yugoslavia in their relations with the Soviet Union). It is not a preoccupation of this work to systematically explore the cold war in its East-West dimensions. A number of important works have surfaced along those lines and could serve as important sources of information on the dimensions and implications of the East-West cold war confrontation (Millar, 1981; Malcomson, 1985; Calleo, 1987; Lynne-Jones, 1991; Medhurst, et al, 1990; Kanet and Kolodziej, 1991). The most important concern here is an evaluation of the impact on Africa as a victim of this confrontation and how governments and leaders were caught in the drama, often as willing participants, to the detriment of the continent's progress and economic development.

THE COLD WAR AND AFRICA

After the attainment of formal political independence by majority of African states in the 1960s, a collaborative effort toward completing the task of continental liberation, unity and economic cooperation was initiated. This culminated in the establishment of the Organization of African Unity (OAU) in May of 1963. Respect for territorial integrity and national sovereignty was enunciated as founding principles for progress and peace on the continent. The question whether the notion of the nation-state should be entertained in the African context, where states have come into being as an accident of history and not on any conceivable notion of national or ethnic identity, was ignored. Yet, those principles and objectives were crippled in the intense wave of cold war rivalry between the Soviet Union and the United States, and the ideological divisions that it brought to the forefront of African politics. It suddenly became fashionable for national leaders to identify themselves with one bloc or the other. In some respects, this was a tactical ploy by leaders to attract international support and financial largesse in their post-independence reconstruction. To a larger extent, however, external actors were looking for more than mere diplomatic arrangements. The manifestation of this was the actual entanglement of foreign missions in the domestic politics of their hosts often leading to *coup d'etats*, assassination attempts on radical leaders, the signing of agreements to provide military bases, joint military exercises and exchange programs. The attempt to establish areas of influence to promote perceived interests in the conflictual climate of great power rivalry generated a dynamic of dependency and foreign control and soon relegated any independent action by national leaders to the background.

To some close observers, 1975 marked a turning point in Africa in that "sub-Saharan Africa was transformed into an arena of East-West confrontation with, as a new dimension, the presence of Cuban troops capable of overturning situations that the USSR formerly could only suffer" (Chaliand, 1982). Before this time, Gerard Chaliand believes, Africa had been of limited and marginal interest for the great powers. It is, however, true that the former colonial powers and other middle powers in the 1960s began a new era of relations with the newly independent countries, consolidating existing structures of economic inequality and extending diplomatic relations to African countries of strategic importance to them (e.g., Nkrumah, 1965; 1970). Such diplomatic overtures sometimes proved disastrous to fledgling governments on the continent with allegations of superpower or great power involvement in plots of destabilization.

The exit of Portugal from Africa in the mid 1970s and the radical post-Haile Selassie regimes in the Horn of Africa (Ethiopia and neighboring Somalia) transformed African politics into one of crises and a cold war zone for the superpowers. With regard to the Soviet Union, the significance of Africa was not necessarily economic (they have abundant and adequate mineral reserves of their own). However, within the cold war setting, it was to serve as easy access for 'military bases, telecommunications stations, listening posts' in such strategic areas as the Southern African hemisphere via the Indian Ocean and the Middle East. The Red Sea and the Mediterranean were thus vital in these calculations just as Angola in the South, Berbera (Somalia) and Eritrea on the horn were of critical importance. Beneath this strategy lay the grand design to extend Soviet influence and communist ideals as a counteraction to Western influence. Securing cooperation from African governments required granting financial and military assistance and supporting the African liberation struggle. Between 1972 and 1976, Soviet military aid to Africa rose from $25 million to $1000 million dollars with Ethiopia alone taking $1000 million in 1979. By the same year, Moscow and its allies had about 12,000 military instructors and 40,000 civilian advisors on the continent (Chaliand, 1982 p. 42). In comparison to the United States, however, the Soviets appeared to be conservative in making economic commitments. While the United States' direct financial aid to Africa between 1970 and 1976 totaled $2000 million (with $300 million going to 29 countries in 1979 alone under bilateral agreements), the Soviets provided only $200 million (Chaliand, 1982 p. 42).

The United States was equally active in the military sphere with arms sales to Africa totaling $26 million by 1979 from a high of $62 million in 1976 (Chaliand, 1982, p. 50). The explanation for this downturn in military expenditure was the ascendancy of President Carter to power and his new foreign policy directed toward pacifism and human rights promotion. There was, however, no sense of accountability by African governments for these seemingly huge financial transfers since the original purpose was to elicit political loyalty rather than to promote economic development and social progress. Corruption, nepotism and abuse of power reverberated across the continent. Equally, the high expenditure on arms by donor countries and African governments benefited dictatorial and inept regimes. Internal fighting generated enemies which were often opposition elements and alienated groups in society demanding accountability and representation in government. Often than not, the military capitalized on these developments with consequences of authoritarianism and political instability. Such countries as Ghana, Nigeria, Democratic Republic of Congo (Zaire), Burkina Faso, Togo, Niger, Mali, Sudan, Uganda among others were soon afflicted with military dictatorships on the grounds of civilian ineptitude and corruption.

Indeed, the post-colonial structures and conditions provided the Western powers with unchallenged opportunities to construct neo-colonial relationships faster and which tended to enhance their national interests in terms of investments and trade. France in particular acted as if Francophone Africa was an extension of metropolitan France. By 1980, France reportedly was exporting 55% of its total industrial goods marked for the Third World to Africa. With regard to financial assistance, it provided annually an estimated $1000 million to African governments (Chaliand, 1982 p. 52). With this financial clout, the French interfered with impunity in the domestic affairs of 'Francophone' Africa often alluding to its military agreements with these countries as legitimate grounds for intervention, if only to prop up regimes that it favored.

Portugal on the other hand, at least until the rise of Antonio de Spinola in 1974, persisted in its belief that Angola, Cape Verde Islands, Guinea-Bissau and Mozambique were integral components of a decaying Portuguese empire. Considered at the time by many as the most backward country in Western Europe in terms of industrialization and economic development, it had to cling to its colonial territories for resource transfers in order to survive. Meanwhile, her colonial war against African liberation fighters with support from its NATO partners had adverse repercussions for its economy. Then came the coup and the inevitable happened. It did not only set the tone for changing its colonial policy in Africa but afforded the superpowers the opportunity to occupy the political vacuum created by her exit from the continent. Angola soon became the flagpole around which the ideological battle and superpower rivalry for the control of Southern Africa revolved. With Apartheid South Africa steadfastly anchored in the pursuit of its nationalist interests in the sub-region, the hypocrisy and double standards of the Western powers provided the support she needed to intimidate and fracture the solidarity of the front-line states.

In particular, the African liberation struggle offered the most fertile opportunity for imperialist adventure on the continent. The attainment of independence by the Portuguese colonies of Angola and Mozambique soon deteriorated into an intense military and ideological confrontation. Elsewhere in the sub-region, Southern Rhodesia (Zimbabwe), Namibia and the Republic of South Africa were still engulfed in wars of liberation. These nationalist leaders were conveniently branded as either communists or terrorists by Western leaders while those willing to accept Western support were labeled as patriots and representatives of democratic forces. Tacit American financial and military support for the questionable, if not treasonable, activities of Jonas Savimbi in Angola is an example and will certainly go down in history as the closest that ideology blinded Western leaders into turning a country into killing fields. Savimbi is neither a patriot nor a democrat. He is simply power-hungry and would like to see himself become president of Angola at whatever cost. The controversial linkage of the exit of Cuban forces from Angola to the resolution of the Namibian independence question was another. In reality, both were by-products of the super-power conflict for space and influence.

At the same time, there were separatist movements and ethnic conflicts in areas such as Southern Sudan, Eritrea, Western Sahara, the Ogaden Region of Somalia and Chad. All these created an atmosphere of instability on the continent through external intervention in the form of arms sales, the erection of military bases and military assistance.

The dynamics of these conflicts generated an attraction for middle-level powers within and without the region to play their cards in accordance with perceived interests. Cuba with Soviet support was very active in Angola, Ethiopia and briefly in Somalia. The Libyans and the French were at cross-purposes in Chad. The French and the Belgians were in Democratic Republic of

Congo (former Zaire). Morocco was hyper-belligerent against the Polisario Front in Western Sahara. South Africa as a regional power clung to Namibia and conducted periodic destabilizing raids into the front-line States of Zambia, Mozambique. Elsewhere; Israel up to 1977 was active in Ethiopia and had established military links with South Africa. Congo (Zaire), with covert assistance from the United States served occasionally as a conduit pipe to Savimbi's UNITA rebels in Angola. On top of all these, Britain, under Margaret Thatcher, was shouting itself hoarse that economic sanctions would hurt South African blacks even more, thus obfuscating UN and Commonwealth resolutions that would have speeded up the international movement against Apartheid. South Africa, in the process gained from Western covert collaboration in their effort to defeat Soviet communism.

It would seem as if the process of decolonization and the attainment of formal political independence by African countries meant control over the continent's destiny, resources and external relations. In the same vein, with a seat in the General Assembly and a periodic opportunity for membership in the Security Council, African countries might have felt they could quickly achieve the leverage to translate opportunities into national progress. Both assumptions were wrong and it became obvious that superpower and great power rivalry within and without the United Nations was played in any arena that provided an outlet for subversion and control. The voting behavior of the United States and some of its allies in the Security Council and the UN General Assembly best describes the hypocrisy of the West at this crucial time of the African liberation struggle and the fight against Apartheid. The OAU appeared impotent in the face of all these developments but not without the decisiveness to assert its support for and offer of financial and material contributions to genuine liberation movements.

Groups such as the PAIGC (Guinea-Bissau), MPLA (Angola), SWAPO (Namibia), ANC and PAC (South Africa), Patriotic Front--the ZANU and ZAPU-- (Southern Rhodesia), the Polisario Front (Western Sahara) and FRELIMO (Mozambique) benefited from these enormously and attained international recognition through the OAU's commitment. The most unfortunate part, however, was the loss to Africa of some of its illustrious sons and statesmen through assassinations often carried out with the complicity of security forces. Of particular mention are leaders who dedicated their lives to the liberation struggle and for African emancipation. Such individuals include Edourdo Modlane and Amilcar Cabral of Guinea-Bissau, Agostinho Neto of Angola, Samora Machel of Mozambique and the young and dynamic South African, Steve Beko. The loss of lives among the African youth, particularly hurriedly-trained guerrilla fighters who were pushed to the battle front, number in the thousands; their sacrifice is, however, worth the recompense of freedom.

Issues of ideology did not stop at the battlefront but in national reconstruction and economic development as well. It became fashionable for African countries, despite their rhetoric on non-alignment and neutrality, to adopt rather incoherent ideological perspectives in their dealings with external powers. Suddenly, countries such as Nkrumah's Ghana, Nasser's Egypt, Nyerere's Tanzania, Modibo Keita's Mali, Sekou Toure's Guinea, Kerekou's Benin and Boumedine's Algeria were 'socialist' and looked to the Eastern bloc of countries and China for economic assistance and trade. The Soviets even briefly established some presence in the Congo Republic, Democratic Republic of Congo (Zaire), Sudan and Somalia, but with little success. The foreign and economic policy pronouncements of these countries took on an anti-Western and anti-imperialist orientation with disastrous consequences for pragmatic policy formulation. Similarly, a group of other African countries revealed an amenable disposition toward the capitalist path of development. Countries such as Kenya, Morocco, Cote d'Ivoire, Senegal, Gabon, Liberia, periodically Nigeria, and later Sudan saw themselves in this light and were treated by the West as such. One of the implications of this phenomenon was that it crippled national unity since it was easy for governments of the day to brand fellow nationals or critics as dissidents and work tirelessly for their liquidation.

The capacity of governments to silence their critics with arrests, death threats and assassinations was tremendous and rampant. With lack of any effective opposition, government officials found it easy to embark on the accumulation of personal wealth, expensive lifestyles and conspicuous consumption. Public corruption and economic waste was on the rise and institutional decay quickly set in. The disaffection with policies and the general state of affairs normally attract a swift response from the military and other disgruntled elements in society, often acting together or in association with external forces.

The problem of political instability in Africa, arising as it does from the frequent intrusion of the military into politics, and always with ample justification, has tended to destroy any credibility for civilian rule. Of course, there are other reasons why party politics have so far proven unworkable in Africa (issues of ethnicity, weak and fragile middle classes, lack of the requisite political culture, of compromise and consensus, and questions of tradition). However; the fact that between 1956 and 1984 no less than 55% of *all coups d'état*, as well as a third of all attempted coups and plots world-wide occurred in the West African sub-region alone is a frightening reality (McGowan and Johnson, 1986).

The cold war ideological confrontation in Africa had other dimensions to it. Geo-strategic and economic considerations have been important factors for intervention in certain parts of the continent. For instance, the material resourcefulness of the continent had always constituted an appeal to multi-national conglomerates and their governmental sponsors. Africa is by far the leading supplier of raw materials globally. It produces 85% of the world's mineral exports (65% of Western Europe's, 15% of Japan's and 5% of North America's). According to estimates, Africa supplies a significant proportion of the world's production in such minerals as diamonds (75%), gold (70%), cobalt (70%), vanadium (50%), platinum (46%), chrome (36%), manganese (30%) and copper (20%) (Chaliand, 1982 p. 33). This is enormous wealth with high concentration within the Southern African sub-region--Angola Namibia, Republic of South Africa, Zambia and Zaire. Large reserves of hydrocarbons, phosphates, iron and uranium are also located in the Maghreb and surrounding countries of Algeria, Libya, Morocco, Mauritania, Niger and Western Sahara. The exploration of oil has equally reached appreciable levels in countries such as Nigeria, Gabon, Angola and Libya. Certainly, these are crucial products for the mainstay of industrial economies, particularly European countries already acquainted with the African geo-political turf and its strategic significance. Even a new entrant such as the United States with 98% of its manganese requirements coming from abroad, had half of this resource imported from Africa in the 1970s. According to Chaliand (1982, pp. 36-38), "the mineral stake is inseparable from the geopolitical stake in Africa." Of special mention is the strategic importance of South Africa in particular. It is the only country that produces enriched uranium and heavy water (nuclear technology) in Africa with about 13,000 tons in 1985 only behind the United States with 40,000 tons. In addition, South Africa produces about 27% of the world's chrome (possessing 70% of the world's reserves) and 25% of manganese, which are of vital military utility to the West. All together, Africa produces about a third of the world's raw materials outside the former communist world. The necessity to capture these markets from Communist control during the cold war was obviously a major attraction.

It would seem befitting to close the discussion with the summary observation of Zaki Laidi (1990 pp. xvii) on how the superpowers finally collaborated to make their formal exit from the continent after years of rivalry:

> On December 22 1988, the United States and the Soviet Union sponsored an Angolan-Cuban-South African accord anticipating the total though gradual withdrawal of Cuban troops from Angola by July 1991, as well as South Africa's departure from Namibia. Thus, ended not only the last chapter of decolonization in Africa but also one of the most acute African crises. In many respects, the Soviet-American benediction in Southern Africa confirms the crucial role the superpowers have taken on in the exacerbation and the denouement of African crises since 1975.

It is clear however that the political situation in Angola and Mozambique is still unstable since these countries are permanently engulfed in civil strife. Infrastructural provisions have been completely destroyed, economic development is at a standstill and a large pool of young men have become amputees, a result of the civil wars. The independence struggle is completely meaningless under such circumstances and the gains of a “peaceful” cold war international system to these societies are catastrophe.

POST-COLD WAR AFRICA: THE BALANCE SHEET

Today, the international community could look back on the cold war years with a sigh of relief, not regret. Humanity may have escaped the possibility of nuclear Armageddon. Nuclear competition and ideological confrontation did not provide the world with peace and stability, it gave the world tension and hatred, death and destruction. It is only the few ideologues and beneficiaries of those frightening years that would think otherwise. From Eastern Europe to the fringes of sub-Saharan Africa new realities have emerged, yet pain and anguish, products of the ideological struggle between two organizing world systems, are still visible. The Soviet Union is no more and in its place new societies have been born with the natural desire to live in freedom and liberty. The same desire permeates the thoughts of all that cherish these values globally. The perennial attempt to project individual rights and freedoms as the preserve of particular ideological persuasions, and on that basis having the prerogative to sell these to the rest of the world is false.

What is evidently clear in analyzing the continent's predicament is the fact that Africa, from colonial times through the cold war has not been left alone to develop naturally. Its people, its resources and its unique character have regularly been defiled and destroyed by external actors. Outsiders have periodically come in preaching peace and love only to contemptuously and deceitfully condemn the people to servitude and indignity. With independence came an opportunity for African countries to embark on economic reconstruction and cultural emancipation. Unfortunately, the tide of history militated against this noble course. The cold war bipolar international structure in place and its dynamics derailed the process of reconstruction and African leaders folded up in the embrace of neo-colonial relations with its attendant costs (Ofori-Amoah, 1995 pp. 15-24).

The celebration of the end of the cold war is for the West a time to proclaim yet another victory. The victory is the global reach of capitalism and the power of the free market. The victory is seen as the possible growth and flowering of liberal democracy in every nook and corner of the world (Art, 1991). Even to some, recent developments marked by the demise of communism constitute the "end of history," (Fukuyama, 1989) but to the rest of humanity it is the distortion of history. It is equally interesting to consider the response of Samuel Huntington to Fukuyama's gyration and nostalgia over the victory of liberal democracy and free market enterprise (Huntington, 1989). In a real sense, Africa's path of growth and development is forever distorted; the current state of affairs is neither victory nor success. This is not the place to analyze the woes and tribulations of capitalism worldwide or its debilitating impact on the continent. Nor is this the place to evaluate the future of democracy on the continent. One Africanist recently concluded that "a region of the capitalist world that is basically unable to reproduce itself economically, and hence is collapsing socially, [cannot] be expected to sustain civil, egalitarian political processes. . . ." (Leys, 1994). Yet, his own observations on the sordid conditions prevalent in typical Western societies which have managed to reproduce themselves economically only to create more 'Harlems' would seem to contradict his convictions about the workings and dynamics of capitalism as a viable social system to be replicated in Africa.

The enticement that it is the only way out for Africa is less an issue than the uncritical acceptance of wholesale platitudes and all foreign prescriptions. It carries with it the conviction that Africa is moving abreast with the rest of the world. Yet, it is the same world leadership that destroyed Africa in the first place. Angola, Mozambique, Ethiopia and of recent, Somalia, Liberia and Rwanda are testimonies to the fact that their problems and shortcomings arise directly or indirectly from the vestiges of neo-colonialism and the cold war struggle.

The solution to Africa's problems does not lie in societal competition laced in ideology and external sponsorship. Africa has to come back home and take a closer look at itself. South Africa, after its first ever multi-party elections, seems to be setting the tone for the rest of the continent. National reconstruction requires reconciliation, compromise and consensus under what is described as 'consociational' democracy or arrangements (Lijphart, 1968a, 1968b). It is a framework that sets conditions to be met and include the ability of leaders to recognize the dangers inherent in a fragmented system, commitment to system maintenance, ability of elites to transcend sub-cultural cleavages and most of all, meeting the demands of all sub-cultures with appropriate solutions (Dahl, 1971, p. 114). This gives all contending forces within the polity equal participation and sharing derived from their input into the menu.

General conclusions drawn in this work are not purported to suggest that all of Africa's woes and problems are externally generated. There are compelling endogenous forces as well. In particular, Africa's human factor, "the spectrum of personality characteristics and dimensions of other human performance that enable political, economic and social institutions to function and remain functional over time," is in decay (Adjibolosoo, 1994 p. 26). Thus, the cold war might have ended but the struggle for survival on the continent would continue unless Africa focuses on the development of appropriate human factor characteristics, without which no economic development can take place. Among these characteristics are accountability, responsibility, integrity, honesty, tolerance, dedication, a disciplined labor force, respect for the rule of law, respect for human dignity and the respect for sanctity of life (Adjibolosoo, 1994; 1995).

Much of this development of the appropriate human factor must begin with leadership. African leaders realize that leadership demands selflessness and accountability, as well as pragmatic and rational policy choices. Democracy is not a myth nor is it alien to Africa's shores. It has its African content; the problem is how to give it a politico-cultural context. The military should learn to be tolerant of civil society from which its power emanates. For at the end of the day, it is not how much firepower that bellows from the barrel of the gun that matters but the extent to which a society sustains itself materially without recourse to external assistance.

African leaders must realize that to govern is not a birthright but an opportunity to demonstrate a commitment to noble values that enhance social progress and national unity--of justice, freedom, equality and respect for life. While we criticize external actors, Africa's own sons ignominiously destroy the continent's soul. One shudders to recall the record of the Bokassas, the Idi Amins and the Nguessos. Yet, recent atrocities in Liberia, Rwanda, Somalia and a dozen other countries arising from ethnic intolerance would seem to suggest that African leaders have learned little. At the end of the day, it is the choices of leaders on the continent that would make the difference. The rest of the world comes in when the opportunity is granted. For once, and for the sake of human progress, let those choices reflect independence, self-reliance and integrity.

African leaders must also see the significance of the end of the Cold War for Africa. First, previous policies by governments and leaders on the continent were largely carried out to please external actors and financiers regardless of the impact on individual countries and societies. Second, the end of the cold war has certainly created a shift from Africa by the big powers to other important areas and interests (Ofori-Amoah, 1995). Thus, most Western leaders are content to resolve their long neglected domestic problems. This policy also translates into investing in areas that would bring economic returns and benefits for their own citizenry. In this regard, geo-strategic calculations of the type seen in strictly ideological terms are a nullity. The politics of economic survival has obviously superseded that of military security and has forced Western countries to invest more in foreign markets that would bring bigger returns. Eastern Europe, Russia, Southeast Asia and parts of Latin America are safer risks than the soft, mini-states of Africa.

However, African leaders should welcome all these as an opportunity to close their ranks and embark on cultural and economic emancipation. They must realize that the end of the Cold War accords an independent action on the part of national elites and leaders to pursue national development goals devoid of ideological strings and persuasions. The disintegration of communist Europe and the Soviet Union nullifies the efficacy of rigid state control of society, bloated bureaucracies and central planning. Leaders should thrive to streamline their administrations and restore integrity into government. The interests of state elites should not be perceived and enforced as those of entire societies. Political pluralism should be advanced and the needs of sub-cultures and groups should be catered for so as to annihilate the current culture of political alienation. Attempts should be made to attract fuller participation of the people in the decision and policy-making processes. This could be achieved through the creation of institutional and political frameworks that can enhance genuine cooperation on the continent, and education of people with the appropriate human factor characteristics that allow such frameworks to function.

Unfortunately, African countries have so far undermined this opening to embark on any serious objectives for socio-economic and political transformation. For once, the issue should not be how much capital Western governments are willing to transfer to African economies through IMF and World Bank collateral. The focus should be on creating sustained and viable economic structures for the integration of African markets. The ECOWAS in West Africa and the SADCC in Southern Africa (of which the Republic of South Africa recently became a member) are rare potentials for regional economic integration in over all terms. The current leadership on the continent should, as a matter of necessity, think of replicating such schemes through out the continent. The gains to be derived from economic cooperation and the understanding to work together to achieve set goals might be the vehicle toward future political integration. I would even go as far as to suggest a federation of African states on sub-regional basis in order to pull existing resources together for meaningful economic and social transformation. The present zest on the part of military and political elites to be crowned as heads of state of non-viable, fragile, hugely indebted and weak African states only exposes Africa's weakness to the outside world and condemns Africans to perpetual ridicule.

If such economic giants as Germany, France, Great Britain, the United States and Canada, with high levels of material and social attainment, find wisdom in economic integration (the European Union in Western Europe and NAFTA in North America), why not fragile African economies which naturally should gain more by pulling the continent's resources together? The creation of authentic mechanisms for intra-African trade, monetary union and pragmatic allocation of sub-regional industries is a must. The dividends will be far greater than perpetually transferring raw materials to external markets for meager returns. Economic integration should dictate the future of African development, and political integration should be a desirable goal.

It is therefore discouraging to see energy and resources being wasted on ethnic conflicts due to the individual quest for political power. The diversion of hard-earned foreign exchange on peace-enforcement, as is currently done in Liberia by the ECOWAS, is a costly political enterprise Africa could ill-afford at this time of need and scarcity. Ethnic intolerance has translated into civil conflict, often exacerbated by the desire for power and prestige by national leaders. Presiding over looted treasury while whole societies live in misery and poverty is not the way forward in the post-cold war international environment. Avarice, corruption, nepotism and autocratic tendencies should give way to integrity in decision-making and policy choice by leaders. Not any kind of leadership though; leadership that is freely and democratically bestowed and stands to be accountable to the people.

African governments have to realize the difficult circumstances of the 'nation-state' in Africa in terms of cultural heterogeneity, ethnic sensitivities, artificial boundaries and the overall structure of economic under-development. The occupants of governmental power should not undermine or under-rate the potency of ethnic identity. Ethnicity as a force in African politics should not be contained as a disease but cultivated as a resource for nation-building by pulling together the strengths of all as bricks, supporting each other in order to obviate weaknesses. The ability of elites to create institutional frameworks, which could unite divergent forces and allowing them to feel as essential elements in the political processes, becomes paramount.

The African military and their civilian accomplices should realize that political legitimacy does not emanate from the use of force against civil society but from loyalty that is readily given because the people view it as being in their best interest to be part of the political process. State-hood, and for that matter nationalism in the African context, has to be created and cultivated before it can be enforced. The current trend on the continent by leaders to put personal and group interests ahead of the larger interest and to use force to attain power against the popular will bears serious and adverse consequences. It negates all the gains that well-thought out policies through reconciliation, compromise and consensus could bring in the aftermath of the cold war.

African leaders should see beyond ideology and metropolitan politics as was the case in the past and focus more on our own strengths. It is an interdependent global system, some would argue, with no place for autarky. But pursuing self-reliant policies and placing Africa's interests first do not signify withdrawal from the international system. After all, interdependence within a strictly liberal democratic tradition accords hierarchy not equality; it advocates freedoms but not justice; it pursues the profit motive but not equal gain or fair play. These are some of the drawbacks, which need to be redressed through authentic African responses. It is time Africa breaks with traditional concepts and practices of international politics, which limit independent action and place the continent at the manipulation and exploitation by external forces.

NOTE

1. See the Secretary-General of the United Nations, Boutros-Boutros Ghali's Report to the Security Council and the General Assembly of 17 June 1992 titled "*Agenda for Peace*." For an assessment of the global security situation and the UN activities, see Pastor, R. 1993. "Forward to the Beginning: Widening the Scope for Global Action." *International Journal*, Autumn, XLVIII.

ACKNOWLEDGEMENTS

I am indebted to Gerard Chaliand whose work has served as a useful source of statistical information for this chapter.

REFERENCES

Adjibolosoo, S. 1995. The Human Factor in Developing Africa. Westport, CT: Praeger Publishers.

Adjibolosoo, S. 1994. "The Human Factor and the Failure of Economic Development and Policies in Africa." In F. Ezeala-Harrison and S. Adjibolosoo, eds. *Perspectives on Economic Development in Africa*. Westport, CT: Praeger Publishers.

Art, R. 1991. "A Defensible Defense: America's Grand Strategy After the Cold War." *International Security*, Spring, 15 (4): 5.

Calleo, D. P. 1987 *Beyond American Hegemony: The Future of the Western Alliance*. New York: Basic Books.

Chaliand, G. 1982. *The Struggle for Africa: Conflict of the Great Powers*. New York: St. Martin's Press.

Dahl, R. A. 1971. *Poliarchy: Participation and Opposition*. New Haven and London: Yale University Press, p.114.

Fukuyama, F. 1989. "The End of History." *The National Interest,* (16) Summer: 3-8.

Gaddis, J. L. 1991. "The Long Peace: Elements of Stability in the Post-Cold War International System." In Sean M. Lynne-Jones ed. *The Cold War and After - Prospects for Peace*. Cambridge and Massachusetts: The MIT Press.

Gaddis J. L. 1987. *The Long Peace: Inquiries into the History of the Cold War*. New York: Oxford University Press.

Huntington, S. 1989. "No Exit: The Errors of Endism." *The National Interest,* (17) Fall: 3-11.

Kanet, R. E. and Kolodziej, E. A. eds. 1991. *The Cold War as Cooperation*. London: MacMillan.

Krauthammer, C. 1991. "The Unipolar Moment." *Foreign Affairs*, 70 (1): 23.

Laidi, Z. 1990. *The Superpowers and Africa: The Constraints of a Rivalry*, 1960-1990. Chicago and London: University of Chicago Press.

Leys, C. 1994. "Confronting the African Tragedy." *New Left Review*, (204) March/April: 40.

Lijphart, A. 1968a. *The Politics of Accommodation*. Berkeley: University of California Press.

Lijphart, A. 1968b. "Typologies of Democratic Systems." *Comparative Political Studies,* 1, April: 3-44.

Lynne-Jones S. M. 1991. *The Cold War and After: Prospects for Peace*. Cambridge and Massachusetts: The MITT Press.

McGowan, P. and Johnson, T. eds. 1986. "Sixty Coups in Thirty Years: Further Evidence Regarding African Military Coups d'etat." *Journal of Modern African Studies*, 24.

Malcolmson, R. W. 1985. *Nuclear Fallacies: How We Have Been Misguided Since Hiroshima*. Kingston and Montreal: McGill-Queen's University

Press.

Mazrui, A. 1977. *Africa's International Relations: The Diplomacy of Dependency and Change*. London: Heinemann, p. 281.

Mearsheimer, J. L. 1990. "Back to the Future: Instability in Europe After the Cold War." *International Security*, Summer, 15, (1)

Medhurst, Martin et al. eds. 1990. *Cold War Rhetoric: Strategy, Metaphor and Ideology*. New York: Greenwood Press.

Millar, T. B. 1981. *The East-West Strategic Balance*. London: Allen and Unwin

Nkrumah, K. 1965. *Neo-Colonialism: The Last Stage of Imperialism*. London: Nelson,.

Nkrumah, K. 1970. *Africa Must Unite*. New York: International Publishers.

Nye, J. S. 1985. "Non-Proliferation Treaty: The Logic of Inequality." *Foreign Policy*, Summer: 123-131.

Ofori-Amoah, B. 1995. "The Saturation Hypothesis and Africa's Development Problems: On the Nature of development Theory and Its Implications for the Human Factor in Africa's Development." In S. Adjibolosoo, ed. *The Significance of the Human Factor in African Economic Development*. Westport, CT.: Praeger (pp. 15-24).

Pastor, R. 1993. "Forward to the Beginning: Widening the Scope for Global Action." *International Journal*, Autumn, XLVIII.

Waltz, K. 1964. "The Stability of a Bipolar World." *Daedelus*, Summer;

PART V

STRUCTURAL ADJUSTMENT AND DEVELOPMENT

12

THE MYTH OF DEVELOPMENT UNDER GHANA'S STRUCTURAL ADJUSTMENT PROGRAM: EVIDENCE FROM THE FORMAL WOOD-PROCESSING SECTOR (1983-1991)

J. Henry Owusu
Department of Geography
University of Connecticut

INTRODUCTION

It is generally agreed among students and practitioners of African development that the essential features of Africa's central problem of persistent underdevelopment are largely defined by the structure of the economies in the region (United Nations/Economic Commission For Africa 1986; Sawyerr, 1990). Indeed, it was to address such structural problems constraining the region's development that, in accord with the demands of the World Bank, the International Monetary Fund (IMF) and other donor agencies, almost every country in sub-Saharan Africa (henceforth Africa) adopted and implemented a form of orthodox Structural Adjustment Programs (SAPs)[1] in the 1980s.

SAPs are a set of economic policies and prescriptions, promoted and sponsored by the IMF and the World Bank, which generally involve the retreat of government activism in favor of a free and competitive market system and the creation of an enabling environment for investments by local and foreign capital. As a development strategy, SAPs are "based on the postulate that economic efficiency and rational management along the lines of market mechanisms should constitute the sole scale upon which all national considerations of production, administration and culture are measured" (Ould-Mey, 1996, p. 16). This approach, according to the sponsors and proponents of the program, constitute the best remedy for Africa's development problems (Steel, 1988, Younger, 1989, World Bank, 1989). For these external sponsors of the program, "adjustment is needed in order to restore the long-run conditions for stable economic growth. . . so that market mechanisms may at last come to equilibrium. . . . [I]t . . . . stresses the logical necessity of equilibrium growth" (Schwarz, 1990, p. 23).

In this chapter, I argue that the use of SAPs, as a *strategy* for fashioning the development of nationally integrated economies in Africa, as envisaged by the Lagos Plan of Action (LPA)[2] is a misconception. As a result the claims of the program's "success" in Ghana and the program's developmental role in Africa by the IMF and the World Bank, is mythical.[3] The rationale for this argument is fourfold. First, the IMF, the World Bank and donor countries and agencies are neither charitable organizations, nor are they neutral in their activities. These institutions exist to serve the basic interests of their constituents. Thus, rather than fashioning structures for self-sustaining, self-reliant national economic development, SAPs have an inherent bias towards reinforcement of existing patterns of external dependence and intra-national regional disparities, and stymies integration intra-nationally (Palloix, 1975, 1977; Dicken, 1986; Sawyerr, 1990, p. 28). Second, as pointed out by Amin (1990) and Barker et al (1986), the theory of comparative advantage, which is based on the principle of *laissez-faire* and which constitutes the basis for SAPs, was primarily designed for free trade between countries with comparable levels of industrialization. It is not a strategy for industrializing underdeveloped countries, particularly in the face of uncontrolled imports from developed countries and truncated international markets. Third, the *laissez-faire* principle itself also provides the necessary conditions for a process of cumulative downward causation to occur at both the international and intra-national levels for African economies (Myrdal, 1957). Fourth, SAPs *assume* that classical instruments of control of money supply, credit squeeze, exchange rate and interest rate adjustments, and trade liberalization which may be valid in well-structured economies, could bring about positive results in African economies (UN/ECA, 1986, p. i). However, the fundamental structural bottlenecks of African economies such as their externally dependent status and poor sectoral linkages internally--reflecting the "weak and disarticulate structures"--make SAPs unsuitable, as a development policy for African economies.

In view of all these, the adoption of SAP in Ghana could be seen as essentially metonymical,[4] a move on the part of the government and the program's sponsors to achieve hidden policy objectives or to promote hidden agenda. In the rest of this chapter, I provide evidence to support these views. I do this in three stages. First, I discuss the general perspectives of the proponents and critics of orthodox structural adjustment. Second, I provide an overview of the Ghanaian political economy to identify the political and economic developments that culminated in the adoption of the SAP by the Ghanaian government. Third, I provide evidence from Ghana's formal wood processing industry to show that economic development impact of SAP is much less than claimed by the program's sponsors. Finally, I offer some concluding thoughts regarding the use of SAP by African countries for economic development.

COMPETING PERSPECTIVES ON ORTHODOX STRUCTURAL ADJUSTMENT PROGRAMS

Two main but competing perspectives are identifiable with respect to the developmental role of SAPs in Africa. The first is the perspective of the proponents, representing mainly the views of the IMF/World Bank internalists. The second perspective is that of the critics, composed of both World Bank in-house and structuralist criticism.

The Perspective of the Proponents

The proponents of SAPs believe that the "invisible hand of the market" is the surest path to removing the developmental bottlenecks in African economies, because market forces make production, exchange and distribution in economies more efficient through competition (see Storper and Walker, 1989, p. 36). They proceed from the basic neo-classical/liberal premise that Africa's development problems were primarily internally generated and sustained (World Bank, 1981; Green, 1987 and 1991; Steel, 1988; Younger, 1989; and Schwarz, 1990). To them therefore, the solution has to begin internally, utilizing the principle of comparative advantage in the exploitation and export of primary products. To overcome the lack of domestic capital, the production and processing of such exports must be operationalized with international capital, since "growth with debt" incurred through such facilities as sector adjustment loans (SECALs), enables the borrowers to increase their capacity and to expand with the aid of net foreign savings.

The prescriptions of the proponents relate to such issues as the use of an incentive system, the development of an infrastructural base, currency devaluation and an exchange rate system, geared at "getting the prices right." Accordingly, the SAP proponents argue that policies involving the improvement of the incentive system, rehabilitation of the basic infrastructure and the creation of a favorable economic environment to expand production and exports, *inter alia*, should:

1. Enhance production linkages by strengthening and increasing the connections between the primary-stage processing firms and the suppliers of non-primary inputs including equipment and spares. This should make transportation and communications much easier; and

2. Promote service and marketing linkages to the primary-stage processing firms, by making it easier for the providers of such services as financial, maintenance and technical inputs, to link up better with them.

The proponents of SAPs hold the view that the low volume and efficiency of investment that characterized African economies, were largely caused by the disruption of the market mechanism of prices by government controls which paralyzed market incentives. In terms of the efficient operations of firms, therefore, adjustment should weed out inefficient firms or those, which integrate in an inefficient way since market forces will force them to fold up or devise new strategies to deal with the competitive, volatile and uncertain environments. In such environments, producers will have to devise new forms of organizational structure either directly out of their own experiences or indirectly through observation of the experiences of other firms (Dicken and Lloyd, 1990, p. 305).

The supporters also argue that financial markets negatively impact on manufacturing industries if their efficient operation is impeded by government regulation of interest rates and controls on entry. Industry, the argument goes, suffers because such regulation inhibits the free flow of capital through the economy (Hamilton, 1989, p. 1523). The free flow of capital is also linked to the issue of overvalued currencies of African economies. According to the proponents, the overvalued pre-adjustment currencies of African economies stimulated production for the domestic market while they discouraged production for the world market. To the proponents, therefore, overvalued currencies adversely affected traditional export sectors of the African economies at least, with respect to foreign capital investment. This is because there tended to be an anticipated devaluation of the overvalued currencies, which kept foreign capital overseas. Consequently, the proponents of SAPs expect that devaluation of the pre-adjustment overvalued currencies of African economies will halt the capital flight, reduce imports, and engender a reallocation of factors of production to the sectors producing tradable goods and services.

The proponents also argue that an unregulated exchange rate policy is necessary for African economies under adjustment because overvalued currencies constrain export growth and indirectly slow down the possibility of obtaining much-needed foreign exchange to meet debt service obligations (Lensink, 1996). In sum, the proponents argue that government interference with the market *via* various types of legislation diminishes African economies' gains from trade since they cannot pursue their comparative advantage. These arguments, however, are all disputed by the critics, who are basically structuralists.

The Perspective of the Critics

The critics focus primarily on the nature of the process whereby economic growth is achieved such as equity issues; and on indigenous rather than external control of national destiny. From their structuralist viewpoint, the critics' position begins with the premise that Africa's developmentally problematic structures result from the incorporation of the region's pre-capitalist economies into the global market system (Slater, 1975; Mabogunje, 1981; Sawyerr, 1990). For example, in the case of Ghana, the problems emerged from the way Britain organized the Gold Coast as a tributary colony to expand her own economy, leaving a legacy of a "warped" economy with "untransformed structures," an economy with a one-sided external orientation and dependence (see Sawyerr, 1990).

Within the above context, SAPs are seen by the critics as a neo-colonial mechanism for opening up African economies and their markets to Western business interests (Hamilton, 1989, p. 1529). For example, the technological requirements for the rehabilitation of the primary-stage processing industry, compels the adjusting African countries to purchase production, transportation and telecommunications equipment, as well as their spare parts, thereby reinforcing their dependence on imported technology and, to some degree, on foreign technicians and other related personnel. The procurement of such equipment and spares is normally tied to bilateral and multilateral loans schemes as the SECALs, a process aided by the reduction or removal of foreign exchange controls, the lifting of restrictions on imports and the free repatriation of profits by foreign investors (Sawyerr, 1990).

SECALs thus worsen the balance of payments situations, and force African firms to produce more at lower prices to defray debts and service charges. The procurement and debt repayment processes are, therefore, seen as mechanisms for supporting the economies of, and firms in the donor countries. Hancock (1989, p.156-70) notes that Britain, for instance, allocates some £850m per annum to its bilateral aid programs. Out of that, some 80% is typically used by the recipient countries to buy British goods and services. He documents that according to the Overseas Development Administration (ODA), multilateral agencies can normally be relied upon to purchase British goods and services with a value equivalent to 120% of Britain's multilateral contributions. For the US, he notes that, through the World Bank, 82 cents of every tax dollar contributed are immediately returned to American businesses in the form of purchase orders.

In Ghana's formal wood-processing industry, for example, such overdependence on expensive imported technology and equipment makes matters worse by the necessity to lay workers off in the industry, in the name of efficiency, despite Ghana's huge reserves of unutilized and underutilized labor. In that respect, Barker et al. (1986, p. 7) suggest that productive resources available to such industries are not fully utilized, as required, in the Ricardian sense of the comparative advantage theory. Furthermore, the few skilled employees in such industries are exploited as noted in Emmanuel 's (1972) theory of unequal exchange, on top of the high costs incurred by the dependence on expensive imported equipment (Sawyerr, 1990. p. 28).

The critics also point out that the flexible exchange rate system emphasized under the program, hurts African industries because:

1. It has the tendency to push the price of foreign exchange beyond the reach of local entrepreneurs who want to import capital goods or equipment, thereby biasing the pattern of imports away from such essential imports; and

2. It floods African markets with relatively cheap imported finished consumer goods and industrial inputs that could otherwise be produced domestically. Such cheap imports also reduce the few existing linkages among domestic industries and prevent the emergence of potential ones. Furthermore, they reduce capacity utilization among domestic industries, and deepen the external dependency of domestic industries. These result from the fact that the cheap imports tend to have a ready market and thus yield high profits more quickly. Importers of such commodities are thus able to generate huge amounts of the local currency and therefore outbid the importers of the essential machinery and industrial equipment in cases where foreign exchange is auctioned. Their competition also tends to bid up the price of foreign exchange (see Sawyerr, 1990, p. 31-33).

With regard to the infrastructure rehabilitation measures under SAPs, the critics note that the restoration or development of basic infrastructure has a heavy bias towards infrastructure related to export production (Sawyerr, 1990). Even though they concede that the restoration of such infrastructure is indispensable to economic recovery at any event, they point out the negative implications. The rebuilding of infrastructure like harbors, railroads and trunk roads, which tends to attract disproportionate amounts of the new public investments under SAPs, invariably reinforces the commitment to, and dependence on, the export of primary products. While the assured supply of such products certainly benefits the industrialized economies, the benefits to African countries--in terms of continued and increased production for export, are less clear in the long run. Even in the short run, the critics argue, the normal low export prices should give cause for worry. Moreover, the critics argue further, the nature of investments in such infrastructure and the procurement methods adopted in connection therewith usually involve the importation of machinery and other finished goods, contractors and consultants from the Western industrialized countries.

In other words, those measures favor the Western industrialized countries over African economies. In fact, in the case of African economies, even in the export of primary-stage processed natural resources, the unfavorable production and market conditions are almost the same as for unprocessed commodity exports. Roemer (1981, p. 432), for example, argued that refining industrial raw material for export (as in the production of lumber and furniture parts based on the buyers' specifications) may even increase the risk of adverse external shocks. This is because the exports then become "specific products" produced by "specific techniques" and thus become subject to greater risks of substitution by new products or obsolescence in the face of new technologies.

As part of the goal of national and regional integration under the Lagos Plan of Action, geographic and sectoral linkages are expected. However, on issues relating to such linkages, the focus has traditionally been abstracted from its broader context, namely, the asymmetrical power relationships that exist between firms located in the peripheral regions such as Africa and those in the core regions. This separatism is just as geographic space is usually separated out, and excluded in neo-classical economics. Linkages, therefore, have tended to be perceived purely in terms of geographic proximity *viz.*, intra-nationally rather than at the international level (see Dicken and Lloyd 1990, p. 332-333).

The critics of SAPs argue that the negative effects of the asymmetrical power relationships pertaining to export processing thus cannot be ignored under structural adjustment. This is because, export-oriented producers of lumber and furniture-parts, for example, under the program constitute "process and components subcontractors" relative to the "principal firms" overseas. In other words, they engage in "specialty" and "cost-saving" subcontracting.[5] Under such production arrangements, Sayer (1986, pp. 47-48) notes that both functionally and geographically, "the relationship between firms and their suppliers tends to be distant, how suppliers operate is of no concern to the purchaser, provided the price is right, and this lack of inter-firm contact together with the infrequent nature of deliveries, allows suppliers to locate considerable distances away from the purchaser, if by doing so they can minimize labor costs and other expenses." Such African subcontracting firms, therefore, stand at a disadvantage in cases where the principal firms engage in dual or multiple sourcing and play them against one another with respect to prices. Also, because export processing demands efficient production, it does not have the protective feature of import substitution that may help develop neophyte entrepreneurs and managers (Roemer, 1981, p. 431).

Mytelka aptly sums up the critics' position regarding SAPs as a development strategy in Africa. She notes that "[S]tructural adjustment programs that lead to more debt are thus not a solution. They are part of the problem. It is time therefore to move beyond mere palliatives, such as increased bank lending or direct foreign investment flows, to a more fundamental rethinking of the mass production model" (Mytelka, 1989, p. 107).

To the critics therefore, SAPs simply do not address some basic structural issues in African development. They point out that the state is indispensable in addressing those basic structural problems and that the strategies for addressing the structural problems should take cognizance of the unique history and the specific context of the adopting economy (UN/ECA, 1986; Mytelka, 1989).

THE POLITICAL ECONOMY OF GHANA'S STRUCTURAL ADJUSTMENT PROGRAM

Given that the Ghanaian economy is heavily dependent on exports to the developed world, changes in the former cannot be isolated from the broader global economy. My discussion is, therefore, predicated on the view that the Ghanaian political economy, and for that matter, its structural and spatial characteristics--in terms of production and exchange--resulted primarily from its incorporation into the global capitalist system (Frank, 1969; Wallerstein, 1974; Slater, 1975). This process of incorporation entailed the formal political and economic organization of a pre-capitalist African economy into a primary export one. Exports are oriented to the demands of the dynamic 'center' of the global capitalist economy namely, Western Europe and the US (and now also, Japan), based on market principles and a relatively high level of technology.

The incorporation process, described by Frank (1969) as "the development of underdevelopment," had two dimensions: external integration into the global economy and an internal disintegration (Slater, 1975) as reflected in some of the patterns in the export-processing industry such as dependence on external capital, technology and markets, on the one hand, and the lack of production linkages such as downstream processing (secondary- and tertiary-stage production), on the other.

As a result of the incorporation process, post-colonial governments have had two options with respect to relations with the 'center' (Ninsin, 1990). These are:

1. To sustain the capitalist economy of the periphery together with its superstructural political apparatus dominated by the national bourgeoisie--an option that demands a mandatory accommodation with international capital; and

2. To delink[6] or rupture the economic and other links with international capital. The purpose of this is to create a new structural basis and impetus for autonomous national development. This approach involves a radical restructuring of the old socio-political relations. However, given the resilience of the capitalist law of value, there is a real prospect of collapse with this option, if the delinking movement lacks a firm socialist content, *vis-à-vis* a mere popular one (see Tandon (1985).

These options have confronted post-colonial governments of Ghana in the face of a declining economy and have major implications for industry. The two options were thus instrumental in shaping policies and actions designed to arrest the country's development problems prior to 1983. They also informed and influenced the PNDC government's policy measures under Ghana's SAP, the Economic Recovery Program (ERP) and it is within that context that the program is seen to be a metonym.

The ERP as a Metonym

Ninsin (1990) has shown that the rise of J. J. Rawlings to power, as the leader of both the Armed Forces Revolutionary Council on June 4, 1979 and of the PNDC on December 31, 1981 is explicable only within the context of Ghana's political and economic unrest. According to Ninsin, Rawlings and the PNDC government, unlike previous administrations, "correctly comprehended the dual character of the crisis: political and economic" acknowledging that "the first arose from the second." Rawlings realized from the experiences of the previous regimes that the justification and legitimization of the PNDC regime politically rested primarily on the restoration of the country's economic health. This realization came after he ran into problems by tackling the political aspect of the crisis first (Ninsin, 1990).

To reverse the order and give priority to the economic aspect, the colonial "old wine" of producing raw materials and semi-processed items (such as lumber) for export was, under the circumstances, indispensable. However, it had to be put in a "new wineskin," (i.e., the adoption of a structural adjustment program under the auspices of international capital through the IMF and the World Bank).

The previous administration of the People's National Party (PNP) under Dr. Hilla Limman, which was constitutionally elected in August 1979, did nothing to address the then explosive economic and political situation. Essentially it pursued the same policies as Acheampong's National Redemption Council by refusing either to devalue the currency, reduce borrowing sharply or, until shortly before its overthrow, to raise significantly the producer price for cocoa, thus deepening the social and economic crisis (Huq, 1989, pp. 16-17). Under those circumstances,

> [W]orkers and progressive organizations responded to the damaging social effect of the economic crisis with sustained and widespread political agitation and open denunciation of the government. It was clear that parliamentary (liberal) democracy had failed to open the domains of power to the popular masses as a way of giving public policy a popular content. Its only justification, it seems, is that it was appropriate for promoting bourgeois rule and alienating the masses from the instruments of rule as well as from the material means of labor and of life (Ninsin, 1989, p.135).

It was under those circumstances that Rawlings ousted the PNP regime and proceeded immediately to resolve the political crisis by first disorganizing the bourgeois institutions of rule and then reconstituting them to incorporate the masses. In this wise, Defense Committees were formed in work places (Workers' Defense Committees) and residential areas (People's Defense Committees) under the national umbrella of an ultra-leftist National Defense Committee.

In order to preserve its political power, at a time when it was most vulnerable to any form of manipulation by international capital, the PNDC had to proclaim the primacy of economics over politics. It then adopted the metonymical policy of economic recovery for the production of wealth, under the auspices of none other than the IMF and the World Bank. Ostensibly, the wealth subsequently produced could eventually be enjoyed by all Ghanaians, including the workers. In his radio and television broadcast to Ghanaians on May 2, 1983, regarding the newly adopted ERP, Rawlings asserted that it was "the only viable option open to us." The only way to stop the downturn in the economy was to "stimulate production--particularly in the foreign exchange earning sector of the economy--by providing it with adequate financial incentives in the form of bonuses for foreign exchange earnings from legal exports." The "basic objective," according to Rawlings, was "to establish the right environment to do business and to make investments; both foreigners and our own citizens can then take advantage of the environment" (Ghana Investment Centre, 1990, p. 7). In other words, it became cogent, expedient and imperative to create an enabling economic environment and political stability for production. Such conditions, with Western support, are necessary for the operations of international capital. The ERP, as Ghana's SAP was thus initiated in April 1983 under those political and economic circumstances.

THE CASE OF GHANA'S FORMAL WOOD-PROCESSING INDUSTRY

For the World Bank, the forestry sector offered the greatest immediate potential for growth and foreign exchange earnings (World Bank, 1984). The sector had readily available and vast natural resource base, capable of spinning off linkages within the domestic economy and generating foreign exchange to meet the nation's external commitments. At the same time it was capable of satisfying the nation's role in the international division of labor as a producer of raw and semi-processed raw materials for the industrialized West. Thus, the sector was given immediate priority by the government under the ERP.

ERP Policies and Actions Affecting the Industry

Government policy under the ERP, with respect to the wood-processing industry was to ensure improvement in the industry's deteriorating facilities and proper husbandry and efficient utilization of the country's forest resources (Forestry Commission, 1988, p. iv). The government aimed at "achieving a quick increase in production of the private companies through providing them with spare parts, equipment and materials," supporting the rehabilitation of selected mills, while at the same time re-organizing those that were state-owned

(Govt. of Ghana, 1984, p. 11). The government also moved to alleviate some immediate physical constraints in the form of production equipment shortages, transport equipment and spare parts, with the assistance of SECALs from the International Development Association to fund the export rehabilitation project. There were other SECALs from such international organizations as the Overseas Development Administration (ODA), through which the British government provided the PNDC government with some £8.7 million in 1984 and 1985, as a grant tied to the purchase of timber sector equipment from UK manufacturers. Some of the SECALs were offered with a food aid program for the employees of the beneficiary companies to make them more attractive, thus exploiting the food crisis at the time.

Effects of the ERP on the Industry's Output and Exports

As shown in Figure 12.1, in general, production and exports in the industry were tremendously boosted. The production of logs increased steadily but dramatically, registering a change of 290% over the short period of 1983 through 1990. As a proportion of total production, log exports increased from 13.8% in 1983 to 15.3% in 1990.

Primary-stage processing, or the production of lumber, continued to dominate in the industry. Its volume of production also increased steadily but dramatically, registering an increase of 218% over the period. In terms of exports, despite a policy of curtailing log exports in favor of processed-wood, there was a 354% increase in volume. The volume of lumber exports increased steadily, by 325%. Relative to total output, the volume of lumber exports increased steadily from 25.9% in 1983 to 37% in 1990. These were in contrast with the annual minimum of 51% that characterized the 1960's. Processing further downstream (e.g., into furniture and fixtures, plywood and veneer), however, continued to be small in terms of size and growth, with the volume of exports increasing by only 148%.

Primary-stage processing was given priority for several reasons. First, the SECAL program was primarily aimed at rehabilitation of industry to meet development expectations under the Lagos Plan of Action. Second, the policy of phasing-out of log exports naturally meant domestic processing of wood. Third, lumber production was the next least expensive activity investment-wise, and had a ready market.

FIGURE 12.1
VOLUME OF WOOD AND WOOD PRODUCTS EXPORTED IN CUBIC METERS (1982-1991)

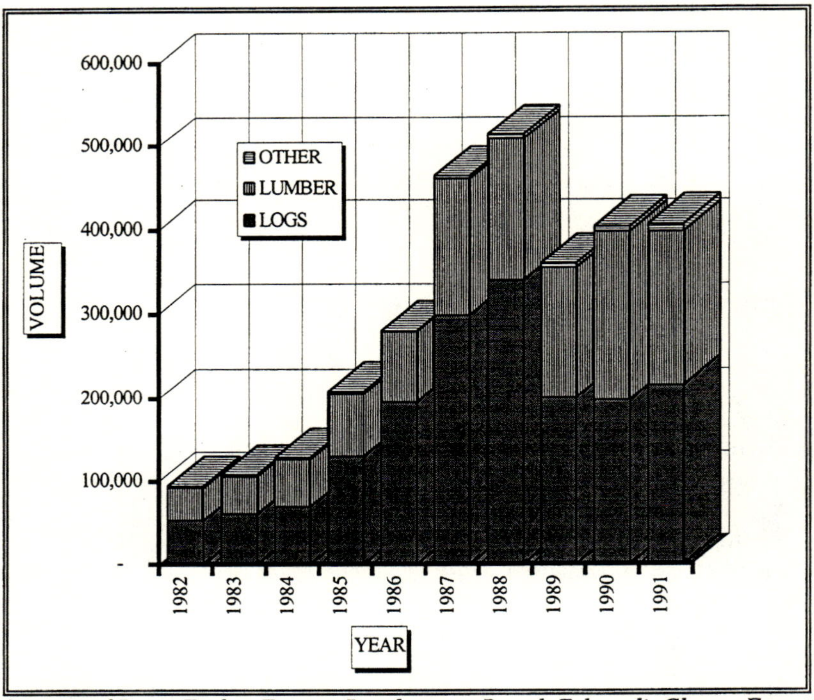

Sources of Data: Timber Exports Development Board, Takoradi, Ghana; Forest Products Inspection Bureau, Takoradi, Ghana; Ministry of Lands and Mineral Resources, Accra, Ghana.

In addition to these incentives under the ERP investment code, such as the flexible exchange rate system, provisions for profit retention abroad, and tax exemptions based on the volume of output exported, served to encourage lumber producers, all the more, to export their output.

Furthermore, most of the sawmillers were beneficiaries of the sector adjustment loans, and in the face of a series of devaluations and rising interest rates, they were under tremendous pressure to increase their lumber exports in order to generate enough money to meet their debt obligations (see Owusu, 1994).

In generating foreign exchange through the industry for the country, the ERP was a big success for the government and the sponsors, largely as a result of the pressure on the SECAL-beneficiary firms to service their debts. The increased volume of processed-wood exported (e.g., lumber and furniture parts), particularly lumber as opposed to logs, dramatically increased the government's income in terms of the foreign exchange generated (see Figure 12.2).

FIGURE 12.2
INCOME FROM WOOD AND WOOD-PRODCUTS EXPORTED IN US DOLLARS (1982-1990)

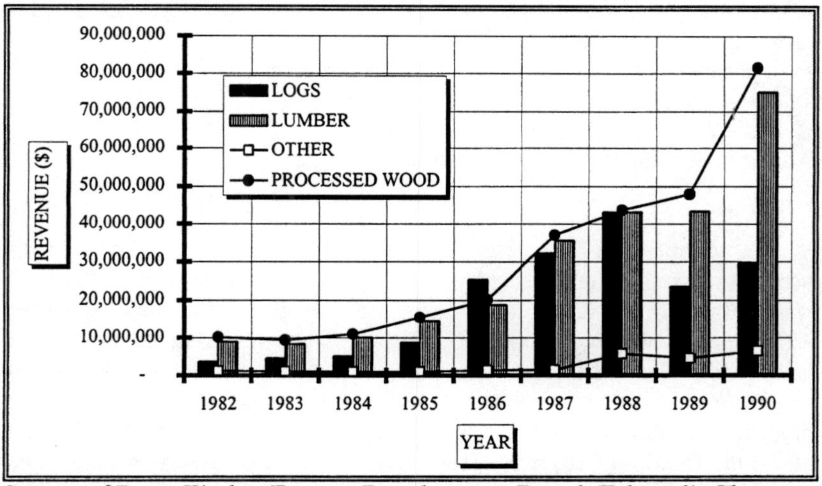

Source of Data: Timber Exports Development Board, Takoradi, Ghana.

The foreign exchange generated by the industry at the end of 1988 was enough to absorb the nation's annual debt interest payment. In 1991, there was enough income from the sector to meet the annual debt interest payment, and to contribute US $58.363m of that year's principal amount of US $122.714m. To achieve this, however, the government squeezed the firms, with the concurrence of the donor countries, by lending the SECALs to them as commercial loans, at interest rates of 31-35% and with a 4-year repayment period beginning within 12 months of receiving the loan despite the frequent devaluations. Meanwhile the government had taken the SECALs from the donor countries at rates between 8% and 10% with a 10-year moratorium. The dramatic generation of foreign exchange was also assisted by rehabilitation of the basic economic/physical infrastructure, such as roads, telecommunications and harbors. These sped up the processes of production, transportation and export of the processed-wood.

Whilst the SECAL-beneficiary firms had to struggle to generate foreign exchange to keep up payments on their loans, they in the process, generated funds for the government to defray debts owed to the donor countries. By June 1990, after eight years of the ERP, Ghana had been able to pay up all its remaining recorded arrears in foreign debt, thus restoring normal economic relations with the creditors. In terms of foreign exchange generation, therefore, the forestry sector became a net contributor to the payment of foreign debts, a departure from the pre-ERP pattern.

In spite of this, the foreign exchange spent on acquisition of imported inputs continued to be high. Besides, within the context of nationally integrated development, adjustment-related changes in the wood-processing sector in terms of linkages; accommodation of international capital; and self-reliance, were far from positive. Let us take a closer look at these in turn.

Adjustment-related Changes and Industrial Linkages

As regards intra-sectoral linkages, the traditional and principal linkage between sawmills (primary-stage processing) and wood processors downstream was broken. In the main, the sawmills preferred to sell their lumber on the export market in order to boost their export retention quotas, minimize their taxes (which were based on the volume of exports), and ensure that significant amounts of savings were kept off-shore "for contingencies." Downstream, the producers of furniture and fixtures (secondary-stage processing) could not afford the world market prices. They faced cash-flow problems resulting from the financial structure reforms, particularly, the frequent and massive devaluations, and high interest rates. The commercial banks were also, unwilling to grant these downstream wood processors long-term loans because of financial sector restructuring under the ERP. The crucial linkage between sawmills and processors downstream was, therefore, substituted with an intense external forward linkage, whereby the sawmills served as 'subcontractors' producing for 'principal firms' abroad. Secondary-stage formal wood-processing also, became involved in an external forward linkage since the main export items were furniture-parts, which were assembled outside Ghana. This made the secondary-stage formal wood-processing firms too, 'subcontractors' producing for 'principal firms' abroad. The economic benefits of intra-sectoral linkages were therefore shifted from Ghana to donor countries abroad, primarily the countries of the European Economic Community (now European Union) which received a minimum of 81% of the exports per annum.

The external shift of inter-sectoral linkages was further exacerbated by the effects of the frequent and massive devaluations associated with the adjustment program. For example, many of non-wood items used to produce furniture and fixtures such as nails, glue and varnish were obtained on the import market since local products could not compete with the cheap imports. These foreclosed potential linkages, reinforcing pre-ERP patterns such as lack of inter-firm linkages and dependence on imported inputs.

Inter-sectorally, linkages occurred to a limited degree. A more developed linkage was established with the engineering sector, in which truck-trailers were manufactured to haul logs and lumber from the bush to the mills and to the ports. There were also, improved linkages with the transport and telecommunications sector *via* increased use of the road and railway systems to the ports, and telecommunication systems for internal and external business transactions, which were all indispensable for the export promotion program, emphasized under the ERP.

Linkage with the informal sector also intensified. It involved the sale of sub-standard quality wood ("rejects") by the sawmills to the informal sector, which was then reprocessed and resold to firms producing furniture in the formal sector for the domestic market. The formal sector furniture production firms were willing to purchase lumber from the informal sector because they could not afford the world market prices charged by the sawmillers who wanted to enjoy such benefits as tax rebates based on volume exported and overseas profit retention as provided under the investment code.

The geographical and structural pattern of the location of wood-processing firms in urban/metropolitan areas persisted, thereby precluding further spatial integration. New centers of production, which could serve as propulsive growth poles, did not emerge to generate further linkages through a process of cumulative upward causation as posited by Myrdal (1957) and Boudeville (1966). Other areas were, therefore, denied potential linkages that might have emerged through neighborhood and demonstration effects from the location of firms outside the urban/metropolitan areas. As a result, there continued to be movement of population from rural areas to the urban/metropolitan centers putting further strains on the inadequate socio-economic infrastructure and services.

Adjustment-related Changes and Accommodation of International Capital

The exploitative role of international capital was reinforced during the period, for raw materials and labor continued to be exploited in a more intensive manner in Ghana. In the case of raw materials, the steady and dramatic increase in the volume of processed and unprocessed wood exported confirms the reinforcement. Indebtedness particularly from the sector adjustment loans and the frequent devaluations, that made exports cheaper, compelled firms to produce and export more processed wood in order to survive. As was the case prior to the ERP, the bulk of the increased exports went to the donor countries, particularly the then EEC countries which received a minimum of 81% per annum, and as much as 95% in 1986. It should be borne in mind that the lumber and furniture parts, which constituted the bulk of the exports, are essentially raw materials for firms in the metropolitan or donor countries. Moreover, despite the policy of phasing out the export of unprocessed wood, the volume of logs exported increased. These raw materials became so cheap as a result of the frequent and massive devaluations that they were often resold on the world market (Barker et al., 1991, p. 5). Suppliers from other African countries and other tropical Third World countries also helped to inundate the world market with cheap supplies, thereby depressing the prices further. Some buyers, therefore, stocked up the cheap wood as an operational strategy, which further depressed prices by diminishing the demand relative to the supply. Stocking up supplies, this way, as part of the principal firms' "just-in-case" strategy, thus rendered the Ghanaian producers very vulnerable to external shock. As subcontractors, therefore, the Ghanaian producers constituted potential "shock-absorbers" for the European principal firms.

It was also, to facilitate the exploitation of Ghana's timber, as a raw material, by the donor countries that the Ghana Timber Marketing Board was replaced by the twin bodies--the Timber Exports Development Board and Forest Products Inspection Bureau--whose setup and organizational structures were recommended by Silviconsult, a consulting firm appointed by the World Bank (this meant that Silviconsult's recommendations would be consistent with the economic interests of the World Bank). The operations of these two principal organizational bodies of the industry streamlined timber export processes to make them easier and more efficient. Their operations were enhanced by the activities of other related bodies, such as the Ghana Investments Center, which promoted the very liberal investment code; and the Ghana Export Promotion Council, which *inter alia*, promoted labor training for wood-processing.

The rehabilitation aspect of the program was also very heavily biased towards the restoration of basic infrastructure related to the export of raw materials. While it is true that the restoration of such infrastructure is indispensable to economic recovery in any event, the ports, the railroad system, the trunk roads from the forests to the ports, and telecommunication system attracted disproportionate amounts of new public investment. At the Donors' Conference[7] in November 1983, for instance, it was decided that two-thirds of the government's foreign exchange expenditure over 1984-85 was to be spent on rehabilitating the railroad network, roads and the Tema and Takoradi ports, while as much as $13 million was allocated for the rehabilitation and development of posts and telecommunications (Government of Ghana, 1984, p. 13).

Such rebuilding of infrastructure tends to reinforce the commitment to, and dependence on, the export of primary products as Sawyerr (1990, p.30) pointed out. For one thing, the nature of investments in such infrastructure and the procurement methods adopted involved importing of machinery and other finished goods as well as contractors and consultants from the donor industrialized countries. For another, while the assured supply of raw materials certainly has benefited the donor countries, the benefits to Ghana of continued and increased production of primary commodities for export are unclear in the long run. Even in the short run, the low export prices give cause for concern.

The wood-processing sector also served as a market and dumping ground for products from the donor countries. The SECALs were provided as a convenient way of sustaining and, indeed, reinforcing the market. For Britain, in particular, the sector adjustment loans advanced to rehabilitate the forestry sector was a very convenient strategy of using the Overseas Development Administration and credit from the Export Credit Guarantee department to bail out the then ailing British Leyland Corporation. This strategy was especially successful with the system of tied-purchases and credit line system as described by Hancock (1989). In addition to selling products like trucks and wood-processing equipment, some of which were inappropriate for conditions in Ghana, spare parts for their maintenance subsequently had to be obtained from the same sources. In certain cases, technicians from the seller-companies had to be brought in--at the expense of the buyers--to either install or repair the machinery or equipment, some of which broke down quite frequently. The tied-purchase and credit line systems have effectively propagated an international "junk-yard," whereby inappropriate and substandard machinery and equipment or technologies are dumped in developing countries for profit. The same system also reinforced the dependency of the wood-processing industry on foreign technology and inputs.

The uninterrupted movements of capital into and profits and rent obtained from the industry out of the country were facilitated by the removal of exchange controls, the operation of private foreign exchange bureaux (forex bureaux) and the export profits retention scheme. Also, the Ghana Investment Promotion Center Act guaranteed the unconditional transferability of capital, profits and dividends. Thus, there were no restrictions on the conversion and transfer of foreign currency. Other enabling mechanisms included provisions under the investment code, which gave very liberal tax exemptions to foreign investors.

Security for international capital for moving profits out of the country was ensured with Ghana becoming a signatory to the Multilateral Investment Guarantee Agency (MIGA). This agency insures international capital against delays in currency transfers, if such delays are attributable to the host government; expropriation and similar measures; breach of contract; or war and civil disturbances. Also, Ghana signed the Bilateral Investment Promotion and Protection Agreements with a number of countries to give further protection to investors from those countries (UNIDO, 1991, p. 52).

The wood sector and the wood-processing industry thus continued to be aligned to the interests of metropolitan/donor countries in such a way that the asymmetrical colonial relations were sustained and reproduced. The "open" nature of the economy/sector, therefore, stymied nationally integrated development.

Adjustment Related Changes and Self-Reliance

On the whole, there was an increase in job-creation/employment both for the skilled and unskilled. The Ghana Investment Center, in its investment promotion activities, was able to create 7,213 jobs over the three-year period (1988-90) alone relative to a few jobs the sector lost between 1983 and 1986. There was also a systematic effort, albeit on a small scale, to mobilize humanpower towards the development of the industry, for example through the training activities of the Timber Export Development Board and the Ghana Export Promotion Council, and there was, less dependence on expatriate personnel than there was prior to the adoption of the ERP. The industry thus became relatively more self-reliant with respect to personnel.

Nevertheless, there was by no means any independent technological progress, given the continued and intensified dependence on foreign technology, machinery and equipment. This situation was exacerbated by the import of technology, machinery and equipment procured with adjustment loans. Other contributory factors were the cancellation of the import licensing system and tax exemptions on imported machinery and equipment. All these killed the motivation for local engineers and technicians to develop indigenous technology, quite apart from the local perception of inferiority associated with made-in-Ghana technology, machinery and equipment, a mentality that became ingrained in colonial times. Although some improvisations and adaptations were made in the informal sector, in places like the Kumasi "Suame Magazine"--an agglomeration of informal fitters and artisans patronized by the formal sector--they do not constitute real technological progress because they were not novelties. On top of these, old and used machinery and equipment continued to be imported as before the ERP, thus providing opportunities for some overseas firms to dispose of their old machinery and equipment based on obsolete technology at a profit. All these undermined the quest for self-reliance.

With respect to imported inputs and foreign exchange conservation, the dependence on foreign inputs--technology, machinery and equipment, and non-wood material inputs--certainly did not foster economizing on foreign exchange. With the trade liberalization policy and easy access to foreign exchange through the forex bureaux, it became easy for merchants engaged in importing non-wood inputs to flood the domestic market with such items as nails, varnishes and glues--items which could be produced locally. Since such inputs have a ready market, they move quickly on the market, yielding high profits for the merchants as noted by Sawyerr (1990, p. 33). This was more so prior to 1992 when foreign exchange was auctioned. The merchants were, therefore, able to mobilize large amounts of the local currency, the *cedi,* to outbid the local manufacturers who wanted to import capital goods and equipment. Apart from bidding up the price of foreign exchange, competition from the merchants tended to push the price of foreign exchange beyond the reach of importers of capital goods and other items essential to the industrial recovery of the economy and the social well-being of the people. In other words, the liberalization measure under the ERP biased the pattern of imports away from essential items. It flooded the market with finished consumer goods. It squeezed out local manufacturers, contributed to the collapse of local industry; and deepened the economy's dependence on imports (see Sawyerr, 1990, p. 33).

As for the application of the wood resources to meet the needs of Ghanaians, as expected under a policy of self-reliance, the sector indeed, generated foreign exchange for the country. The wood sector contributed immensely to the payment of national foreign debts and other foreign transactions necessary for the survival of the country. However, it was the high quality wood that was exported. Domestic needs were largely satisfied by second- or lower-grade wood because local consumers could not afford the high quality wood at international market prices.

Significantly, international capital has been ambivalent about the environmental costs associated with the increased export of such tropical wood overseas (see Hayter, 1989, p. 117). Yet the apparent benefits from such exports to the Ghanaian economy and the donor countries may be overshadowed by heavy environmental costs, with global implications in the long run (George, 1992).

In fact, George (1992) argues that there is a direct relation between the high foreign debts of developing nations like Ghana, and the process of deforestation in the tropical world, linking the environmental damage to the export-oriented adjustment program pushed by the World Bank and the IMF. For example, in 1982, just before adjustment, Ghana's outstanding external public disbursed and undisbursed debts were $1,114.020m and $1,503.523m respectively, with a service interest of $27.778m. By 1991, they had soared to $2,756.985m and $3,270.553m, with a new service interest of $70.637m (World Bank, 1985; 1991). To meet such debt obligations, Ghana had no option but to increase her wood exports along with other primary exports (see Owusu, 1995). It is therefore, not surprising that the World Bank suggested to the PNDC government, at the beginning of the adjustment program that "the forestry sector offered the greatest immediate potential for growth and foreign exchange earnings" (World Bank, 1984, p. xxi). Although rapid growth may be achieved and foreign exchange earnings increased dramatically, the long run environmental costs from destroying Ghana's rain forest could defeat the very purpose of self-reliance.

CONCLUSION

In this chapter, I have shown that nationally integrated development under the World Bank/IMF-sponsored SAPs is a myth. I argued that Ghana's SAP was essentially metonymical: it was adopted by the then PNDC government to achieve two objectives simultaneously--perpetuating itself in power and accommodating international capital. Indeed, the adjustment program has not only ensured the survival of the PNDC government, but also has been tremendously beneficial to international capital. However, relative to the development of a nationally integrated economy in Ghana, as envisaged under the Lagos Plan of Action, evidence from the formal wood-processing sector validates the main argument of the critics that SAPs are mechanisms for the production and reproduction of conditions of foreign dependence. From its inception, the ERP had an inherent bias towards the reinforcement of the colonial patterns rather than fashioning a nationally integrated development.

In fact, as a development policy for African economies, SAPs, like the classical "Trojan horse," are a trap; they snare adjusting economies, through such mechanisms as SECALs, into accumulating substantial external debts--a trap that constitutes a powerful basis for international capital to engage in non-political, non-military manipulation of political and economic decision-making in adjusting countries (Sawyerr, 1990, p. 28). For African countries, therefore, SAPs are essentially a form of neo-colonialism.

As the evidence shows, the notion that orthodox SAPs offer the best remedy for Africa's development problems is based primarily on the self-interest of the Western industrialized economies. That the program has been a "success" in Ghana as claimed by its sponsors is therefore a myth.

NOTES

1. In my discussion, the acronym, SAP, refers to orthodox structural adjustment programs in contrast with the Economic Commission for Africa's Alternative Framework to Structural Adjustment Programs for Socio-Economic Recovery (AAF-SAP).
2. *The Lagos Plan of Action for the Economic Development of Africa - 1980-2000* (OAU, 1982), as ratified in the Final Act of Lagos (Annex I), is an agreement by the Heads of State and Government of the OAU reached at a meeting in Lagos, Nigeria in 1980 devoted to the economic problems of Africa. It is a detailed analysis and prescriptions in respect of natural resources, agriculture, industry and technology, among other things. It also provides guidelines regarding measures for the basic restructuring of the economic base of the continent to achieve self-sustaining development by the end of the century. The LPA thus serves as a standard development frame of reference for Africa because "development", as a concept, is otherwise subject to very elastic interpretations.
3. According to an IDA Report (The Evolving Role of IDA, p. 9), "the experience of Ghana demonstrates how economic performance can be turned around with a combination of good policies and donor support". *The Financial Times* of London's issue of July 20, 1989, also in a special supplement on Ghana, described Ghana as a 'Star Pupil' of the structural adjustment process.

The Ghanaian experience is thus an appropriate model for the evaluation of the program in Sub-Saharan Africa.

4. Gore (1984, p. 258) describes development policies as metonymical when they are used by a government, policy makers, or a group of political actors, in tandem with their development objectives to achieve hidden policy objectives or to promote a hidden agenda.

5. The relationship between the principal firm overseas and the subcontractors may be short- or long-term, or in certain cases single batch. The principal firm may also provide detailed designs or specifications, or in other cases provide technical, financial or general assistance or advice.

6. According to Samir Amin, one of the main proponents of delinking, the measure does not mean autarchy. Rather, it is "the refusal to submit to the demands of the worldwide law of value, or the supposed 'rationality' of the system of world prices that embody the demands of reproduction of worldwide capital. It presupposes the society's capacity to define for itself an alternative range of criteria of rationality of internal economic options, in short a 'law of value of national application'" (Amin, 1990, p. 71).

7. The important donors for Ghana are: Canada, France, Germany, Italy, Japan, Switzerland, United Kingdom, USA, Arab Bank for Economic Development in Africa, African Development Bank, EU, European Investment Bank, IFAD, UNDP, WFP, and World Bank.

REFERENCES

Amin, S. 1990. *Maldevelopment: Anatomy of a Global Failure.* London/Tokyo: United Nations/Zed.

Barker, C. E., Bhagavan, M.R., Mitschke-Collande, P. V. and Wield, D.V. 1986. *African Industrialization: Technology and Change in Tanzania.* Brookfield, VT: Gower.

Barker, K., Boateng, P. and Moreno, A. 1991. *Timber and Wood Products Section of Export Diversification in Ghana.* Report prepared for the US Agency for International Development, Bethesda, Maryland Development Associates Inc.

Boudeville, J. -R. 1966. *Problems of Regional Economic Planning.* Edinburgh: Edinburgh University Press.

Dicken, P. 1986. *Global Shift: Industrial Change in a Turbulent World.* London: Paul Chapman.

Dicken, P. and Lloyd, P. 1990. *Location in Space: Theoretical Perspectives in Economic Geography.* New York: Harper Collins.

Emmanuel, A., 1972. *Uneven Exchange: A Study of the Imperialism of Trade.* New York: Monthly Review Press.

Forestry Commission. 1988. *A Review Report on the Economic Recovery Programme: The Forestry Sector, 1982-87.* Report prepared by the

Forestry Commission for the Ministry of Finance and Economic Planning. (April). Accra: Government of Ghana.

Forest Products Inspection Bureau. 1991. Export Permit for the Year 1991. Takoradi, Ghana: FPIB.

Frank, A. G. 1969. *Latin America: Underdevelopment or Revolution*. New York: Monthly Review Press.

George, S. 1992. *The Debt Boomerang: How Third World Debt Harms Us All.* Boulder: Westview Press.

Ghana Investment Centre. 1990. *The Investor: A Journal on Investment in Ghana*. I. (1). Accra: GIC.

Gore, C. 1984. *Regions in Question: Space, Development Theory and Regional Policy*. London: Methuen.

Government of Ghana. 1984. *Economic Recovery Program, 1984-86: Review of Progress in 1984 and Goals for 1985, 1986.* Report Prepared for the Second Meeting of the Consultative Group for Ghana. (Paris, December, 1984; November, Accra).

Green, R. H. 1987. *Stabilization and Adjustment Policies and Programs. Country Study 1: Ghana*. Annankatu, Finland: WIDER.

Green, R. H. 1991. *Reduction of Absolute Poverty: A Priority Structural Adjustment.* Institute of Development Studies. Discussion Paper 287. Sussex: IDS.

Hamilton, C. 1989. "The Irrelevance of Economic Liberalization in the Third World." In *World Development*. XVII. (10): 1523-1530.

Hancock, G. 1989. *Lords of Poverty: The Power, Prestige, and Corruption of the International Aid Business*. New York: The Atlantic Monthly Press.

Hayter, T. 1989. *Exploited Earth: Britain's Aid and the Environment*. London: Earthscan.

Huq, M. M. 1989. *The Economy of Ghana*. London: Macmillan Press.

Lensink, R. 1996. *Structural Adjustment in Sub-Saharan Africa*. New York: Longman.

Mabogunje, A. L. 1981. *The Development Process: A Spatial Perspective.* New York: Holmes and Meier.

Myrdal, G. 1957. *Economic Theory and Under-Developed Regions*. London: Duckworth.

Mytelka, L. K. 1989. "The Unfulfilled Promise of African Industrialization." *African Studies Review,* XXXII (3): 77-137.

Ninsin, K. A. 1990. "Ghana Under the PNDC: Delinking or Structural Adjustment?" In Azzam Mahjoub, ed. *Adjustment or Delinking? The African Experience.* The UN Univ./Third World Forum: Studies in African Political Economy. Tokyo/London: UN Univ. Press/Zed.

Organization of African Unity. 1982. *Lagos Plan of Action for the Economic Development of Africa, 1980-2000.* Geneva: International Institute for Labor Studies.

Ould-Mey, M. 1996. *Global Restructuring and Peripheral States The Carrot and the Stick in Mauritania.* Lanham, MD: Rowman & Littlefield.

Owusu, J. H. 1994. *Ghana's Economic Recovery Program and Changes in the Structural and Organizational Patterns of the Formal Wood-Processing Industry (1983-1991)*. Ph.D. Dissertation, University of Iowa, Ann Arbor, Michigan: University Microfilms International.

Owusu, J. H. 1995. "Structural Adjustment and African Development: Evidence From Ghana's Formal Wood-Processing Sector." *Review of Human Factor Studies*, 1 (2): 60-79.

Palloix, C. 1975. "The Internationalization of Capital and the Circuit of Social Capital." In H. Radice, ed. *International Firms and Modern Imperialism.* Harmondsworth: Penguin.

Palloix, C. 1977. "The Self-Expansion of Capital on a World Scale." *Review of Radical Political Economics,* IX: 1-28.

Roemer, M. 1981. "Dependence and Industrialization Strategies." *World Development,* IX (5): 429-434.

Sawyerr, A. 1990. *The Political Dimension of Structural Adjustment Programs in Sub-Saharan Africa.* Accra: Ghana Universities Press.

Sayer, A. 1986. "New Developments in Manufacturing: The Just-in-Time System." *Capital and Class,* XXX: 43-72.

Schwarz, G. 1990 "Stabilization Policies Under Political Transition: Reform Versus Adjustment in Brazil 1985-89." *The Developing Economies,* XXXVIII (1) March.

Slater, D. 1975. "Underdevelopment and Spatial Inequality: Approaches to the Problem of Regional Planning in the Third World." *Progress in Planning,* 4 (2).

Steel, W. F. 1988. "Recent Policy Reform and Industrial Adjustment in Zambia and Ghana." *The Journal of Modern African Studies,* 26: 157-164.

Storper, M. and Walker, R. 1989. *The Capitalist Imperative. Territory, Technology and Industrial Growth.* Cambridge, Mass.: Blackwell.

Tandon, Y. 1985. "Some Theoretical Aspects of the Delinking Debate and the Experience of Zimbabwe and Uganda in this Context." Mimeo.

Timber Export Development Board, (Undated). *Ghana: Forests, Wood and People.* London: TEDB.

UNIDO, 1991. *Investor's Guide to Ghana.* Report Prepared in Cooperation with the Government of Ghana., Vienna: UNIDO.

United Nations Economic Commission for Africa, 1986. *African Alternative Framework to Structural Adjustment Programs for Socio-Economic Recovery and Transformation (AAF-SAP).* New York: E/ECA/CM.15/6/Rev.3.

Wallerstein, I. 1974. *The Modern World-System.* New York: Academic Press.

World Bank, 1981. *Accelerated Development in Sub-Saharan Africa* Washington, D.C.: World Bank.

World Bank, 1984. *Ghana: Policies and Program for Adjustment.* Washington D.C.: World Bank.

World Bank, 1985. *Ghana: Towards Structural Adjustment, Vol. II: Statistical*

Appendix. (Oct. 7). Report No. 5854-GH. Washington, D.C.: World Bank.

World Bank, 1989. Sub-Saharan Africa: From Crisis to Sustainable Growth, A Long Term Perspective Study. Washington, DC: World Bank.

World Bank, 1991. *Ghana: Progress on Adjustment.* (April 16, 1991) Report No. 9475-GH. World Bank Western Africa Department. Washington, D.C.: World Bank.

Younger, S. D. 1989. "Economic Recovery Program - A Case Study of Stabilization and Structural Adjustment in Sub-Saharan Africa." In *Successful Development in Africa - A Case Studies of Projects, Programs and Policies.* Economic Development Institute of the World Bank: Analytical Case Studies. #1.Washington, D.C.: World Bank.

13

GHANA'S ECONOMIC REFORM PROGRAM: A MODEL FOR OTHER AFRICAN COUNTRIES?

Joe W. Essuman
Department of Business and Economics
University of Wisconsin Center-Waukesha

INTRODUCTION

The economies of Sub-Saharan Africa have witnessed sustained stagnation since the mid-1970s. The result is that the engine of economic growth and development has stalled in many African states over the past two decades. Africa's economic crisis has been manifested in sluggish growth, rising rates of inflation and balance of payments problems.

Since the beginning of the 1980s, economic malaise has culminated in the implementation of stabilization and adjustment programs in many African countries geared toward the correction of policy distortions and structural imbalances. In recent years, there has been growing controversy relating to the record of structural adjustment programs (SAPs) in Africa. Many African leaders, neo-structuralists, and dependency theorists, attribute the plight of Africa's adjustment experience to external reliance and exogenous shocks. On the other hand, the IMF/World Bank perspective places much more emphasis on internal economic factors. In fact, a thread loosely woven through many IMF/World Bank publications suggests that domestic-policy shortcomings underscore the magnitude of Africa's economic crisis and her frustration with structural adjustment.

Controversy over the effectiveness of Africa's structural adjustment continues unabated. Alternative policy frameworks to structural adjustment programs in Africa include ECA/OAU's Lagos Plan of Action (LPA) for the Economic

Development of Africa (1980), and ECA's African Alternative Framework (AAF) to Structural Adjustment Programmes (1989). In contrast to the World Bank's advocacy for the traditional export-led development strategy, the LPA recommends a shift of emphasis to a strategy of collective self-reliance. The AAF, like the LPA, which preceded it, calls on African governments to shift away from export-led development toward a strategy of collective self-reliance. Both the LPA and AAF are premised on longer-term view of development as opposed to the shorter-term policy reform paradigm, which characterized earlier World Bank reports. While SAPs emphasize budgetary balance, servicing of external debt, curtailment of subsidies, public sector retrenchment, levying of user fees, trade liberalization, and currency devaluation, the AAF implores lending agencies and donors to pay greater attention to Africa's special circumstances. It urges agencies and donors to be more sensitive to the vulnerabilities of Africa's economies before they impose harmful conditionalities on them. In essence, the ECA emphasizes human-centered development and poverty alleviation, through education and training, employment, accessibility to productive land, food production and distribution, and the provision of health care and physical infrastructure, particularly in the rural areas. While differences in prescription still exist, there has been an appreciable convergence of views in recent years, culminating in the publication of the World Bank's latest report on SAPs in Africa: Adjustment in Africa, Reforms, Results, and the Road Ahead (1994)

Meanwhile, Ghana is often cited as the one African country whose macroeconomic reforms have resulted in an appreciable economic growth. In fact, Ghana's reform program is now seen as a model for other African countries, and Ghana is often showcased as the World Bank and IMF's star pupil in Africa. There is a widespread view that the primary achievement of Ghana's economic reform program has been the correction of previously distorted prices. Although specific features of adjustment programs vary widely from country to country to reflect diverse needs, Ghana's experience does offer important lessons for other African countries.

This chapter highlights Ghana's adjustment experience, and addresses the misconception that Ghana's economic reform program represents a blueprint for other African countries. The chapter contends that in spite of the up-beat commentary on Ghana's reform effort by the World Bank and the IMF, the impact of the Economic Reform Program on the human condition in Ghana is negligible. The chapter concludes that even though Ghana is often regarded as the World Bank/IMF's star pupil in Africa, its reform program may not be a model for other African countries due largely to differences in the economic, political, physical, and institutional circumstances.

THE ROOTS OF GHANA'S ECONOMIC CRISIS

Ghana's economy stagnated during the 1970s and was characterized by shrinking outputs and declining per capita income. By the early 1980s, Ghana had experienced a long period of declining growth and inherited a set of economic institutions, which served only to accentuate her economic problems. The economy had stalled and was virtually dysfunctional. Real per capita income fell by over 30% during the decade. The situation was aggravated by a severe drought, growing external imbalances, and the unexpected task of accommodating the return of one million Ghanaians from Nigeria.

This economic malaise was the result of the cumulative adverse effects of a combination of internal and external factors. Infrastructural bottlenecks, and particularly the breakdown of the transport sector, undermined haulage to the ports. Moreover, an overvalued exchange rate for the cedi discouraged production of exports, including cocoa, and encouraged smuggling and deterioration of productive assets. A wide array of interventionist policies by successive Ghanaian governments suppressed market forces and paved the way for a thriving underground economy, which resulted in rent-seeking activities.

In the view of the World Bank, "the key weakness of past policies was the combination of virtually absolute protection with an overvalued exchange rate and grossly inadequate export incentives. This system led to misallocation of resources and robbed Ghana's industry of the stimulus of expanding markets and bracing competition."[1]

The government of Ghana itself attributed the poor performance to both internal and external factors, which included the "maintenance of a fixed and highly overvalued exchange rate that discouraged exports and produced huge profits for traders of imported goods; large deficits in the Government's budgets which resulted in inflationary pressures which further distorted effective exchange rates; the imposition of price controls at the manufacturing stage which discouraged production, while deriving excessive profits to the unregulated small-scale trading sector; misallocation and use of import licenses which created further inefficiencies and denied critical inputs and equipment to high priority areas."[2] Large fiscal deficits financed mainly through borrowing from the domestic banking system fanned inflation, which reached 120% in 1983. Pervasive government intervention in the economy via a complex web of price, distribution and import controls fueled relative price distortions and undermined incentives to save, produce and invest.

The external factors were identified by the Ghanaian government as "the sharp increase in petroleum prices in 1979, followed by a world recession and declining export prices, which created a major deterioration in the terms of trade."[3] However, compared to the domestic conditions, the external environment was generally favorable to Ghana (e.g. the buoyancy in the international cocoa market).

Against this backdrop of structural deficiencies and sustained economic decline, Ghana launched perhaps the most radical structural adjustment program on the continent of Africa, with the assistance of the IMF and the World Bank, in April 1983.

GHANA'S ADJUSTMENT PROGRAM

In order to ensure the success of the initial stabilization program, a series of structural reforms had to be initiated over the medium term:

Exchange Rate Reform

At the core of the adjustment strategy was the establishment and maintenance of a "realistic and market-determined exchange rate."[4] In 1983, the cedi was overvalued by as much as 400%. This was the result of government policy that pegged the cedi at the rate of C2.75 to the US dollar in the face of an inflation rate of 122.8%. In essence, the government was subsidizing imports and surcharging exports. Adjustment of the distorted exchange rate was to become the centerpiece of external sector reforms. The IMF had initially prescribed a one-time devaluation of the cedi to ensure the timely elimination of distortions in the economy. However, the Ghanaian government opted for a system of multiple exchange rates in order to avoid public outcry against "devaluation" and also to save political face. Initially, the exercise consisted of a system of bonuses for exporters and surcharges for importers that raised the effective official exchange rate from C2.75 = US$1 to C25 = US$1. This new rate represented a depreciation of over 89%. Though the Minister of Finance defended the exercise on the grounds that the "distorted exchange rate served only to reward the privileged few who had access to foreign exchange,"[5] the initial reaction to the measures was ferocious. There were widespread protests by students and many urban workers. The General Transport and Chemical Workers Union labeled the exercise "inhuman."[6]

The unwieldiness of operating the system of bonuses and surcharges compelled the Ghanaian government to unify the exchange rate in October 1983, and to further devalue the cedi to C30 = US$1. The cedi was progressively devalued until it reached C90 = US$1 by January 1986. In the face of popular resentment against the continual exchange rate adjustment, the Ghanaian government, the Provisional National Defense Council, (PNDC) found it politically infeasible to initiate further devaluation by administrative decree. Ghana's Trade Union Congress (TUC) registered its abhorrence to the government's "submission to the dictates of the IMF and the World Bank," and behooved the PNDC to "wrestle the country's economy from the grip of these financial institutions."[7]

With the view to depoliticizing subsequent exchange rate adjustments, the PNDC initiated a market-driven system in September 1986 by which the allocation of foreign exchange was to be determined by the highest bid in a weekly currency auction system. This second-tier official market covered virtually all international transactions other than cocoa, petroleum, essential drugs, and government debt-service payments on debts incurred prior to January 1986. The second-tier rate was determined in weekly auctions at which only the public sector and private importers of non-consumables could compete. The auction excluded importers of consumer items under the Special Import License (SIL).

One of the main objectives of the currency auction system was to eliminate the parallel market and encourage remittance of funds by Ghanaians working abroad through official banking channels. By the end of 1986, the spread between the official and parallel market rates had witnessed a significant reduction of 20-25%, from the level of 100% prior to the introduction of the auction.

The second stage, which was launched in February 1987, abolished the two-tier system and merged the two markets into a single-tier exchange rate system. The value of the cedi continued to be determined by auctions, but all transactions were at the auction rate.[8] Access to the auction was therefore widened to include more and more categories of consumer goods and debt-service payments. The result was that practically all consumer goods could be funded via the auction by end-March 1988. This paved the way for the abolition of the import licensing system by January 1989.

Ghana's exchange rate reform involved not merely adjustment of relative prices, but also locally-developed strategic reforms of fundamental economic institutions. However, the "ability to pay" criterion which governed the auction system was not necessarily the best approach to ensure the most efficient utilization of scarce foreign exchange from the point of view of development. In the Zambian experience, for example, it turned out that 90% of the foreign exchange went to only 100 firms. Of these, 99% were foreign-owned. In abolishing the auction system, the Governor of the Bank of Zambia explained that these foreign companies had taken advantage of their superior liquidity position to obtain most of the foreign exchange auctioned. This would not have been so serious if their import priorities were in consonance with those of the economy. However, he pointed out that many of the expatriate firms expended the scarce foreign exchange frivolously on some goods that were readily available locally, including dog food! (African Concord, 16.7.87)

In the face of Ghana's exchange rate reforms, a considerable black market for foreign exchange continued to thrive, partly because of the uneasiness of many Ghanaians to "advertise" their cedi holdings by using the auction. In response, the government of Ghana decreed in 1988 that hard currencies could be freely traded via foreign exchange bureaux. Under this policy, any corporate or natural person could be licensed by the Bank of Ghana to buy and sell foreign exchange at freely negotiated rates. The Minister of Finance explained that this would "depoliticize" the exchange system.

The introduction of the foreign exchange (FOREX) bureaux implied the absorption of the parallel market. However, segmentation between the official weekly retail auction and the FOREX bureaux (since the bureaux were not permitted to purchase foreign exchange at the retail rate) culminated in a high spread between the bureaux and the auction rates. When the spread narrowed two years after the establishment of the FOREX bureaux, the Bank of Ghana abolished its retail auction in early 1990, and instituted a weekly wholesale auction in which all authorized dealers could participate, including the FOREX bureaux.

Ghana now has in place a flexible exchange rate regime under which the exchange markets are unified in a composite exchange system combining a weekly wholesale auction with an interbank and retail foreign exchange market. The weekly wholesale auction rate applies to official transactions including customs valuation, while other rates apply to all other transactions. The government announced in early 1995 that the stabilization of the cedi was still a top priority. Ghana's experience with deregulation suggests the need to reorientate institutions, attitudes, and perceptions of bureaucrats and the public at large. For example, public patronage of the foreign exchange bureaux was initially restrained by fears of possible arrest of patrons.

Rehabilitation of the Export Sector

In view of the central role that cocoa plays in the Ghanaian economy, it was the focus of long-term reform. The devaluations automatically increased the local currency equivalent of the cocoa producer price which increased from C12,000 per ton in 1982-83 to C140,000 per ton in the 1987-88 season. The objective had been to reduce the share of the total price appropriated by the state and to improve the real returns to the producer. The percentage of the world price received by farmers shot up from approximately 22% in 1983 to an estimated 41% by 1987.[9] The percentage of the free-on-board price received by producers increased from 35% in 1984 to 54% in 1990. In addition, cocoa purchases by the Ghana Cocoa Marketing Board (Cocobod) increased from 168,100 tons in 1983 to 288,800 tons in 1988.[10] This increase in deliveries to the Cocobod seems to have stemmed from a decline in cross-border cocoa smuggling (particularly to the Ivory Coast) in response to producer price increases, rather than an increase in production, since the gestation period for the cocoa crop is approximately seven years.

Attempts were also made to reform the Cocobod in order to reduce its operating costs. The resulting redeployment exercise cut the payroll of the Cocobod from 100,000 to 42,000 employees, of which approximately 20,000 were found to be "ghostworkers." Moreover, some of the Board's functions (e.g. production, marketing, transportation, research and extension) were transferred to other state institutions or to the private sector, as part of an overall attempt to demonopolize domestic marketing. However, the Cocobod continues to exert a major influence on producer prices.

Aside from cocoa, other programs have been launched to rehabilitate the mining and timber industries with the support of IDA credits. Meanwhile, gold has overtaken cocoa as Ghana's biggest export earner, with timber ranking third.

Growth in industry and manufacturing increased by 8.2% and 4.9% respectively between 1981-86 and 1987-91. An export earning retention scheme allows certain exporters to retain a proportion of their foreign exchange proceeds for the procurement of critical inputs and other needs. Ghana recorded a trade surplus with Britain for the first time in 1994. Total exports grew at an average annual rate of 8.1% during 1987-91, compared with 4.5% during 1981-86. However, at 15% of GDP, Ghana's export ratio is still relatively low.

Decontrol and Reform of Prices

Shortly after the 1983 budget, the government of Ghana moved to eliminate price controls on almost all commodities. Primarily, the elimination of these controls and the abolition of most of the ineffective and corrupt price-control bureaucracy was an acknowledgment by the military government, PNDC, that the vast majority of urban residents were already paying black-market prices. According to the World Bank, the objective of the exchange rate and price reforms was to "shift incentives further from trading and rent-seeking activities to production to permit producers to obtain a larger share of scarcity rents and to enable them to generate the liquidity necessary for expansion of production." [11] The lifting of price controls allowed traders to market their goods in public, and resulted in the re-emergence of markets in many Ghanaian cities. An important advantage of shifting from controlled to market-based systems is that it removed a major source of patronage and corruption.

Agricultural Reforms

A general criticism of adjustment programs is their focus on export crops, and their virtual neglect of food crops. Although Ghana's adjustment experience has been hailed as a success story, its reforms within the agricultural sector did not commence until the late 1980s. Since 1986, however, increased resources have been devoted to the provision of inputs (e.g., fertilizer and seeds). The development of infrastructure, especially the construction and repair of feeder roads, has improved supply response and impacted positively on both export crops (particularly, cocoa) and food agriculture. Besides, non-governmental agencies and organizations have been very successful in their promotion of peasant food agriculture. As a result of these developments and improved weather conditions, Ghana in 1989 produced 77% of the total amount of maize, rice, sorghum, and millet that it needed, the highest level of self-sufficiency since 1975.[12] Increases were also registered in the production of starch staples such as cassava, cocoyam, and yams. [13]

Nonetheless, Ghana lagged behind other African countries with respect to its agricultural performance. For example, during 1987-91 Ghana registered a modest 2% annual growth in its agricultural sector compared with 3.9% and 5.3% annual growth recorded for Nigeria and Tanzania respectively. Significant bottlenecks still exist in the agricultural sector. There is the need for increased investments in research and extension services, and improvements in small-scale irrigation and rural infrastructure, with the view to improving the structural conditions in the agricultural sector. Improvements in human capital and infrastructure and the strengthening of institutional capacity are critical to improvements in living conditions and poverty alleviation.

State Enterprise and Public Sector Reform

Comprehensive reforms in the public sector had to be initiated to ensure the success of Ghana's adjustment program. To this end, blatant state interventions in the economy (e.g., price controls and foreign exchange allocation) had to be eliminated. The government also took action to reduce the size of the civil service. The structural adjustment program aimed at eliminating approximately 36,000 redundant positions from an estimated total civil service of approximately 540,000 workers.

The reform efforts also included improvements in the efficiency, productivity and profitability of state enterprises. Large blocks of shares of nationalized companies have already been sold to private interests. The sale of the Ashanti Goldfields Corporation fetched the government over $350 million. Ghana earned C63.2 billion from divesting 107 companies, six years after the government instituted the Divestiture Implementation Committee (DIC). In view of what critics claim to have been a rather slow process of divestiture, the government is considering the involvement of merchant banks in the sale of enterprises in order to speed up the divestiture exercise.

Monetary and Fiscal Policies

The stabilization and structural adjustment programs summoned a set of very conservative monetary policies, including strict credit ceilings, and an increase in interest rates from 14% in 1983 to 26% in 1987, with the objective of attaining positive real interest rates and stimulating savings. With the view to containing inflationary pressures, the Bank of Ghana increased the minimum base lending rate from 36% in 1994 to 39% in January 1995.

Public sector finances were rigorously managed with the objective of drastically reducing the budget deficit. The government attempted to reduce current expenditures through the elimination of subsidies, massive public sector retrenchment, reduced deficit financing, broadening of the tax and revenue base, and repricing of government services. As a result of these policy reforms and an inflow of external funds, government deficits which averaged 5.4% of GDP between 1980 and 1982 was eliminated by 1986.[14] However, budget deficits have since re-emerged, and inflation continues to pose a major problem. The rate of inflation averaged 24.9% and 27% in 1994 and 1993 respectively.

Fiscal policy played a key role in promoting stabilization and rehabilitation. While a policy of fiscal restraint was adopted to provide essential support for demand management, the budget was used as a vehicle for mobilizing domestic resources to finance outlays for rehabilitation and raising the domestic savings rate. These objectives were premised on a comprehensive tax reform effort for the purpose of raising revenue, promoting equity and reducing economic disincentives at the same time.[15] The ratio of taxes to GDP was raised by 10% as a result of a comprehensive tax reform. Ghana introduced the Value Added Tax (VAT system in March 1995 with the view to improving and widening the tax structure. However, the administrative and operational difficulties associated with the VAT led to soaring prices for food and services. The hasty implementation of the tax culminated in price hikes of between 300% and 400%. However, a good part of the price hike could be traced to greed, misunderstanding, and corruption. In the interim, a series of demonstrations dubbed "Kume Preko" (i.e. You might as well kill me) were staged by workers and opposition groups to protest the economic hardship in Ghana. The demands of the protesters included a 70% salary increase and a repeal of the Value Added Tax system. Critics of the government argued that a combination of low literacy rate and large informal sector did not represent the ideal conditions under which a very sophisticated and unfamiliar tax could be hastily implemented. The rather unpopular VAT, which was levied at the rate of 17.5%, has since been repealed.

OVERALL EFFECTS OF GHANA'S ADJUSTMENT PROGRAM

The accomplishments of Ghana's structural adjustment program, or economic recovery program as it is called in Ghana, have been widely acknowledged by donors and lending agencies. Although the program is incomplete, it is claimed to have achieved many of its immediate objectives, at least in terms of standard economic aggregates.

Compared to the growth rate of 2.3% recorded for the entire continent of Africa (excluding Nigeria) between 1980 and 1987, the Ghanaian economy grew spectacularly at an average rate of about 6% between 1983 and 1988. The entire continent, including Nigeria, grew by only 0.5% each year.[16] Over the last decade, the growth rate of the Ghanaian economy averaged 5%.

However, these growth statistics ought to be taken in context, since statistics do not necessarily reflect improvements in the human condition. While there has been a modest increase in the real per capita income of Ghanaians, this only returns the country to where it had been in 1981. The average Ghanaian's income was approximately 140% higher in 1971 than it was in 1989.[17] Wages remained uniformly low, and even the best-paid civil servants earned little more than $50 a month in 1990.[18] The national daily minimum wage was increased from C790 in 1993 to C1200 in 1995. However, the cedi price of the US dollar depreciated from an annual average rate of C815 = $1 to C1034 = $1, while the rate of inflation increased from 21.5% to 24.9% over the same period. Urban workers have witnessed dramatic declines in their living standards. The result is that many families have had to resort to a variety of disturbing survival strategies.

In spite of the overall increase in economic growth, significant sectors of the Ghanaian economy have not returned to the levels that prevailed in 1977. For instance, the level of total manufacturing, even after five years of reform, was only 62.1% of its 1977 level.

Moreover, the massive depreciation of the cedi, tight credit restrictions, and high interest rates have combined to create a liquidity crisis for importers and the industrial sector. Even commercial banks have complained of liquidity problems, and have often declined to lend to importing firms because the costs of imports in the depreciated currency often exceeded their total equity. Struggling under the liquidity squeeze, high input costs, and a depressed domestic market, Ghana's manufacturing sector has had to face competition from a flood of consumer imports made possible by liberalization. Nonetheless, the IMF was not disposed to easing the tight limits on credit, on the grounds that this may prove inflationary. Thus, a cost explosion and tight liquidity have combined to reduce the ability of the private sector to contribute to economic recovery through the absorption of redundant public sector employees.

Similarly, the attempt to expand cocoa exports through dramatic increases in the producer price has coincided with large market surpluses and a major slump in world prices, creating "a chocolate lover's dream and a cocoa producing country's nightmare."[19] Okogu (1989, p38) argues that the development path being carved out by Ghana's adjustment measures appears to be destined, if it succeeds, to intensify the dependence of African economies on the outside world, and deepen the raw-material-producing relationship which has been the lot of African countries from colonial times. In response to improved incentives, the supply of primary products has expanded and resulted in falling world prices. Export income declined from $1.1 billion in 1983 to $0.986 billion by 1992.

Another area of concern lies in the external debt implications of Ghana's structural adjustment program. Concessional new financing has only served to defer Ghana's external debt problem. New capital inflows have been offset almost dollar for dollar by outflows for debt servicing and repayment arrears.[20] Ghana's total debt and debt-service ratio stood at $3,800 million and 24.3% respectively in 1992. At the end of 1994, Ghana's total official external debt, including obligations to the IMF, was estimated at $5,001.08 million. Of this amount, short-term debt was estimated at $267.6 million, while medium-term debt stood at $1,191.01 million. Obligations to the IMF under medium-term facilities, such as structural adjustment, enhanced structural adjustment, trust fund loans, etc., amounted to $700.3 million. In contrast, the domestic debt was put at C531.1 billion.

Ghana's reform effort has again been criticized for its dependence on World Bank and other donor aid. Critics claim that the level of influence exercised by the World Bank over Ghana's policy process is by all accounts very high indeed. [21] Similarly, Hutchful (1989, p. 112) argues that "what has emerged in Accra is a parallel government controlled (if not created) by the international lender agencies." However, given the depth of Ghana's economic stagnation, the deterioration of infrastructure, and the structural bottlenecks in many facets of the Ghanaian economy, it is difficult to imagine how the economy could have risen by its own bootstraps from its virtual comatose condition.

In Ghana, as in many other countries where structural adjustment programs have been launched, there have been both winners and losers of economic reform. While those connected with export industries (e.g., cocoa farmers, gold miners) have benefited somewhat from Ghana's massive devaluations, additional problems have been created for food production and industrial activity. The progressive increases in the producer price of cocoa could cause a diversion from food to cocoa production, and undermine local food sufficiency. In spite of the significant attempts at market liberalization and price incentives, food agriculture has not enjoyed any credible commitment from the government. Although there have been increases in food output, they have resulted largely from improved weather conditions rather than any articulable policy reforms. To ensure long-term recovery, a strong agricultural sector with domestic linkages is needed.

Other reforms, such as increasing the user fees for medical services and education seem to have affected mostly the poor. After a series of dramatic price increases resulting from the "cost recovery" reforms, public utilities have been experiencing problems in the collection of payment from hard-pressed consumers and businesses. This development has affected access to basic services. The currency devaluations, levying of user fees, curtailment of subsidies, and retrenchment of the public sector, may have had the collective effect of reducing access of vulnerable groups to education and health care, and exposing many to unemployment, malnutrition and other socio-economic quagmire.

Those who lost their jobs in the retrenchment exercise could also be considered losers although, in most cases, it could be argued that there was no economic justification for their jobs in the first place. It could also be contended that some of the reforms have not been biased against the poor, since they arguably did not have access to some of the imported goods before the devaluation. Though the abolition of price controls affected urban workers, it is doubtful that many were actually available to them at the official prices.

Aware of the possible dislocations that could occur from the reforms, the government of Ghana became the first in Africa to initiate what has been called a "Program of Action to Mitigate the Social Costs of Adjustment" (PAMSCAD). The program, which initially attracted $85 million from foreign donors, set a precedent for economic adjustment programs elsewhere by gearing its projects to easing the social costs of adjustment, and helping the most vulnerable. Its projects include a large-scale redeployment of former civil servants, who lost their jobs from the retrenchment exercise. Though PAMSCAD confronts a difficult task, the government of Ghana has noted that it contributes to the political viability of the entire reform exercise. [22]

Ghana has yet to go the full distance in restructuring its economy. It still intervenes heavily in the marketing of export crops. Partly due to the monetization of fiscal deficits, the financial position of the banking sector is still weak. There is still an appreciable degree of government interference in the management of the financial sector. A large share of bank lending still goes to public enterprises, crowding out private sector borrowing. These developments are illustrative of the fact that Ghana's reform program is not yet complete. Further reforms are needed in the educational, tax and banking systems, as well as in state-owned enterprises. However, few African countries, besides Ghana, come close to having adequate monetary, fiscal and exchange rate policies.

In spite of the so-called positive impact of structural adjustment on the Ghanaian economy, Ghana is still dependent on raw material exports, especially cocoa. The manufacturing sector still lacks foreign direct investment, due in part to intense global competition for investment funds. Foreign investors generally are attracted to Asia and Eastern Europe compared to Africa.

Given the economic malaise of the last 20 years, one cannot indict the reform effort for failing to provide good remedies. Perhaps the most realistic evaluation of Ghana's adjustment experience is that a moderate improvement has been achieved in the economy, and that some progress has been made in the attempt to lay a foundation for sustained economic growth in the future.

LESSONS FOR OTHER AFRICAN COUNTRIES

Though the success of Ghana's adjustment program has been acknowledged by lending agencies and donors, Ghana's adjustment experience has not been problem-free. For one thing, the pace of private sector investment has been slower than anticipated, particularly outside the mining sector. In spite of the positive reviews of Ghana's reform efforts, there are some unique features and circumstances that must be considered before any attempt is made at using Ghana's experience as a blueprint for other African countries.

To begin with, the Ghanaian economy had collapsed to such a great extent by 1983 that there probably would have been very few losers from structural adjustment. With the economy in a virtual comatose, few people were actually benefiting from the status quo. Consequently, the level of opposition to the reform program was relatively lower than might have been the case if many people may have had a stake in maintaining the status quo.

Besides, the government of Ghana was able to survive the initial ferocious reaction to the reform program partly as a result of sheer luck. The government withstood several coup attempts that failed. It was this ability to face up to the political limits usually associated with Fund programs that set the PNDC apart from previous Ghanaian governments and other regimes in Africa. It is important to note that the ability of the erstwhile military government to administer painful adjustment prescriptions was unencumbered by political ramifications. However, after the rebirth of a multi-party political system in 1992, the Ghanaian economy witnessed a slump. Critics of the government attribute this to feet-dragging by President Rawlings, the former military leader, to mobilize support for the 1996 elections. Unemployment hovered around 30%, inflation was estimated at about 30%, and the base-lending rate was set at 35%. Against this backdrop, the Rawlings administration was compelled to increase government spending and slow down the pace of economic reforms in an attempt to mobilize mass support for the president's re-election bid in November 1996. Rawling's critics claimed that he had been overwhelmed by the frustration of operating under a constitution after presiding over a decade of military dictatorship. Thus, the extent to which other countries can emulate the Ghanaian model depends on the prevailing political system and climate in each country.

Moreover, the populist style and charisma of the Ghanaian leader, Jerry Rawlings, seem to have also mobilized some initial support, at least among urban residents. However, in 1995, after over a decade of reforms under the auspices of the World Bank and the IMF, Ghana was hit by a spate of anti-government protests involving civil servants, nurses, teachers, university lecturers, and judicial-service workers. Unions organized a series of protests to support their demands for a 70% pay hike and a repeal of VAT. The workers complained that they had nothing to show for over a decade of World Bank and IMF sponsored belt-tightening reforms.

Also, the economy of Ghana had plunged into such depths that 1983 was essentially an economic trough. In the circumstance, Ghana inadvertently was able to experience a subtle economic upturn soon after it launched its reform program. However, stabilization and structural adjustment programs may actually reduce growth in the short term, especially in Africa where supply response may be particularly low, in view of structural rigidities and socio-economic bottlenecks. In the circumstance, some of the lessons of Ghana's reform experience may not apply to other countries whose economies may be healthier relative to the Ghanaian economy in 1983. Under these circumstances, successive reforms would involve higher adjustment costs.

Some critics have advanced the argument that the dependency of Ghana's structural adjustment on IMF-Bank funding and oversight has "turned Ghana into a laboratory for extensive neo-classical experimentation, unencumbered by the distraction of popular democracy. . . . Popular enthusiasm, the greatest asset of the (Ghanaian) regime, has once more been replaced by what Rawlings bemoans as the 'culture of silence."[23]

In spite of these limitations and criticisms, Ghana's experience does offer some useful lessons for other African countries embarking on economic recovery programs. First of all, Ghana's experience suggests that structural adjustment and, in particular, the emphasis on "getting prices right" can be very effective in eliminating gross distortions in the economy and to laying the foundation for economic growth. The primary achievement of Ghana's reform program has been to correct previously distorted prices to promote economic growth. The Ghanaian experience demonstrates that the elimination of price distortions can have some immediate positive effects. In the short run, however, the condition of the average citizen is likely to deteriorate. In spite of the bustling economic activity, many Ghanaians still grumble about the rising cost of living and the drop in real incomes. The Ghanaian currency has been devalued by 200-fold in the last decade, and the World Bank estimates that it will take several decades for average per-capita income to rise above the poverty line.

While there is a similarity of objectives and instruments of structural adjustment, the political strategies for the reforms are essentially different. Because no two countries share the same economic conditions, no two adjustment programs are the same. There is, therefore, the need for individual African governments to map out appropriate local reform strategies, and to mobilize the necessary political support for them. To some extent, the reform efforts in Ghana have been successful partly because of locally-developed strategies to deal with the expected political fallout of the controversial issue of devaluation. The lesson here for other African countries is that a 'gradualist' approach as opposed to a 'faster-track' approach to exchange rate reforms may be realistic for both economic and political reasons.

Ghana's experience also provides specific lessons for other African countries in such areas as improvements in infrastructure, fiscal performance and the distribution of adjustment costs and benefits. An important step in combating inflation and exchange rate depreciation may be an independent central bank. As at now, the Bank of Ghana is virtually an extension of the government.

Another lesson provided by the Ghanaian experience relates to how long it takes for an inert economy to begin to move again, even in the face of strong reforms. The World Bank now acknowledges that it was initially overly optimistic in its expectation of the time required to implement structural reforms, and that the early programs were often too complex, and the conditions too wide-ranging, for successful implementation. Consequently, there is now a concerted effort by the IMF and the World Bank to move away from overly ambitious short-term programs towards medium-term adjustment. The more there is a genuine meeting of minds between governments and international agencies, the greater the likelihood of success in achieving the stated objective of conditionality.

Perhaps, it is also important to note that the Ghanaian government sought to avoid "overloading the stabilization phase with too many structural adjustment measures. For example, the exchange rate was not floated until the authorities were convinced that excess demand for foreign exchange had attenuated."[24]

Most importantly, Ghana found that the international community was extremely forthcoming with new aid. The World Bank was enthused by the idea of using Ghana as a test case to demonstrate how its structural adjustment policies could work in the African setting. Aid from the Bank was very significant in providing crucial resources to jump-start the Ghanaian economy. In particular, the

Bank's funding was critical to many specific projects. From the level of $9.20 in 1983, total per capita foreign aid jumped to $27.50 in 1987, with most of the aid coming from the World Bank and the IMF.

A more relevant question as far as other African countries are concerned, is whether or not the Bank can provide the same level of resources in a timely fashion and on appropriate terms to countries embarking on similar reform programs. In Zambia and other African countries the failure of donors to provide promised funding has been a factor in the failure of some structural adjustment programs.[25] Even the then Finance Minister, Dr. Kwesi Botchwey, who spearheaded Ghana's reform effort expressed frustration with the conditionalities of international financial institutions. He noted that some $200 million in loans and $100 million in grants were withheld from Ghana in 1994. Though aid is not essential for some of the needed reforms, it is especially difficult to expect African governments to commit themselves to major programs and policies while the essential decisions on official development assistance are kept to vague promises.

In the face of mounting external debt, tough rescheduling postures by creditors, underdevelopment, poverty and the long-term nature of Africa's problems, non-concessional debt is not realistically helpful. Since the capacity of African countries to service these debts in the future is rather murky, debt relief ought to be an integral part of the co-operation needed from the international community.

CONCLUSION

In general, structural adjustment has posed a political threat to many African governments some of whom have found ways to avoid full compliance with the inherent conditionality. In the circumstance, the application of structural adjustment programs of the type launched in Ghana has remained rather limited, and the results have been mixed. The criticism that structural adjustment programs are likely to perpetuate the neo-classical foundations of African economies has intensified.

Given the nature and influence of exogenous shocks and the limited availability of domestic resources, external support for structural adjustment is critical to ensure a real chance of sustainable success. Under the auspices of the World Bank and the IMF, Ghana seems to have turned its battered economy around. The general supply situation has improved, significant growth rates have been recorded, infrastructures have been fixed, and industrial production has been stepped up. Ghana's reform experience seems to suggest the following lessons for other African countries:-

1. Maintenance of a realistic exchange rate facilitates international competitiveness, encourages exports, discourages smuggling, and the proliferation of parallel markets, and reduces rent-seeking and distortions emanating from import licensing. Low budget deficits, if sustained, are

helpful in reducing inflation. Inflationary pressures in the Ghanaian economy were attenuated until the recent increases in government spending.

2. Promotion of competition encourages efficiency and improves the supply situation. Competition may be harnessed through trade reforms, deregulation, and privatization.
3. Minimization of pervasive government intervention in markets (e.g., price controls and foreign exchange allocation) reduces relative price distortions, facilitates the re-emergence of markets, improves the supply situation, and reduces government bureaucracy.

However, in spite of the vaunted achievement of Ghana's Economic Recovery Program, the momentum for growth has slowed down. The rate of unemployment currently stands at 30%, the cost of living has soared, the inflation rate is about 30%, and the daily minimum wage of about $1.10 can buy only one meal a day for one person. Though the World Bank singles out Ghana as having the best macroeconomic policies in Africa, it concedes in its most recent report on Africa's SAPs, 'Adjustment in Africa (1994, p. 40) that "the average poor Ghanaian will not cross the poverty line for another fifty years."

The applicability of Ghana's adjustment experience to other African countries is essentially a function of the initial conditions on the one hand and the political feasibility of the proposed measures on the other hand. The link between political and economic reforms is critical for sustained economic growth in Africa. In general, the capacity of countries to adjust is constrained by domestic politics.

Sub-Saharan African countries ought to be wary of the bandwagon syndrome. The Ghanaian experience should be seen as offering some guidance in the packaging of country-specific programs rather than a blueprint for all African countries. African governments and donors ought to agree on a set of country-specific priorities, and commit themselves to achieving them over the long term. Ultimately, SAPs that fall short of the economic transformation are of limited usefulness in the African context. Intra-regional co-operation and international co-operation must go hand in hand if Africa is to reverse its decline and move toward self-sustaining development. Meanwhile, the hard reality is that even for those African countries pursuing strong reform efforts, only modest improvements in living standards can be realistically promised to their citizens.

NOTES

1. The World Bank, Ghana: Policies and Programs for Adjustment No.4702-GH, issued on October 3, 1983: "Manufacturing Sector", par. 90.

2. Ibid.

3. "Economic Recovery Programme", November 1983, par. 26-27.

4. World Bank/IDA, "Report and Recommendation of the President of the International Development Association. . . . on a Proposed Development Credit. . .

. to the Republic of Ghana for a Structural Adjustment Program", report No. P-4403-GH (Washington: March 23, 1987), p 14.

5. "*People's Daily Graphic," April 25, 1983.*

6. *"People's Daily Graphic," April 30, 1983.*

7. *"People's Daily Graphic,"* November 10, 1984.

8. Oil and drug imports, as well as debt servicing, were at the first-tier rate of C90 = US$1 before the introduction of the single-tier rate.

9. World Bank, 1989, p. 147.

10. Statistical Service, Quarterly Digest of Statistics, December 1988, p. 5.

11. *West Africa*, January 13, 1986, p. 78.

12. PNDC, "Achievement of the PNDC in the Sector Under Ghana's Economic

Recovery Programme, 1982-1988", Mimeo, May 1989, p. 15.

13. Statistical Service, p. 5, and Kodwo Ewusi, *Statistical Tables on the Economy of Ghana, 1950-1985* (Legon: Institute of Statistical, Social and Economic Research, 1986), Table 53.

14. World Bank, 1989, p. 99.

15. Sheetal Chand and Reinold Van Til, "Ghana: Toward Successful Stabilization and Recovery," *Finance & Development*, Vol.25, No.1, IMF, Washington DC, March 1988, p. 35.

16. "Sub-Saharan Africa: From Crisis to Sustainable Growth," The World Bank, Washington DC, 1989, p. 222.

17. Jeffrey Herbst: "Economic Reform in Africa: The Lessons of Ghana," Universities Field Staff International (UFSI), *Field Staff Reports*, Africa/Middle East, 1989-90/No.15, p. 8.

18. World Development, UNDP, New York, NY, 1990, p. 24.

19. "Cocoa Surpluses a Bitter Blow to Producers," *The Globe and Mail*, Toronto, April 11, 1988.

20. John Loxley, Ghana: Economic Crisis and the Long Road to Recovery", North-South Institute, Ottawa, 1988, p. 34.

21. Loxley, op. cit. (1988), p. 28-30.

22. "Program of Action to Mitigate the Social Costs of Adjustment," Accra, Ghana, 1987, p. 21.

23. See Eboe Hutchful, "From 'Revolution' to Monetarism: The Economic and Politics of the Adjustment Program in Ghana," 1989, p. 123.

24. J. L. S. Abbey, Ghana's High Commissioner to the United Kingdom, IMF Survey, October 30, 1989 Vol.18, No. 29, p. 328.

25. World Bank: "Adjustment Lending: An Evaluation of Ten Years of Experience", *Policy and Research Paper No.1*, The World Bank, Washington DC, 1988, p. 84.

REFERENCES

Chand, S. and Van Til, R. 1988. "Ghana: Toward Successful Stabilization and Recovery." *Finance & Development*, Vol. 25, No., IMF, Washington DC, March 1988, pp. 32-35.

Economic Commission For Africa. 1989. *ECA and Africa's Development, 1983-2008.*

Herbst, J. 1989. "Economic Reform in Africa: The Lessons of Ghana." UFSI Field Staff Reports, Africa/Middle East, 1989-90/No. 15.

Hutchful E. 1989. "From 'Revolution' to Monetarism: The Economics and Politics of The Adjustment Programme in Ghana." In B. Campbell and J. Loxley, eds. *Structural Adjustment in Africa*. New York: St. Martin's Press.

Loxley, J. 1988. *Ghana: Economic Crisis and the Long Road to Recovery*. Ottawa: North-South Institute.

Okogu, B. 1989. "Structural Adjustment Policies in African Countries: A Theoretical Assessment." In B. Onimode, ed. *The IMF, The World Bank and The African Debt: The Economic Impact.* Vol. London: The Institute for African Alternatives.

Organization of African Unity, 1980. *The Lagos Plan For Action for the Implementation of the Monrovia strategy for the Economic Development of Africa, 1980 - 2000*. Lagos: ECA/OAU.

UNDP/The World Bank: African Economic and Financial Data. Washington, DC, 1989.

World Bank, 1992. "World Development Report, 1991." New York: Oxford University Press.

World Bank. 1989. "Sub-Saharan Africa: From Crisis to Sustainable Growth." Washington, DC: World Bank.

World Bank. 1988. "Adjustment Lending: An Evaluation of Ten Years of Experience." Policy and Research Paper No.1, Washington DC.

INDEX

ABOUT EDITORS AND CONTRIBUTORS

Senyo Ben-Sylva K. Adjibolosoo is a Professor of Economics at Trinity Western University, Langley, British Columbia, Canada. Dr. Adjibolosoo obtained his B. A degree from University of Ghana, his M. A. degree from University of York, Canada, and his Ph. D (Economics) degree from Simon Fraser University, Burnaby, British Columbia, Canada. An econometrician by training, Dr. Adjibolosoo devotes all his time to economic development, and is the originator and inspirer of the human factor perspective on development theory and practice. He is the founder and Executive Director of the International Institute for Human Factor Development (IIHFD). He is also the founder and Editor of the Review of Human Factor Studies, which is the journal of the IIHFD. Dr. Adjibolosoo is a prolific writer. His numerous publications, which cover both econometrics and the role of the human factor in economic development, include many articles in such journals as *Communications in Statistics, Scandinavian Journal of Development Studies* and *Review of Human Factor Studies*. In addition, Dr. Adjibolosoo has published over five books in the area of human factor and economic development and has numerous, book chapters. His research continues to focus on the human factor in economic development, in which he continues to conduct and publish cutting edge research.

Francis Adu-Febiri obtained his B. A (Hons) degree from University of Ghana, Legon, his M. A. degree from Simon Fraser University, Canada and his Ph. D (Sociology) degree from the University of British Columbia, Canada. Dr. Adu-Febiri is an Assistant Professor at the Social Sciences Department at Camosun College, Victoria, Canada, where he teaches courses in Introductory Sociology, Canadian First Nations Issues, and Social Science Research Methods. In addition, he teaches Race and Ethnic Relations at University of Victoria. Dr. Adu-Febiri is a Research Associate of the International Institute for Human Factor Development. His research and publications focus on sociology of tourism, political sociology, sociology of development, human factor development, race and ethnic relations, and structural dynamics of African societies. Dr. Adu-Febiri's published research in these area have appeared in *Tourism Recreation Research,* India; the *African Review*, Tanzania; *Berkeley Journal of Sociology*. California, USA; the *Review of Human Factor Studies*, Canada; and *EthniVoices*, Canada. He is currently working on a book: Tourism and Ghana's Development Process: A Human Factor Perspective.

Joe Willie Essuman earned his B. A degree in Economics at the University of Cape Coast, Ghana, and his MA, MS, and Ph.D. (Business) degrees at the University of Wisconsin-Madison. Dr. Essuman is currently an Associate Professor of Economics at the University of Wisconsin-Waukesha, where he teaches Principles of Economics, Money & Banking, and Business Statistics. Dr. Essuman also teaches International Economics and International Finance as an adjunct professor in the MBA program at Concordia University Wisconsin. He also teaches Economic Theory & Practice at Marquette University's College of Professional Studies. Dr. Essuman previously worked as a research officer in the Bank of Ghana. His research interest is in development economics and international finance, with a concentration on Africa.

Boniface Y. Gebe obtained his B. A. (Hons) degree from the University of Ghana and his M. A and Ph. D (Political Science) degrees from Queens University, Kingston, Ontario, Canada. Dr. Gebe's research interests lies in the international relations, and post-cold war developments.

Godson Chintuwa Obia obtained his B. Sc. degree from University of Nigeria, his M. A degree from University of Toronto and his Ph. D (Geography) degree from University of Oklahoma, Norman, Oklahoma. Dr. Obia is currently an Associate Professor of Geography, Eastern Illinois University, Charleston, Illinois, where he teaches courses in World Geography, African Geography and Culture, Economic Geography, Human Impacts on the Environment, and Spaceship Earth. His research focus is on Agricultural Policy and Land Use Studies, Environmental Issues, and Rural Sustainable Development in Africa Nutrition and Health in Africa, and Local Community Development. Dr. Obia has published peer-reviewed articles in these areas that have appeared in such journals as *Journal of Third World Studies, Professional Geographer, Applied Geography Conference Proceedings, Small City and Regional Community*, and the *Platte Valley Review*. He is a contributor to a recent book on the Geography of Sub-Saharan Africa. Dr. Obia is a Research Associate of the International Institute of Human Factor Development.

Benjamin Ofori-Amoah received his B. A. degree from University of Ghana, Legon, his M. Sc. (Planning) degree from University of Science and Technology, Ghana, his M. A. (Higher Ed. Adm.) from University of Exeter, UK and Ph. D (Geography) degree from Simon Fraser University, Burnaby, British Columbia, Canada. Dr. Ofori-Amoah is currently an Associate Professor of Geography at the University of Wisconsin at Stevens Point, where he teaches courses in economic, urban, manufacturing, and transportation geography, and community development. Dr. Ofori-Amoah is an Economic Geographer and a Regional Planner with research focus on development theory, development planning, technological change and the human factor. He has published peer-reviewed articles and book chapters on these topics that have appeared in such journals as *Industry and Development, Appropriate Technology, Canadian Geographer, Environment and Planning A, Geoforum, Review of Human Factor Studies* and several books on Africa. Dr. Ofori-Amoah is a Research Associate of the International Institute of Human Factor Development and is the President of the International Institute of Human Factor Development (USA).

Joseph Ransford Oppong is an Assistant Professor of Geography at the University of North Texas, Denton TX. He has a B. A. (Hons) degree in Geography with Sociology from the University of Ghana, and M. A. and Ph.D. degrees from the University of Alberta, Edmonton, Alberta, Canada. Dr. Oppong has taught geography at the University of Alberta and University of Iowa, Iowa City, Iowa. Dr. Oppong is a Medical Geographer and his major areas of expertise include Location-Allocation Modeling, Third World Health Services Delivery, and the Geography of Disease. Current research interests include the Geography of Cancer in Texas, Vulnerability and HIV-AIDS in Africa, Informal Health care in rural Africa, and political ecology of Africa's Refugee and Landmine crisis and the associated health implications. Dr. Oppong was a Director of the Africa Specialty Group of the Association of American Geographers between 1994-97 and is currently a Board Member of the Medical Geography Specialty Group of the Association of American of Geographers. Dr. Oppong has published in several leading journals including *The Professional Geographer, Geographical Analysis, Social Science and Medicine, Applied Geographic Studies*, and *Review of Human Factor Studies*. Dr. Oppong is also a Research Associate of the International Institute for Human Factor Development.

William Yaw Osei is an Associate Professor of Geography at the Algoma University College, Sault Ste Marie, Ontario, Canada. He holds a B. A. degree in Geography from the University of Ghana, an M. A. Degree from Carleton University, Ottawa, and a Ph. D. degree from University of Western Ontario.
Dr. Osei is an all-round geographer with expertise in both physical and human geography. He has taught courses in geomorphology, biogeography, the environment, Africa, world regional geography and economic development. Dr. Osei's current research focus is forestry and rural energy systems in Africa, urban agriculture, environmental rehabilitation of surface mines and wild resources. He has published several articles on wood fuel and deforestation, rural energy technology and sustainable development, socio-economic dynamics of forest loss and the human dimensions in forest management. These articles have appeared in *Geoforum, the Environmentalist,* and the *Review of Human Factor Studies.*

John Henry Owusu holds a B A. degree from University of Science and Technology, Ghana, an M. S (Geography & Regional Planning) from the Indiana University of Pennsylvania, and an M. A. and a Ph. D degree in Geography from the University of Iowa. Dr. Owusu is an Assistant Professor of

Geography at the University of Connecticut, Storrs, Connecticut where he teaches Geography of Economic Development, Geography of Africa and Geography of Latin America. Dr. Owusu is a Development Geographer with a research focus on industrialization and development in Sub-Saharan Africa, particularly Ghana. His publications are mainly in the area of structural adjustment programs (SAP) and African development, with a primary focus on the economic and spatial effects of adjustment on Ghana's formal wood-processing sector. Dr. Owusu is a Research Associate of the International Institute of Human Factor Development.

STUDIES IN AFRICAN ECONOMIC AND SOCIAL DEVELOPMENT

1. Richard Vengroff and Alan Johnston, **Decentralization and the Implementation of Rural Development in Senegal**
2. Olayiwola Abegunrin, **Economic Dependence and Regional Cooperation in Southern Africa: SADCC and South Africa in Confrontation**
3. Charles O. Chikeka, **Britain, France, and the New African States: A Study of Post-Independence Relationships, 1960-1985**
4. Daniel Teferra, **The Making and Economy of Ethiopia**
5. Santosh Saha, **A History of Agriculture in Liberia, 1822-1970: Transference of American Values**
6. Santosh Saha, **A History of Agriculture in West Africa: A Guide to Information Sources**
7. Kwaku Osei-Hwedie, **A Search for Legitimate Social Development Education and Practice Models for Africa**
8. Emmanuel Ike Udogu, **Nigeria and the Politics of Survival as a Nation-State**
9. Aloy Chife, **The Political Economy of Post-Cold War Africa**
10. Benjamin Kline, **Profit, Principle and Apartheid, 1948-1994: The Conflict of Economic and Moral Issues in United States-South African Relations**
11. Senyo B-S. K. Adjibolosoo and Benjamin Ofori-Amoah (eds.), **Addressing Misconceptions About Africa's Development: Seeing Beyond the Veil**